Critical Incident Stress Debriefing: *CISD*

An Operations Manual for the Prevention of Traumatic Stress Among Emergency Service and Disaster Workers

Second Edition, Revised

Jeffrey T. Mitchell, Ph.D.
University of Maryland Baltimore County
and
George S. Everly, Jr., Ph.D., F.A.P.M.
Union Memorial Hospital, Baltimore
Loyola College in Maryland

Chevron Publishing Corporation
5018 Dorsey Hall Drive
Suite 104
Ellicott City, MD 21042

About the cover:
A San Jose, California paramedic / firefighter comforts a police officer who risked his life attempting to rescue a child, but was beaten back by intense heat and smoke. The child died in the blaze.

Editorial / Production Supervision
and Interior Design: *Douglas Lamb*
Editorial Assistance by: *Scott C. Donohue, B.S., NREMT-P*
Cover Design and Layout: *Caroline J. Zimmerman, B.A.*

© *1995, 1996 by Chevron Publishing Corporation*
Reprinted 1997
Ellicott City, Maryland 21042
(410) 740 - 0065

Printed in the United States of America

ISBN: 1-883581-02-8

" ... but this I do know
you who will be truly happy
are those who will have sought for and found
a way to serve."

- Albert Schweitzer

DEDICATIONS, *Second Edition*

To my mother and my sister, June, who both taught me all about caring in the earliest days of my life and practiced that same care for my father in his final days.

(JTM)

To my children Marideth, George and Andrea, may you know only health, peace and happiness.

(GSE)

ACKNOWLEDGEMENTS

Lists of acknowledgements always run the risk of failing to adequately recognize the contributions of some very important people. To mitigate those risks, the authors would like to point out the fact that this book could never have been possible without a constant stream of feedback from over 400 Critical Incident Stress (CIS) teams in twelve nations.

Many thousands of bits of information in verbal and written form had to be processed by the authors to formulate the chapters in this book. Some of the ideas were "authored" by participants in CIS courses. Others came from members of CIS teams, law enforcement agencies, fire service personnel, nurses, physicians, disaster workers, personnel in emergency medical services, school systems, mental health services and industries. These people and many more actively and enthusiastically contributed their feedback and helped to create a movement, a change in Critical Incident Stress Management (CISM) and the eventual writing of these pages. Naming each individual and acknowledging each and every contribution is clearly an impossible task, which shall not be attempted.

Each of you who has given to us, should know in your hearts the contributions you have made. Please know you are in our hearts and we acknowledge and appreciate all you have given to us and to Critical Incident Stress Management.

Thank you for your support and loyalty. We are grateful.

J.T.M. and G.S.E.

Contents

TABLES

Chapter 13

Chapter 14

Appendix A

FIGURES

Chapter 1

FUNDAMENTALS OF CRITICAL INCIDENT STRESS DEBRIEFINGS (CISD)

INTRODUCTION

This book is designed to be an operational treatise on how to preserve and enhance the most important resource any organization possesses - the human resource. Preserving and enhancing human resources is a difficult enough task in the face of the normal stress and strain of living in the 1990s. It becomes even more challenging when the human resources routinely face risks and working conditions well-outside the usual realm of human endeavor. Having made that assertion, several professions immediately come to mind: emergency service personnel, public safety personnel, nurses, physicians and disaster workers. Few are likely to argue with the assertion that these individuals routinely find themselves in uniquely stressful, high risk and potentially traumatizing pursuits as part of their paid or volunteer careers.

While there have been substantial advances in the treatment of occupational stress and post-trauma disorders in recent years (see Everly and Lating, 1995), there is a compelling logic that argues for efforts to be directed toward prevention of occupational stress and post-trauma syndromes. This is so, especially among the high risk professions we have just enumerated (Butcher, 1980; Kentsmith, 1980; Yandrick, 1990; Mitchell and Bray, 1990). The Critical Incident Stress Debriefing (CISD) process is specifically designed to prevent or mitigate the development of post-traumatic stress among emergency services professions and other high risk disciplines. In this text we will review not only CISD but other interventions found useful in preventing or mitigating the effects of excessive stress and trauma.

DEFINING THE VICTIM

The first point that needs to be made is that emergency service personnel find the notion of being a victim inherently repugnant when applied to themselves or their families. This is easy to understand. Emergency service personnel are the rescuers, not the rescued! Nevertheless, by virtue of their high risk professions they and their families may at some time become victims of stress and trauma. Indeed, the most significant of all recognized risk factors for the development of post-traumatic stress or Critical Incident Stress (CIS) is the direct, or indirect, exposure to a highly traumatic event. But some differentiations can indeed be made in how we define victims. Depending upon the nature of the exposure to the traumatizing event, we can classify potential victims in three categories:

1. **"Primary Victims**," that is, those individuals most directly affected by a crisis, disaster or trauma; typically thought of as the "direct victims" of the trauma.

2. **"Secondary Victims**," that is, those individuals who are in some way observers of the immediate traumatic effects that have been wrought upon the primary victims. Emergency response personnel, rescuers and bystanders would be examples.

3. **"Tertiary Victims**," that is, those affected indirectly by the trauma via later exposure to the scene of the disaster / trauma or by a later exposure to primary or secondary victims. Typically tertiary victims were not exposed to the immediate "first hand" aspects of the traumatization thus they were not exposed to the "shocking immediacy." Family members of victims or rescuers might be examples of tertiary victims.

The focus of this text will be upon the prevention or mitigation of post-traumatic stress among emergency service, hospital personnel, disaster response workers and public safety personnel who are most likely to become "secondary victims." Of course, emergency personnel and related professionals may find themselves as primary or tertiary victims, or some combination as well, but they are most prone to becoming secondary victims.

The principles of CISD, defusings and related interventions can be of value with not only secondary victims but primary and tertiary victims as well when modified by a knowledgeable professional who has been trained in applying the techniques.

Before detailing various interventions, let us first lay some important ground work.

CRITICAL INCIDENT STRESS MANAGEMENT (CISM)

The field of critical incident stress management (CISM), as we know it today in the emergency services professions, was born largely with the 1983 paper "When Disaster Strikes ... The Critical Incident Stress Debriefing," authored by Jeffrey T. Mitchell. This seminal paper described the creation of the Critical Incident Stress Debriefing (CISD) for the mitigation of post - traumatic stress reactions.

Although the field of CISM may have been born of the CISD process, it is certainly far more than that. CISM represents an integrated "system" of interventions which are designed to prevent and/or mitigate the adverse psychological reactions that so often accompany emergency services, public safety and disaster response functions. CISM interventions are especially directed towards the mitigation of post-traumatic stress reactions.

As discussed in this volume, CISM includes, but is not limited to:

1. Pre-incident education and trauma immunization programs

2. One - on - one crisis intervention

3. CISD

4. Defusings

5. Demobilizations

6. Family and significant others support programs

7. Stress management and trauma management education programs

8. Peer support programs (which may consist of several of the aforementioned interventions)

9. On-scene support processes

10. Informal group discussion

11. Follow up programs

12. Other programs as required

As the reader will note, CISM is more than just a technique. It is a system of well-integrated interventions. CISM is a philosophy and a belief in the importance and value of the human resource.

AN INTRODUCTION TO CRITICAL INCIDENT STRESS DEBRIEFING

Critical Incident Stress Debriefing (CISD) is a proper noun referring to a form of structured psychological debriefing conducted in small groups. Contrary to common usage, CISD is not a generic term for debriefings, rather it refers to a formal, structured protocol originally developed by the senior author (JTM) as a direct, action-oriented crisis intervention process designed to prevent or mitigate traumatic stress subsequent to a traumatic event. Debriefing models other than the CISD do indeed exist. CISD is simply the best known and most widely utilized (Meichenbaum, 1994). While originally designed to be applied among public safety, disaster response, military and emergency service personnel, CISD can be used with virtually any population, including children, when employed by a skilled intervention team. CISD is only one formalized intervention within a broader category of stress-related psychological interventions referred to as CISM. Let us take a closer look at these concepts.

CISD after unusually distressing events is a standard operating procedure in many fire departments, law enforcement agencies, hospitals, dispatch centers, emergency medical services units, corrections facilities and other public safety and emergency services organizations. There are over three hundred critical incident stress intervention teams in the United States alone and at least another one hundred in other parts of the world including Australia, Canada, Germany, Great Britain, Sweden, New Zealand and Norway.

A wide range of emergency personnel have benefited from the services of these specialized teams. Today, it is not uncommon to come in contact with physicians, police officers, fire fighters, paramedics, nurses, emergency medical technicians, disaster workers, wilderness searchers, wild land fire fighters, corrections officials, mental health professionals, life guards, school and industrial groups, among many others, who have been helped through one or more CISDs. In some areas critical incident teams are regularly serving commercial, industrial and community groups. This is a book for all of these organizations and individuals. This is a book for those who have chosen to serve others.

This fundamentals chapter is essential to assure that the reader has an understanding of the basic terms and concepts utilized in the CISD process. Progress through the remainder of the book will be enhanced by the knowledge gained in this chapter. It is highly recommended that even those experienced in CISD read through this chapter before launching into the chapters which follow. Over the years new CISD concepts have been formed and many new procedures have been established. This chapter presents the latest thinking on CISD and sets the stage for the chapters which follow.

In order to assist the reader in comprehending the principles and practices delineated in the subsequent pages, we will begin with an introduction and brief review of 27 key terms and concepts. They are listed in Table 1.1.

TABLE 1.1

BASIC TERMS AND CONCEPTS

- Crisis Event
- Stress
- Stressor
- Target Organ Strain
- Critical Incident
- Trauma
- Traumatic Stress
- Critical Incident Stress
- Post-Traumatic Stress Disorder
- Debriefing
- Critical Incident Stress Debriefing (CISD)
- Formal CISD
- Informal Discussion
- Specialty Debriefing
- Critical Incident Stress Team
- Team Leader
- Peer Support Personnel
- Professional Support Personnel
- Community Response Team (CRT)
- Combined Emergency Services CIS Team
- Critical Incident Stress Management (CISM)
- Defusing
- Demobilization
- Individual Consultations
- On-scene Support Services
- Spouse and Significant Other Support Services
- Follow up Services

BASIC DEFINITIONS

Table 1.1 encapsulates the basic terms that we will be addressing in this section.

CRISIS EVENT .... An event which produces a temporary state of psychological disequilibrium and a subsequent state of emotional turmoil. A crisis represents a disruption in psychological homeostasis or balance (Mitchell, 1981).

STRESS .... A response characterized by physical and psychological arousal arising as a direct result of an exposure to any demand or pressure on a living organism. The more significant the demand, the more intense the stress reaction will be. Some stress is actually positive. Stress reactions which are moderate are actually helpful in that they motivate us to make positive changes, grow and achieve goals. When stress is helpful, it is called "**Eustress.**" When stress reactions are prolonged or excessive, they can cause harm. The destructive nature of stress is called "**Distress.**" Stress is perhaps best thought of as the sum total of "wear and tear" (Selye, 1956, 1974) and as such may be thought of as accelerating the aging process.

STRESSOR .... A stressor is any event acting as a stimulus which places a demand upon a person, a group or an organization. Mild stressors produce a mild stress reaction and severe stressors produce excessive stress reactions. More will be said about stress and stressors in chapter 2, the Nature of Human Stress.

TARGET ORGAN STRAIN .... The adverse effect of stress on the mind and/or the body. It is often described as the symptoms of wear and tear on the somatic and psychological systems. Target organ strain can result from excessively intense stress and/or excessively chronic stress (Everly, 1989).

CRITICAL INCIDENT .... A turning point event. A critical incident is often called a crisis event. A critical incident is any event which has a stressful impact sufficient enough to overwhelm the usually effective coping skills of either an individual or a group. Critical incidents are typically sudden, powerful events which are outside of the range of ordinary human experiences. Because they are so sudden and unusual, they can have a strong emotional effect even on well-trained, experienced people. If the critical incident is extreme in nature, it may serve as the starting point for the psychiatric disorder called "Post -traumatic Stress Disorder."

TRAUMA .... A trauma is any event which attacks the psyche and breaks through the defense system with the potential to significantly disrupt one's life, perhaps resulting in a personality change or physical illness if it is not managed quickly and/or effectively. To cite the American Psychiatric Association (1987), a trauma is "a psychologically distressing event outside the range of usual human experience" (APA 1987, p. 247). Such events are typically thought to "overwhelm" one's normal coping mechanisms. According to the American Psychiatric Association's latest taxonomy of diagnostic terms (APA, 1994) the traumatic event will engender intense fear, helplessness or horror.

TRAUMATIC STRESS .... The stress response produced when a person is exposed to a disturbing traumatic event. "Traumatic Stress" is often used as a synonym with the term "Critical Incident Stress" (Mitchell, Bray, 1990; Everly, 1989); the traumatic stress reaction may be immediate or delayed.

CRITICAL INCIDENT STRESS .... The reaction a person or group has to a critical incident. Critical incident stress is characterized by a wide range of cognitive, physical, emotional and behavioral signs and symptoms. Most people recover from critical incident stress within a few weeks. Another term for critical incident stress is "Traumatic Stress."

POST-TRAUMATIC STRESS DISORDER (PTSD) .... A formally recognized psychiatric disorder which may result from an exposure to a critical incident or "traumatic event" (APA, 1980, 1987, 1994). Post-Traumatic Stress Disorder is identified by three characteristic clusters of symptoms which follow a psychologically distressing event which is considered outside of the range of ordinary human experience:

1. Intrusive recollective thoughts

2. Arousal

3. Numbing / withdrawal / avoidance

The traumatic event or "critical incident" is one that is markedly distressing to almost anyone and often produces intense fear, terror or helplessness (APA, 1994).

FIGURE 1.1

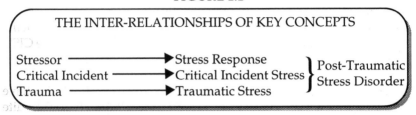

THE INTER-RELATIONSHIPS OF KEY CONCEPTS

Stressor ⟶ Stress Response ⎫ Post-Traumatic
Critical Incident ⟶ Critical Incident Stress ⎬ Stress Disorder
Trauma ⟶ Traumatic Stress ⎭

DEBRIEFING .... Generic term for the CISD process developed by Dr. Jeffrey T. Mitchell (see CISD).

CRITICAL INCIDENT STRESS DEBRIEFING (CISD) .... A group meeting or discussion about a distressing critical incident. Based upon core principles of education and crisis intervention, the CISD is designed to mitigate the impact of a critical incident and to assist the personnel in recovering as quickly as possible from the stress associated with the event. The CISD is run by a specially trained team which includes a mental health professional and peer support personnel from the emergency services (law enforcement, fire service, emergency medical services, nursing, disaster services, physicians, corrections, park services, dispatch, etc.).

"FORMAL" CISD .... It is a structured group process integrating crisis intervention strategies with educational techniques. Another definition of a formal debriefing is a peer driven, clinician guided discussion of a traumatic event with the goal of mitigating the psychological trauma and accelerating recovery from significant stress. A formal debriefing contains seven distinct phases which help to provide the structure of the CISD process. The formal debriefing begins with a set of _**introductory remarks**_ which set the tone for the debriefing, motivate the participants to accept and cooperate with the process and to establish the working rules for the discussion. The second phase of the formal CISD is the _**fact phase**_ in which the participants describe what happened during the incident. The third phase is the _**thought phase**_ and the participants are asked about their first or most prominent thoughts while they were going through the incident. The _**reaction phase**_ is the fourth phase. Here the participants discuss the elements of the situation which were the worst for them. The signals or symptoms of distress which were encountered during or after the critical incident are described in the fifth phase of the formal debriefing which is called the _**symptom phase**_. During the sixth phase, the _**teaching phase**_, team leaders and peer debriefers spend a fair amount of time providing information and suggestions which can be used to reduce the impact of the stress. In the seventh and final phase, *re-entry*, participants' questions are answered and loose ends are tied up. The last phase of the debriefing always ends with a few summary comments from the CISD team members.

INFORMAL DISCUSSIONS .... For centuries, emergency personnel have had informal discussions of traumatic events and these were often quite helpful to the personnel. Friends listening to and assisting each other after traumatic events is encouraged. Trained peer support personnel are often present during these discussions and they can help to guide them along the most helpful paths. Trained peers can also observe when signs and symptoms of distress are present and they can guide the personnel to debriefings or other forms of assistance.

SPECIALTY DEBRIEFINGS .... These debriefing services are provided to people outside of a team's normal area of responsibility. The emphasis in such a debriefing is on the educational aspects of the debriefing rather than on the self disclosure aspects of the debriefing. There is usually more emphasis on the role of the mental health professional and less on the role of the peer support personnel. See "Community Response Teams" below.

CRITICAL INCIDENT STRESS TEAM .... A team which can be best described as a partnership between professional support personnel (mental health professionals and clergy) and peer support personnel (emergency services personnel) who have received special training to intervene in stress reactions. The majority of teams in the United States have been developed to provide support services for emergency personnel. More recently, many teams have been established to serve the needs of industries, school systems and commercial organizations. There are many names applied to critical incident stress teams. They include, but are not limited to:

- Crisis Response Team

- Crisis Events Response Team

- Emergency Services Support Unit

- Critical Incident Stress Debriefing Team

- Critical Incident Stress Management Team

- Critical Incident Response Team

TEAM LEADER .... A mental health professional who leads a CISD. When debriefings are provided to emergency personnel, the team leader works closely with trained emergency service peer support personnel such as police officers, fire fighters, paramedics or nurses. When debriefings are provided to community groups, schools, industries or other non-emergency organizations, the use of peers is limited or non-existent. In those cases, team leaders will pick one or two mental health professionals to assist them.

PEER SUPPORT PERSONNEL .... Peer support personnel are the emergency personnel on a CISD team. They are drawn from the rescue personnel, fire fighters, law enforcement agents, nursing staffs, communications personnel, corrections, FBI, Marshals' Service and the military. Providing peer support personnel from the same professions is extremely important for stress interventions with emergency personnel. In educational, commercial and industrial settings, however, peers are often not part of stress teams. Industrial, educational and commercial organizations' usually rely more heavily on the skills of professional support personnel (mental health professionals). Occasionally, these organizations will utilize Employee Assistance Programs (EAP) or their own medical staffs to assist with trauma interventions.

PROFESSIONAL SUPPORT PERSONNEL .... Professional support staff are under two categories - mental health professionals and clergy. They have special knowledge and skills and have received specialized training within their professional fields. Ordinarily mental health professionals have academic training, diplomas, certifications, licenses or some other form of recognition of their training and skills. For the clergy, it is expected that they are ordained clergy or appointed chaplains with special documented training and experience. Most hold academic degrees from colleges, universities or seminaries.

Likewise, mental health professionals must have the appropriate education, training and experience in the clinical areas to provide critical incident stress interventions. Mental health professionals are the psychologists, social workers, psychiatrists, psychiatric nurses or certified mental health counselors. The typical mental health professional who would serve in a professional support position on a critical incident stress team would have at least a master's degree in mental health. Many have Ph.D.s or other forms of academic education and certification.

It is important that whoever provides critical incident support services, whether they be peer or professional support personnel, be properly trained in critical incident stress management, post-traumatic stress disorder and in the techniques of intervention. Despite the best of intentions, interventions by those who are untrained in critical incident stress, may result in harm to those who are the recipients of such services.

COMMUNITY RESPONSE TEAM (CRT) .... A team of mental health professionals and disaster workers such as Red Cross personnel who respond to the psychological needs of disaster victims and the needs of a community after a major incident. A Community Response Team usually parallels the work of a Critical Incident Stress Management team. However, instead of concentrating its efforts on the emergency workers as a CISM team would, the CRT focuses on the primary victims of the incident. In many places, the CRT receives the same training as the CISM team but does not work with the emergency personnel.

COMBINED EMERGENCY SERVICES CRITICAL INCIDENT STRESS TEAM .... This is a fundamental concept in formulating an emergency services critical incident stress team. It means that there is one CIS team serving the needs of multiple agencies such as law enforcement agencies, hospitals, fire departments, emergency medical service agencies, communication centers, disaster relief personnel, ski patrols, corrections agencies, wild land fire fighters, park service agencies and other first response organizations. Each of the agencies or organizations supply personnel to one combined emergency services CIS team which provides consistent training, supervision, case reviews, support services, in-service education and team building programs for the team members. This combined team then supplies the appropriate personnel to assist any of the first response agencies which might need help after a traumatic event. If a law enforcement agency needs assistance, then law enforcement personnel are chosen from the team pool to assist that agency. Fire personnel are chosen to assist fire agencies; nurses are utilized when nurses have been affected by the trauma and likewise for any of the other organizations. The combined emergency service CIS team keeps the cost of training down because the different agencies share CISM training. It is also a more efficient method to utilize the limited number of mental health professionals who are available to serve the various emergency service organizations. But, most important, a combined emergency services CIS team eliminates the need to use an agency's own personnel to provide services to its own traumatized workers. *This is especially important since it is believed that psychological support services provided by people who are too well-known to the recipients may be psychologically unsound both for the recipient and for the provider of the services.* It should be noted here that a combined CIS team does not eliminate the need for an organization to maintain a psychologist, an employee assistance program, a chaplain or any other human services program. CIS teams are a supplement to ordinary human services and personnel support services not a substitute for those programs.

CRITICAL INCIDENT STRESS MANAGEMENT (CISM) .... A wide range of programs and intervention strategies which have been designed to prevent stress in emergency personnel and to assist them in managing and recovering from significant stress should they encounter it in their work. CISM is much broader than just Critical Incident Stress Debriefings (CISD). It contains many special programs and strategies including pre-incident education, significant other support programs, defusings, demobilizations, debriefings, on-scene support services, follow up services, community outreach programs, individual consults, peer counseling, informal discussions, crisis intervention training, disaster preparedness and disaster assistance programs. The best way to think of CISM is as a comprehensive approach to traumatic stress management. CISD is only one of the many techniques under the heading of CISM.

DEFUSING .... The defusing is a shortened version of the CISD. It has three parts, **Introduction, Exploration** and **Information**. Defusings take place immediately or relatively soon after the critical incident is finished and typically last less than one (1) hour. They are led by trained debriefers from the CIS team. The leader of a defusing may be a peer support person or one of the professional support people on the CIS team. Defusings are designed to either eliminate the need to provide a formal debriefing or to enhance the CISD if it is still necessary to provide one.

DEMOBILIZATION .... DE-ESCALATION .... DECOMPRESSION .... All three words are used as synonyms to mean a brief intervention which is reserved for use immediately after a disaster or other large scale incident. The intervention is designed to provide a transition period from the world of the traumatic event back to the world of routine. As units are disengaged from operations at the scene of a disaster, they are sent by unit to a demobilization center. Here they are given a ten minute talk on critical incident stress, the symptoms they might encounter and some suggestions which will be immediately helpful to them during the next twenty four to seventy two hours or until a formal debriefing can be arranged to discuss the large scale incident. Formal debriefings always follow the demobilization several days later. After the ten minute maximum talk, the emergency workers are then sent to another room in which food and non-alcoholic beverages are served. After a twenty minute rest, the units are either returned to normal duties other than the disaster scene or they are released to go home. In a prolonged disaster (beyond one or two shifts), demobilizations are only provided during the first and possibly the second shift. Then demobilizations cease and one to one services (individual consults) and command advisements continue for the duration of the disaster.

INDIVIDUAL CONSULTATIONS .... One rule of thumb which can be followed when providing CISM services is "More than three, think CISD!" That is, a debriefing is triggered when there are more than three people who need it. When there are less than four people who are affected by the traumatic incident, a different type of service is provided - the individual consult. Defusings, demobilizations and debriefings are group processes. Bringing a whole group of people together when only one two or three are affected will produce a substantial amount of anger among those who are not affected by the trauma. The individual consult is a mechanism under the CISM heading which allows for one (or preferably two) trained peers or mental health professional to work with the few who are distressed. The intervention is far more conversational than the formal group processes of the defusing, debriefing or demobilization. It is possible, however, to use the debriefing model as a guide to discuss the traumatic event during the individual consultation. That is, the individual is first asked what happened, then about how they thought during the situation. Next they are asked about the worst aspects of the event. They may then be asked about cognitive, physical, emotional or behavioral symptoms which occurred. Finally, the helper provides some useful advice and suggestions and wraps up the contact.

ON-SCENE SUPPORT SERVICES .... Whenever direct support services are provided at the scene of a traumatic incident, while the event is still going on, the services are called "on-scene" support services. There are three basic supports which are provided at the scene: 1) *brief crisis interventions with emergency personnel who are showing signs of distress*, 2) *advice and counsel to the commanders* and 3) *assistance to victims, survivors and family members who are directly involved with the incident*. Most on-scene services are provide by trained emergency service peer support personnel. *It is important to remember that no group services are ever provided at the scene since group services at the scene will tend to cause more disruption in the personnel. On-scene support services to emergency personnel are typically limited to one-to-one contacts, not groups.*

SPOUSE AND SIGNIFICANT OTHER SUPPORT SERVICES .... Support for the emergency services personnel is inadequate unless it also includes special support services for the spouses and significant others. Greater emphasis is being placed on the loved ones of the emergency worker. They also hurt and are indirectly negatively impacted by the same traumatic events which affect the emergency services personnel (tertiary victims). Many CISM teams are adding significant others to the teams in order to better serve the loved ones of emergency personnel who have been distressed by the traumatic events. Many special programs already exist to assist the significant others of emergency personnel. There are educational programs, debriefings after traumatic events, small on going support groups, grief seminars and family fairs.

FOLLOW UP SERVICES .... Every time an on-scene support service, a demobilization, a defusing or a debriefing is provided, it is necessary to follow these actionsthat is with one or more types of follow up services. In fact, any intervention from an individual consult to a formal debriefing should receive some type of follow up. Follow up services include telephone calls, station visits, chaplain contacts, ride alongs, small group meetings, contacts with commanders, peer visits, one-on-one services, family contacts, referrals for professional contact and any number of other helpful outreach programs which can be thought of in the aftermath of a tragic event.

GENERAL PRINCIPLES OF CISD

If these basic principles of CISD are followed, they will enhance the services provided and reduce the chance of disruptive mistakes. More will be said on these general principles elsewhere in this book.

GENERAL PRINCIPLES OF CISD:

1. CISD is **not** psychotherapy.
2. CISD is **not** a substitute for psychotherapy.
3. CISD should only be applied by those who have been specifically **trained** in its uses.

4. A CISD is a **group process**.
5. A CISD is a **group meeting** or discussion designed to reduce stress and enhance recovery from stress. It is based upon principles of crisis intervention and education, not psychotherapy per se.
6. A CISD is a **team** approach. A CISD team is comprised of a mental health professional and several peer support personnel.
7. A CISD will **not** solve all of the problems presented during the brief time frame available to work with distressed personnel, but it may mitigate those that persist.
8. **Sometimes** it will be necessary to refer individuals for follow up assessment and / or treatment after a debriefing.
9. It is **not** necessary for everyone in the group to speak during a debriefing for the process to be beneficial.
10. Generally it is best to have a **voluntary** debriefing, but there are times when it is better for the good of the group to require the attendance of all involved personnel.
11. Following most well - defined and delineated acute traumatic events, the **ideal time** for a debriefing is after the first twenty four hours and before seventy two hours. There will of course be some variation on the best time for a debriefing depending on the nature of the event, the level of distress in the personnel, schedule considerations, the needs of the group and the demands of the job. Some debriefings, particularly those for line of duty deaths, may be provided before the end of the first day. Certainly, many debriefings, especially those related to mass disaster, have been given much later than the seventy two hour time frame because circumstances warranted a later debriefing. In the final analyses, debriefings are ideally utilized when the participants are most psychologically receptive.
12. CISD is primarily a **prevention** program but it can be used to mitigate post-traumatic stress as well.
13. Although CISD is a technique which was developed specifically for emergency personnel, it has been applied, with great success, to many types of **non-emergency workers**. CISD has been used on:
    - airline personnel   • bank employees
    - oil workers   • miners
    - factory workers   • parks and recreation personnel
    - business office workers   • retail shop employees
    - and a number of other groups including school children

    As long as the provider has been appropriately trained in the procedures and carefully applies the basic techniques, the procedure should be helpful to distressed groups.
14. CISD accelerates the rate of **"normal recovery**, in **normal people**, who are having **normal reactions** to **abnormal events**."

15. CISD should be considered as only **one helpful technique** under the general heading of CISM.
16. A CISD is best provided by those who are **not** well-known to those who need it.
17. The best CISM teams are **multi-organizational and multi-jurisdictional** in structure.
18. CISD is a crisis intervention process designed to stabilize cognitive and affective processes and to further mitigate the impact of a traumatic event. It is NOT an operational critique of a crisis situation or traumatic event!

SUMMARY

This chapter was designed to review and clarify some basic definitions of terms which will be utilized frequently in this book. It also reviews some core concepts of CISD. It should eliminate much of the confusion which has surrounded terms like debriefing, defusing, demobilization, specialty debriefing, individual consults, follow up services, traumatic stress and other terms which are regularly utilized by CISM teams. Even experienced CISM team members should read back through the chapter occasionally to make sure that they are using the terms properly.

The chapter also offers a summary of 18 basic principles of a CISD. These 18 fundamental principles will be utilized in many other portions of the book.

Chapter 2

THE NATURE OF HUMAN STRESS

Before we delve directly into the "how to" of CISD, it seems a worthwhile exercise to review the nature of stress and psychological trauma. Although it may seem obvious, let us emphasize that if there were no such thing as pathogenic stress nor psychological trauma, there would simply be no need for Critical Incident Stress Debriefing nor Critical Incident Stress Management. Thus CISD and CISM were actually created in response to the fact that excessive stress and psychological trauma are just as potentially disabling as is physical traumatization. Let's look at the basics.

DEFINING STRESS

In 1676, Hooks's Law described a phenomenon in physical science where the presence of a "load" or physical "stress" was capable of causing a physical "strain" upon a given material. In 1926 an Austrian endocrinologist, Hans Selye, identified what he believed was a consistent pattern of mind-body reactions which he called the "nonspecific response of the body to any demand" (Selye, 1974, p. 14). Selye later referred to this pattern as "the rate of wear and tear on the body" (Selye, 1976). Early in his career, Selye was invited to discuss these concepts at the College de France. In search of a term that best summarized the aforementioned concepts, Selye went to the physical sciences and borrowed the term "stress." Thus, from the Selyean tradition, the term "stress" is used to denote the nonspecific response of the body to any demand placed upon it. Having created a new term for the body's response to a demand, it was then necessary to create a new term to describe the demand, or stimulus, itself. Thus, the term "stressor" was created. This relationship is depicted in Figure 2.1.

FIGURE 2.1

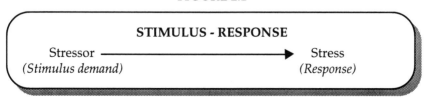

STIMULUS - RESPONSE

Stressor ⟶ Stress
(Stimulus demand) *(Response)*

A major point of confusion is unveiled when authors refer to "mental stress" versus "physical stress." In such references, it is usually clear that the authors have departed from the Selyean notion of the nature of stress as a reaction or response to stressors that may be mental stressors or physical stressors. Despite the substantial historical precedents, there remains less than total agreement on the precise nature of stress.

Rather than discuss the myriad of alternative definitions, we shall define "stress" as it will be used in this book. In line with Selye's definition, stress is a mind-body response which mediates between stressor stimuli (a set of conditions or psychosocial events) and stress-related target organ diseases (see Everly and Sobelman, 1987; Everly, 1989). Figure 2.2 depicts this relationship.

FIGURE 2.2

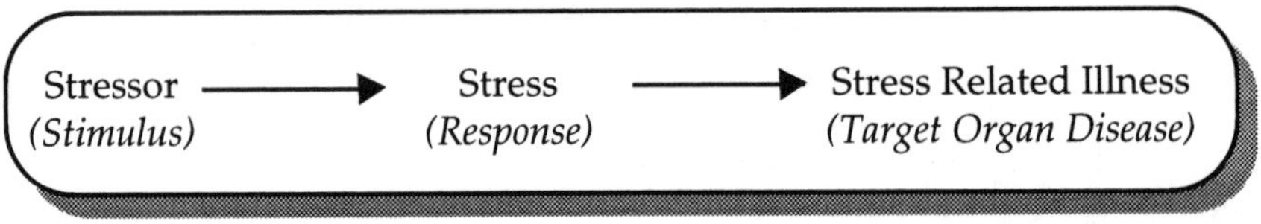

Stressor ———→ Stress ———→ Stress Related Illness
(Stimulus)   *(Response)*   *(Target Organ Disease)*

As Figure 2.2 indicates, the stress response itself serves as a linking mechanism (mechanism of mediation) which explains how stressor stimuli can "cause" or be highly related to stress-related physical disease and dysfunction (target organ effects).

It is important to keep in mind that not all stress is undesirable. This notion is depicted in Figure 2.3

FIGURE 2.3

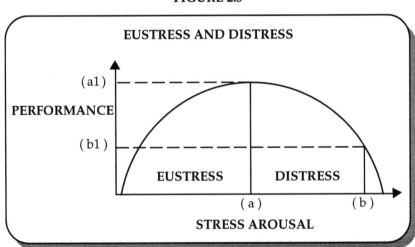

By looking closely at Figure 2.3, we can see that performance actually increases with an increase in stress arousal. This is the motivation underlying coaches' "pep talks" to athletes, or why some people try to "psyche" themselves up before some event which requires increased performance. Point (a) represents the point on the stress arousal axis that leads to maximal performance (a1). Yet look closely at Figure 2.3 and see what happens as stress arousal continues to increase from left to right on the horizontal axis. You can see that performance drops to point (b1) as stress increases to point (b). Selye (1974) refers to positive, motivating stress arousal as "eustress;" stress which leads to dysfunction (e.g., getting "psyched out") or disease, Selye terms "distress." So we see that stress is not always bad. In fact, Selye has argued that the absence of all stress is death.

In the 1940s, 1950s and early 1960s, stress-related diseases were termed "psychosomatic." These diseases were characterized by observable organic tissue pathology which was caused by excessive stress. In 1968, the American Psychiatric Association published the second edition of its Diagnostic and Statistical Manual of Mental Disorders (DSM-II). In this handbook of official psychiatric terms and diagnoses, stress-related diseases were referred to as "psychophysiological diseases." At the same time, neurotic disorders which impaired sensory or motor functions but involved no actual organic tissue damage, were termed "conversion disorders" or "hysterical disorders." Psychosomatic disorders are often confused with conversion reactions. It is important to note that stress-related psychosomatic disorders are "real." They involve actual tissue damage and can even be life threatening in some cases. Conversion reactions are psychological dysfunctions and are not life threatening.

In 1980, the American Psychiatric Association revised its diagnostic manual and created a third edition, the DSM-III. In this handbook of diagnostic nomenclature, stress-related diseases were no longer called psychophysiological, but now came under the diagnostic heading of "psychological factors affecting physical disease." This change greatly expanded the recognition of stress-related diseases. Neurotic-like conversion disorders were changed to a broader heading entitled "somatoform disorders." This taxonomy was retained in the DSM - IV (APA, 1994).

In the preceding section, we discussed basic terms and concepts relevant to the understanding of the human stress response. It is now time to put the "puzzle" together, that is, to explain why psychosocial events in one's environment can extract a "physical" toll from one's mind and body. It has long been known that the stress response is best viewed in the context of a multidimensional systems model. Figure 2.4 presents a detailed systems-based model of the human stress response.

FIGURE 2.4

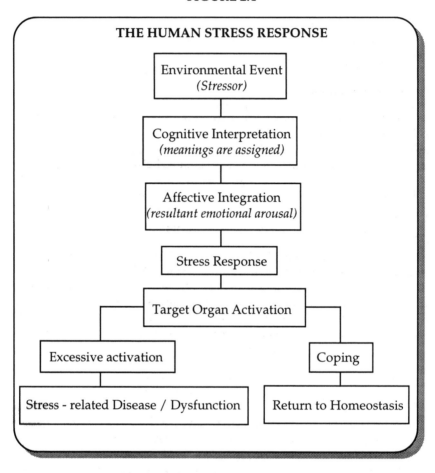

THE HUMAN STRESS RESPONSE

Environmental Event
(Stressor)

Cognitive Interpretation
(meanings are assigned)

Affective Integration
(resultant emotional arousal)

Stress Response

Target Organ Activation

Excessive activation

Coping

Stress - related Disease / Dysfunction

Return to Homeostasis

The systems model of stress presented in Figure 2.4 is an integration of the work of Lazarus and Folkman (1984), Selye (1956), Everly (1989) and Smith and Everly (1992). Let's look at its components:

STRESSORS

Stressors fall into two categories: 1) biogenic stressors and 2) psychosocial stressors (Everly, 1989). Biogenic stressors are stimulants which cause stress by virtue of the biochemical actions they exert on the human body. Preference, or even "addiction" to these substances fails to mitigate their ability to cause stress. Examples of biogenic stressors are:

- Caffeine

- Amphetamines

- Nicotine

- Phenylpropanolamine

- Theophylline

Caffeine is found in coffee, tea, many soft drinks and some medications. A 5 ounce cup of brewed coffee contains about 150 milligrams (mg) of caffeine. Tea (camellia theca) brewed for 5 minutes contains roughly 50-60 mg. A caffeinated 12 ounce soft drink contains between 30-65 mg. A one ounce chocolate bar has a caffeine content of approximately 40 mg. In addition, the following common medications contain caffeine: Anacin (32 mg), Cafergot (100 mg), Fiorinal (40 mg), No-Doz (100 mg), Prolamine (140 mg), Excedrin Extra (65 mg) and Midol (32 mg).[1]

The important point to remember is that, preference notwithstanding, biogenic stressors cause stress arousal. It is believed that dosages in the 200-300 mg over several hours (3 - 6 hrs.) range can be excessive for certain individuals, and can contribute to anxiety and stress-related symptoms (Greden, 1974; Girdano, Everly and Dusek, 1993). Common symptoms of excessive biogenic stressor consumption are sleep disturbances, irritability, jumpiness, nervousness, anxiety and excessive tension.

The second major category of stressors is referred to as "psychosocial" stressors. These stressors, unlike the biogenic variety, do not directly cause stress. Rather, they "set the stage" for stress responses to be initiated through intrapersonal mechanisms. That is, psychosocial stressors appear to be like beauty; they lie in the eye of the beholder. Simply put, although many psychosocial events can be potentially stressful, only those that are interpreted or appraised as being challenging, threatening or otherwise aversive will ultimately become psychosocial stressors. This brings us to the second stage of the model, *cognitive interpretation*.

COGNITIVE INTERPRETATION

The 5th Century Greco-Roman philosopher Epictetus reportedly said, "Men are disturbed not by things, but the views which they take of them." Hans Selye, echoed the same sentiment when he said, "It is not what

(1) *Caffeine content is expressed per standard dosage and without guarantee is belived to be correct at the time of publication. Further questions should be directed to a qualified physician.*

happens to you that matters, but how you take it." Finally, the neurophysiologist Magda Arnold has noted, "the sheer experience of things around us cannot lead to action unless they are appraised for their effect upon us" (Arnold, 1984, p. 125). Simply stated, psychosocial events occur around us every waking moment. These events will not lead to excessive stress unless one or more of them are appraised or interpreted as being: 1) meaningful and 2) potentially challenging, threatening or otherwise aversive. The propensity to appraise / interpret events is a function of learning history and personality. Recent research by Smith and Everly (1992) has noted that interpretational mechanisms play what may be the primary role in occupational stress and illness among accountants.

EMOTIONAL INTEGRATION

Magda Arnold (1970) noted that our emotions are caused by the appraisal of the psychosocial events that we encounter in the world around us. Further, Rosenman (1984) states that emotions are caused by the interpretation of events rather than the events themselves. The belief that emotions are caused by cognitive interpretations is referred to as the principle of "cognitive primacy." Not all authorities are in total agreement that emotions are always caused by cognitions. Nevertheless, there is agreement among authorities performing research in human stress that emotions and stress arousal function in such a manner so as to make cognitive primacy a functional and pragmatic reality if not a phenomenological one (Everly, 1989).

To summarize so far, the world is replete with sources of stress. Most of these potential sources of stress will only become stressors because we choose to, or have learned to, interpret them as challenging, threatening or aversive. Based upon such an interpretation, the mechanisms of human emotion are activated. To this point, however, the "stress response" is not physiologically manifest. On the basis of emotional arousal, the brain employs a "transducer" in order to convert psychological appraisals into somatic realities that affect our physical health. This "transducer" is called the "limbic-hypothalamic" complex. The more stress one experiences, the more likely this limbic circuitry may become neurologically "hypersensitive" (i.e., more easily activated with minimal stimulation over time).

THE STRESS RESPONSE

An understanding of just what the stress response really represents may be derived from the study of neuroanatomy and neuroendocrinology. Let us briefly summarize the core features of the stress response.

The stress response itself consists of three major pathways, or axes: 1) the neural axis, 2) the neuroendocrine axis and 3) the endocrine axis (Everly, 1989). These mechanisms are always activated for they represent necessary aspects of normal human physiological functioning. They become of interest in the study of stress and disease when they become overstimulated and sustain their activation at excessively high levels.

The neural stress axis consists of the nerves of the sympathetic nervous system, the parasympathetic nervous system, (collectively called the autonomic nervous system) and the neuromuscular nervous system (the nerves to the skeletal muscles).

FIGURE 2.5

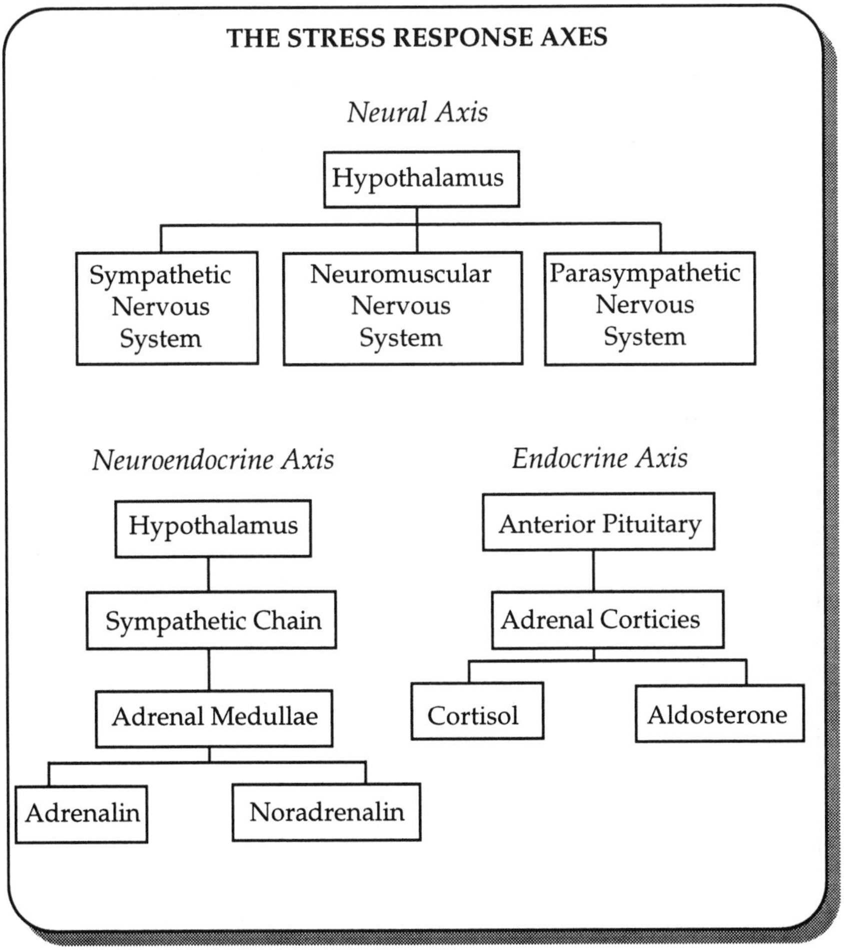

THE STRESS RESPONSE AXES

Neural Axis

Hypothalamus

Sympathetic Nervous System | Neuromuscular Nervous System | Parasympathetic Nervous System

Neuroendocrine Axis

Hypothalamus

Sympathetic Chain

Adrenal Medullae

Adrenalin | Noradrenalin

Endocrine Axis

Anterior Pituitary

Adrenal Corticies

Cortisol | Aldosterone

The neuroendocrine stress axis consists of the sympathetic neural chain and its innervation of the adrenal medulae. Stimulation of this axis results in the release of the hormones epinephrine (adrenalin) and norepinephrine (noradrenalin) from the two adrenal medullae. This axis is responsible for the so-called "fight or flight" response studied by Walter Cannon in the early 1930s.

Finally, the endocrine axis consists of the anterior pituitary gland and its effector mechanisms such as the adrenal cortices which release hormones such as cortisol and aldosterone. Similarly, estrogen, progesterone and testosterone can all be altered during stress. Figure 2.5 shows these three stress response axes.

TARGET ORGAN AROUSAL AND SYMPTOMS

"Target organs" refers to the bodily organs within any given person which may become the somatic "targets" of the stress response.

Given the three stress responses axes just described, the potential range of target organs that could be affected by excessive stress is indeed wide.

Table 2.1 summarizes some of the more common target organ signs and symptoms of excessive stress.

TABLE 2.1

COMMON SIGNS AND SYMPTOMS OF EXCESSIVE STRESS	
COGNITIVE	**PHYSICAL**
Confusion in thinking Difficulty making decisions Lowered concentration Memory dysfunction Lowering of higher cognitive functions	Excessive sweating Dizzy spells Increased heart rate Elevated blood pressure Rapid breathing
EMOTIONAL	**BEHAVIORAL**
Emotional shock Anger Grief Depression Feeling overwhelmed	Changes in ordinary behavior patterns Changes in eating Decreased personal hygiene Withdrawal from others Prolonged silences

THEORIES OF STRESS - RELATED DISEASE

Figure 2.4 presented earlier denotes that when coping strategies are successful, pathogenic stress arousal is reduced. However, if the coping strategies are unsuccessful, target organ activation will continue at excessive levels and target organ disease / dysfunction becomes a matter of time. That is, the target organs simply break down under the prolonged "wear and tear."

There exist several theories concerning just how and why stress leads to specific diseases or disorders. Let's briefly review them.

LIFE CHANGE THEORY

The life change theory argues that "change" causes adaptation. The physiology of adaptation is stress. Too many changes or too extensive a change causes the body to become overwhelmed. The result is a stress-related disease. This major theory was first constructed considering major life changes, for example, moving, divorce, graduation (Holmes and Rahe, 1967), but has been modified to include the effects of minor "hassles" as well (Lazarus and Folkman, 1984). The life events theory fails to enumerate exactly how change leads to disease other than by stating that excessive stress causes the target organ to become exhausted.

WEAK ORGAN THEORY

The weak organ theory states that all of us are either born with, or soon thereafter develop, a "weak," or highly vulnerable target organ. When we become aroused, it is this organ system that bears most of the strain. The more distressed the person becomes, the greater the strain on the weak organ, until it breaks down into a disease state. The key to pathogenesis is simply organ overload due to repeated activation.

HOMEOSTATIC FAILURE THEORY

The homeostatic failure theory was proposed by psychophysiologists in the 1960s and 1970s. It simply states that when aroused during stress, not all organs become equally aroused. Some organs will become more highly aroused and it will take longer to return to their baseline level of functioning. These organs ultimately become diseased from excessive stress (Sternbach, 1966). The key to pathogenesis is organ overload due to a failure to return to baseline levels of arousal quickly.

DISORDERS OF AROUSAL THEORY

One of the most recent theories to explain stress-related diseases is the "Disorders of Arousal" theory. Formulated by Everly and Benson (1989), this theory argues that if an individual is placed under a condition of excessive stress (excessively chronic or excessively high in magnitude), the stress arousal centers in the brain become hypersensitive. This hypersensitivity then leads to a condition where the stress response is too easily activated. This theory argues that all stress-related diseases are caused by excessively intense or excessively chronic arousal occurring within the brain and its effector systems. The target organs then undergo undue strain, that is, "wear and tear" and ultimately breakdown or become dysfunctional as a result.

HYPOKINETIC DISEASE THEORY

Postulated by cardiologists Kraus and Raab (1961), it states that stress is a normal preparatory mechanism that prepares one for physical exertion. It further notes that it is the failure to physically express the stress response that makes it pathogenic, not its mere presence. Thus, conceptually, stress that does not lead to physical activity is more likely to become pathogenic with time.

COPING WITH STRESS: STRESS MANAGMENT

While it is not the purpose of this text to provide an in-depth discussion of stress management techniques (see Mitchell and Bray, 1990; Girdano, Everly and Dusek, 1993), we will briefly highlight some key points.

A review of the myriad of coping strategies designed to manage stress while promoting health reveal four basic strategies:

1. Avoiding Stressors

2. Cognitive Reinterpretation

3. Reducing Arousal

4. Ventilating the Stress Response

AVOIDING STRESSORS

The most powerful means of coping with excessive stress is by avoiding the source of stress or at least reducing exposure to such stressors. Techniques such as problem solving and time management are useful interventions. Something as simple as avoiding or reducing stimulant consumption can be a very powerful means of reducing excessive stress. It is important to keep in mind that the higher the stimulant intake, for example, methylated xanthines, the less stable the nerve cells of the limbic system and sympathetic nervous system (Everly, 1989). Furthermore, the less stable those nerves become, the higher the risk for excessive or traumatic stress sequelae in emergency personnel, or anyone else.

COGNITIVE REINTERPRETATION / REFRAMING

While there can be little doubt that removing a stressor is the most powerful means of coping, many stressors simply don't lend themselves to such an intervention. It has been said that "Stressors, like beauty, reside in the eye of the beholder." Similarly, "There are no things good nor bad, but thinking makes them so, Horatio," said Shakespeare's Hamlet. Cognitive therapies for depression, stress, and anxiety disorders have proven to be powerful and perhaps the most flexible means of coping with stress (Beck and Emery, 1985; Ellis, 1973). Cognitive-based coping strategies would entail the realization that by changing one's appraisal or interpretation of any given stressful or traumatic event, the negative impact of that event upon psychological well-being can be dramatically mitigated. Cognitive coping techniques might include: finding a "silver lining" in a stressor, reinterpreting a "failure" into a "success," using the stressor to "learn a valuable lesson," viewing oneself as "lucky" that the stressor wasn't worse or perhaps seeing stress as a growth experience that "builds character."

REDUCING AROUSAL

The essence of stress is arousal, that is, "wear and tear" (Selye, 1974). The natural antithesis of stress, therefore, is what Herbert Benson has called the "relaxation response" (Benson, 1975). Research has demonstrated the health promoting effects of reducing stress arousal via the relaxation response (Benson, 1983; Benson, Alexander, Feldman, 1975; Everly and Benson, 1989; Everly, 1989). The relaxation response may be defined as a state of lowered metabolic functioning. It can be engendered through a myriad of techniques such as meditation, biofeedback, deep breathing, hypnosis and neuromuscular relaxation techniques (see Everly, 1989 for a review and step-by-step guidelines).

VENTILATING THE STRESS RESPONSE

The ventilation or expression of the stress response is another effective means of coping (Roemer and Borkovec, 1994). Two primary techniques come to mind in this category: catharsis and exercise. Kahn (1966) discovered that expressing emotions served to lower psychophysiologic indices of stress. Similarly, in valuable reviews, Pennebaker (1985, 1990) has shown that verbally expressing emotions helps resolve traumas and reduce stress. With regards to exercise, it has long been known to have health promoting and stress reducing effects when applied in a safe and reasonable manner (de Vries, 1981; Weller and Everly, 1985; Sinyor, et al., 1983). In fact, in their "hypokinetic disease" theory, Kraus and Raab (1961) argue that it is the failure to physically express the stress response that makes it pathogenic!

MALADAPTIVE COPING

Upon occasion individuals will suffer excessive stress and be compelled to use self-defeating, health-eroding coping tactics rather than those described above. Such maladaptive coping tactics include alcohol and drug "self-medication," anger, violence and social withdrawal. Their long-term effects of maladaptive coping will be to create problems above and beyond just stress alone.

SUMMARY

The purpose of this chapter has been to provide a detailed analysis of the human stress response. Let us highlight some of the main points.

1. "Stress" describes the nonspecific responses of the body to any demand placed on it, that is, the "wear and tear" on an individual. It acts as a link between given stressors and target organ symptoms.

2. Not all stress is bad. In fact, to a point, increased stress arousal motivates increased performance. However, as stress continues to increase beyond tolerable limits, dysfunctional consequences appear.

3. Stressors represent environmental events which either cause or set the stage for the stress response. Stressors can be categorized as either biogenic or psychosocial. Biogenic stressors are stimulants which cause stress via the biochemical actions they exert on the human body, for example: caffeine, nicotine, amphetamines and so forth. Psychosocial stressors are environmental events that set the stage for initiation of the stress response. It is one's appraisal or interpretation of these events as meaningful and potentially challenging, threatening or otherwise aversive which creates the stress response.

4. The cognitive-affective domain is crucial to most stress reactions. That is, one's interpretation of events as stressful causes emotional upheaval which results in a physiological stress response.

5. The physical stress response results from over-stimulation (cognitive-affective) of three major axes: 1) the neural axis, 2) the neuroendocrine axis and 3) the endocrine axis. Sustained activation of these axes eventually results in target organ symptoms of ill-health.

6. Coping may serve to mitigate the impact of the stress response on target organs. Coping represents environmental, behavioral or psychological efforts to deal with excessive stress and its correlates.

7. Excessive stress arousal coupled with unsuccessful coping strategies will inevitably result in target organ disease and / or dysfunction. Target organ systems that may eventually be affected by excessive stress include the neurological system, the cardiovascular system, the gastrointestinal system, the neuromuscular system, the immune system, the respiratory system and other body systems.

Chapter 3

PSYCHOTRAUMATOLOGY

INTRODUCTION

Post-traumatic stress reactions may consist of a wide variety of clinical presentations. Such presentations may include brief psychotic reactions, dissociative disorders, adjustment disorders, an acute stress disorder (APA 1994) and perhaps even borderline personality disorder (Herman and van der Kolk, 1987). Certainly the most widely known is Post-Traumatic Stress Disorder (PTSD) (APA, 1994).

Contrary to "historic" opinion, PTSD may be engendered by events other than combat. For example, PTSD may be engendered by:

- A serious accident

- The destruction of one's home or community

- Disasters

- Terrorism

- Natural catastrophes

- Rape

- Criminal victimization

- The threat of harm to oneself or others

- Experiencing / witnessing the actual physical harm to oneself or others (APA, 1987; WHO, 1992; APA, 1994).

Contrary to "popular" opinion, PTSD may occur at a shockingly high prevalence. For example:

- Nearly one-half of all patients admitted to urban trauma centers are likely to suffer from PTSD in addition to their physical trauma, while another 31% of these patients may suffer from a milder variant of post-traumatic stress reaction (Norman and Getek, 1988).

- The lifetime prevalence of PTSD is estimated to be 23.6% for those exposed to noncombat traumatic event (Breslau, et al., 1991).

- It has been estimated that there is an 80% prevalence of PTSD symptoms (any duration) among individuals who are victims of rape, physical injury, and threat of life combined (Kilpatrick, et al., 1989).

- It has been estimated that 16% of urban fire fighters may be at risk to develop PTSD sometimes during their careers (Corneil, 1992).

- Finally it is generally agreed that PTSD goes grossly underestimated because of significant rates of under reporting (Brett and Ostroff, 1985).

With regards to emergency services and disaster response personnel, the epidemiology of PTSD is further obscured by virtue of the fact that there exists an inherent resistance to acknowledge the presence of any psychological discord. Such an acknowledgment, it is feared may result in alienation by peers, the destruction of the personal illusion of invulnerability, and the raising of concerns over some unique weakness or vulnerability being heretofore undiagnosed.

PSYCHOTRAUMATOLOGY DEFINED

The term "psychotraumatology" was coined to define the study of psychological trauma. More specifically, psychotraumatology refers to the study of the processes and factors which:

1. Lie antecedent to psychological trauma

2. Exist concomitant with psychological trauma

3. Develop subsequent to psychological trauma
     (Everly and Lating, 1995; Everly, 1993a).

This term was chosen in contrast to the term "traumatology" (Donovan, 1991) due to the fact that traumatology is already generally accepted to denote the study of "wounds" and thus is already inextricably bound to the practice of physical medicine see Schnitt, 1993.

It is hoped that usage of the term psychotraumatology to define the endeavors enumerated above will reduce semantic confusion and will further assist in the development of the field (Everly and Lating, 1995).

As noted in the previous section, the most common and widely known variant of post-traumatic stress is PTSD. As such it plays an important role in the field of psychotraumatology.

PTSD - BACKGROUND

Post-Traumatic Stress Disorder (PTSD) is the most widely used of the official diagnostic terms employed to denote the psychological sequelae that exist in response to a traumatic event. Nevertheless, the phenomenon was acknowledged to be in existence far before the advent of official diagnostic taxonomies.

Well-documented post-traumatic stress syndromes date back as far as 1666 as a result of the Great Fire of London (Trimble, 1981). But historical records reflective of post-traumatic stress are most commonly found in the archives of war. Army surgeons used terms such as "shell shock," "soldiers heart" and "post-traumatic neurosis" to describe combat related post-traumatic stress. Medical records dating back to the Civil War document the existence of combat related post-traumatic stress. World War I, World War II and the Korean War all added their contributions to the history of post-traumatic stress. Yet is was the Vietnam conflict that ultimately forced modern psychiatry to officially recognize post-traumatic stress as a formal psychiatric disorder. This disorder was named Post-Traumatic Stress Disorder (APA, 1980, 1987, 1994).

As noted earlier in this chapter, PTSD is now universally recognized as a potential response to any form of traumatic event, not just combat. Let's review its nature.

PTSD (309.81) DIAGNOSTIC CRITERIA

PTSD was first officially recognized in the psychiatric taxonomy of the American Psychiatric Association's Diagnostic and Statistical Manual of Mental Disorders (DSM) in the year 1980 (APA, 1980). PTSD has been retained in the subsequent editions of the DSM, specifically DSM-III-R (APA, 1987) and DSM - IV (APA, 1994). Lets examine the four specific diagnostic criteria: the traumatic event, re-experiencing the event, avoidance and numbing reactions and symptoms of increased arousal.

TRAUMATIC EVENT

The sine qua non of the PTSD diagnosis is the existence of a traumatic stressor. Exactly what constitutes a traumatic event may be open to some debate; however, according to the DSM-III-R (APA, 1987, p.250), a traumatic event may be defined as "an event outside the range of usual human experience and that would be markedly distressing to almost everyone."

The DSM-IV (APA, 1994) denotes a traumatic event as "... directly experiencing or witnessing actual or threatened death or serious injury or experiencing a threat to one's own physical integrity or the physical integrity of someone else." In addition, the DSM-IV mandates that the individual's response must be characterized by fear, helplessness or horror. Thus, the DSM-IV has somewhat restricted the definition of a traumatic event and personalized it more so than the DSM-III-R. DSM-IV has also chosen to underscore the critical role that perception or interpretation actually plays in the determination of a traumatic event. A weakness inherent in the DSM IV is the failure to recognize environmental / ecological disasters or catastrophes that don't actually represent a direct threat to human life.

TABLE 3.1

MAJOR FACTORS PREDICTING PSYCHOLOGICAL TRAUMA

- Actual severe physical injury, disfigurement, dismemberment or disability
- Fear of severe physical injury, disfigurement, dismemberment or disability
- Fear of losing one's life
- Torture
- Fear of torture
- Sexual assault
- Fear of sexual assault
- Watching someone else die, experience extreme pain or physical inury
- A belief of failed resonsibility that results in harm to others
- The belief of unjustified survival or escape / avoidance from harm
- The belief of betrayal
- Death or injury to children
- The violation or contradiction of a "core belief" or "critical expectation" (e.g., God, friendship, loyalty, fairness, justice, fidelity or competence)
- Shame associated with factors other than those listed above
- Guilt associated with factors other than those listed above
- War
- Environmental or ecological catastrophe

Note: fatigue, dehydration, extreme heat, extreme cold or certain chemical substances may be presumed to augment the risk of subsequent psychological traumatization from the aforementioned factors

What may be a more realistic definition of a traumatic event comes from the World Health Organization in its International Classification of Disease taxonomy, 10th edition (WHO, 1992). A traumatic event is defined therein as "exceptionally threatening or catastrophic." The ICD-10 goes on to note that predisposing factors may serve to lower the threshold for PTSD but are neither necessary nor sufficient etiologically. Finally, the ICD-10 notes that PTSD may be so chronic as to transition into an enduring personality change as a direct result of the traumatic stressor, a "trauma personality" of sorts.

Table 3.1 enumerated some of the major factors which predict psychological trauma.

RE-EXPERIENCING THE EVENT

The key element of this cluster of symptoms is that the individual experiences intrusive recollective ideation pertaining to the traumatic event. The re-experiencing may take the form of "recurrent and intrusive distressing recollections of the event," "recurrent and distressing dreams of the event, " "a sense of reliving the experience," "intense psychological distress at exposure to ... cues that symbolize or resemble ... the event" or "physiological reactivity on exposure to ... cues ... of the traumatic event" (APA, 1994, p. 428).

AVOIDANCE AND NUMBING REACTIONS

The key element of this cluster of symptoms is that the individual persistently avoids things that are associated with the traumatic event. Numbing of general responsiveness may also be noted.

SYMPTOMS OF INCREASED AROUSAL

The key element of this symptom cluster is the presence of symptoms of increased arousal, or stress, that were not present prior to the traumatic event. Such symptoms might include sleep disturbances, irritability, anger, rage, hypervigilance or exaggerated startle response.

ACUTE STRESS DISORDER (308.3) DIAGNOSTIC CRITERIA

It should be noted that the diagnosis of PTSD cannot be made until the symptoms have persisted for more than one month. The diagnosis of acute stress disorder (308.3) fills the temporal gap from stressor through the subsequent four weeks (APA, 1994). Acute Stress Disorder first appeared in the American taxonomy in the DSM-IV (APA, 1994).

The essential feature of the diagnosis is the development of the characteristic stress, dissociative, recollective ideational and numbing /withdrawal symptom complex as seen in PTSD, but this disorder may be diagnosed as soon as the symptoms have persisted for at least two days. The duration of the symptoms can, obviously, persist for only one month as this is when the PTSD diagnosis becomes relevant.

AN INTEGRATED THEORY OF POST-TRAUMATIC STRESS

In an effort to add greater overall phenomenological significance to the aforementioned diagnostic criteria of PTSD, as well as to attempt to provide greater clinical insight into the disorder, Everly (1993a and 1993b) has constructed a model which integrates the various constituents of the disorder itself. This model is presented in Figure 3.1.

Figure 3.1 demonstrates how the various components of post-traumatic stress may relate to one another (adapted from Everly, 1993a, 1993b).

Let us briefly examine this interpretation of post-traumatic stress.

As noted earlier, the sine qua non of PTSD is the traumatic event itself, that is, some aversive event outside the usual realm of human experience which overwhelms the victim's coping and ego defense mechanisms. As emphasized by Pierre Janet in the late 1800s, to some degree the psychic toxicity of the traumatic event is either augmented or mitigated by the psychological appraisal, or interpretation, of the traumatic event itself by the victim. This is a critical aspect of the model for clinicians to note for it is the alteration of this element that is so important in the recovery process (Everly, 1994).

Phenomenologically, close examination of the model in Figure 3.1 reveals, the intrusive memories of the trauma (which may occur hourly, daily, etc.) combined with excessively chronic and intense levels of arousal (Everly, 1990) constitute the key elements of PTSD. The third major symptom cluster is seen as secondary and reactive to the intrusive memories and arousal. That is, the withdrawal symptoms are seen as resulting from and therefore contingent upon the severity of the interaction between the intrusive recollections and arousal.

Finally, the model (Figure 3.1) extends the symptoms beyond that of merely PTSD and sees other disorders as being potentially trauma related. PTSD, some panic attacks, amnestic syndromes and some substance abuse seem likely candidates for trauma reactive syndromes. Likewise borderline

FIGURE 3.1

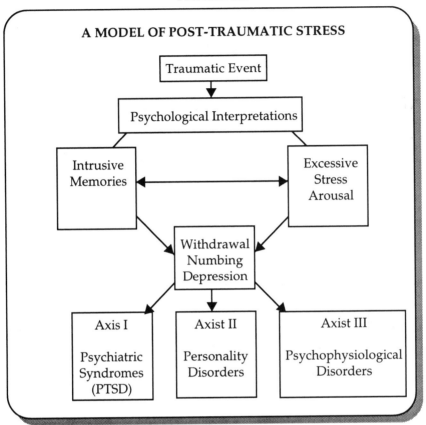

A MODEL OF POST-TRAUMATIC STRESS

Traumatic Event

Psychological Interpretations

Intrusive Memories

Excessive Stress Arousal

Withdrawal Numbing Depression

Axis I

Psychiatric Syndromes (PTSD)

Axist II

Personality Disorders

Axist III

Psychophysiological Disorders

and "multiple" personality disorders may be manifestations of traumatic stress. Trauma may also be capable of creating almost any psychophysiologic reaction or disorder.

Early diagnosis and treatment of PTSD is a desirable goal since the proper treatment depends heavily on a precise diagnosis of the condition. Table 3.2 provides a list of useful diagnostic signs and symptoms of PTSD. These are considered "early warning" signals of the potential for PTSD.

As pointed out in the preceding paragraphs, PTSD is not the only psychiatric manifestation of post-traumatic stress. There will be many victims who will suffer the ill effects of post-traumatic stress yet will not meet all of the diagnostic criteria for PTSD. Table 3.3 lists a variety of potential post-traumatic stress syndromes.

Finally, a wide variety of stress related (psychophysiologic) physical illnesses, for example, acute hypertension, inflammation of the gastrointestinal system, tension headaches, migraine headaches and so forth, may arise as a result of psychological traumatization. Thus, coordination between medical therapeutics and psychotherapeutics is important.

TABLE 3.2

EARLY INDICATIONS OF POSSIBLE PTSD

- Flashbacks

- Traumatic dreams

- Memory disturbances

- Self medication (e.g., alcohol abuse)

- Anger, irritability, hostility which is difficult to control

- Persistent depression, withdrawal

- A "dazed" or "numb" appearance

- Panic attacks

- Phobia formation

TWO FACTOR THEORY OF POST-TRAUMATIC STRESS

While it is clearly important to recognize and understand the signs and symptoms of PTSD diagnostically, these signs and symptoms represent but the "skeleton" of the disorder. In order to be better able to prevent and treat this disorder, we must learn to understand it on a far "deeper" level. We must search for its foundation or core if we are to best target our interventions.

In a phenomenological analysis of PTSD, Everly (1993a, 1993b) has postulated that this disorder actually consists of a two-factor disposition: 1) neurological hypersensitivity and 2) psychological hypersensitivity.

TABLE 3.3

POTENTIAL POST-TRAUMATIC STRESS SYNDROMES

- Acute stress disorder

- Post-Traumatic Stress Disorder

- Complex partial seizures

- Adjustment disorder

- Depression

- Self medicating or substance abuse

- Personality disorders (borderline, antisocial, multiple personality, schizotypal)

- Panic syndromes

- Irratic work-related behavior

- Memory dysfunction without traumatic amnesia

- Amnestic syndromes regarding traumatization

- Virtually any psychophysiologic medical disorder

FACTOR ONE: NEUROLOGIC HYPERSENSITIVITY

Traumatic stress appears to represent a cascade of neural and endocrine events that are capable of altering normal neurologic processing. For example, the physiology of traumatic stress not only results in higher than normal levels of available neurotransmitters, but it may also bias, or predispose, otherwise normal neurons toward a condition of phasic hyperactivity or tonic hyperactivity. This condition has been referred to as neurologic hypersensitivity.

The neurological hypersensitivity just described as being inherent in PTSD is believed to consist of a lowered depolarization threshold within the nerve cells of the amygdala and hippocampal regions (Everly, 1989; Everly and Benson, 1989). There appear to be several mechanisms which potentially underlie the neurologic hypersensitivity in PTSD: 1) a functionally excessive amount of excitatory neurotransmitters available at the synaptic cleft, 2) a functional paucity of the inhibitory neurotransmitter gamma-aminobutyric acid (GABA) and 3) micromorphological changes to the neurons themselves that serve to dysfunctionally facilitate neural excitation, for example, an increase in dendritic spine and a decrease in alpha-2 inhibitory receptors (see Everly, 1993a and 1993b for reviews of primary research). Post (1992) has even postulated that the biochemistry of extreme stress may be able to alter genetic transcription factors so as to create a condition of genetically based neurologic hypersensitivity that may endure indefinitely. Finally, Everly and Horton (1989) found evidence of an immediate to short-term memory consolidation dysfunction in PTSD patients. This dysfunction was in no way content specific to any particular event, task or theme. It may be that the biochemistry of extreme stress can not only create a status of neurologic hypersensitivity, but it may also be capable of destroying brain cells via some excitotoxic mechanism (Sapolsky, Krey, McEwen, 1984; Olney, 1978; McGeer and McGeer, 1988).

Resolution of the neurologic hypersensitivity depends upon lowering the levels of arousal experienced by the individual. Medications and the "relaxation response" have proven useful in this regard.

FACTOR TWO: PSYCHOLOGICAL HYPERSENSITIVITY

The psychological hypersensitivity inherent in PTSD appears to arise from the fact that some aspect of the victim's worldview, that is, "Weltanschauung," has been contradicted. Thus the trauma represents a piece of the puzzle of life that simply refuses to be normally integrated into the overall picture. It was Abraham Maslow (1970) who told us that other than the need for physical survival, the need for "safety" was the most powerful human need of all. In order to make a complex and otherwise indefinable world "safer," humans tend to construct overarching schematic worldviews (ideologies, "Weltanschauung") which help explain the human experience. When something terribly aversive happens that doesn't fit into the scheme, (e.g., a trauma) the effect is post-traumatic stress. The world is no longer safe and will not be safe until some understanding and predictability can be brought to the world again (Everly, 1993a, 1993b, 1994).

Resolution of the psychological hypersensitivity appears contingent upon following one of three possible therapeutic tacts:

1. Integrating the trauma into the existing worldview

2. Creating an "exception to the rule" parallel worldview

3. Abolishing the old worldview and creating a new worldview (Everly, 1994).

PTSD and related post-traumatic stress syndromes have the potential to literally consume an individual's life. The reiterative nature of the disorder is nothing less than a potentially never ending effort to make sense out of the world in the face of traumatic evidence that one's worldview is inadequate and therefore no longer protective. Horowitz (1976) refers to the reiterative quality of post-traumatic stress as the "completion tendency." It seems reasonable that any therapeutic formulation should be directed toward both "factors" in the post-traumatic phenomenon.

A PROGRAM FOR PSYCHOLOGICAL TRAUMA IMMUNIZATION

In the years since the "official" recognition of PTSD and related post-trauma syndromes, we have made tremendous advances in our ability to understand and treat these problems. No longer does PTSD mean an end to a career. Now, the overwhelming majority of individuals who develop PTSD can return to their chosen line of work, often very rapidly. Many individuals never have to leave active duty even temporarily. The key to effective treatment is early aggressive treatment by a knowledgeable psychotraumatologist, (i.e., a mental health professional) who has received specialized training in psychological trauma and who specializes in its treatment.

Having said those words about treatment, however, there exists a compelling logic to aggressively pursue the prevention of PTSD and related syndromes. Peer counseling, crisis intervention, defusings and debriefings are designed to prevent or mitigate PTSD and other stress related syndromes. These techniques can now be structured into a form of "psychological trauma immunization program." Listed below is one approach to such a program.

ORIENTATIONS

Prior to becoming "operational," all recruits, trainees, volunteers and other personnel should receive an orientation, or indoctrination, to the psychological demands or aspects of their "career." Any orientation should include videos, sound tracks and photographs that orient the trainee to the "sights and sounds" of the endeavor they are about to pursue. A basic orientation to stress, anxiety, stress-related physical illness, signs and symptoms of excessive stress and psychological trauma should be mandatory. A brief review of PTSD should be included. Trainees should also receive basic training in personal stress management techniques as reviewed in chapter 2. In fact, any of the adaptive, health promoting stress management techniques briefly enumerated in chapter 2 can be of great value in diminishing the risk of excessive stress before, during and after highly stressful incidents and even disasters.

All responders should be briefed in the staging area before deployment at a disaster scene. They need to be oriented to the nature of the specific disaster facing them. Videos and photographs may be very helpful during the incident orientation. They should also be reminded of signs and symptoms of excessive stress and trauma. This tactic may obviously be impossible if there is no opportunity to prepare prior to tactical engagement. This system is recommended, however, in large-scale disasters.

ON-SCENE CRISIS INTERVENTION

All emergency service workers should be encouraged to use stress management techniques as reviewed in chapter 2 as ongoing means of coping with the stress of high demand shifts, prolonged incidents, or major disaster situations. Every effort should be made to assure that disaster workers are properly fed, sheltered, rested and rotated from difficult tasks to less difficult tasks. They should be regularly monitored for both the physiological and psychological effects of traumatic stress. When necessary, on-scene support personnel should be available to provide quick one-on-one consultations to reduce the harmful effects of stress (Mitchell and Bray, 1990). On-scene support personnel may consist of mental health professionals, peer support personnel or teams of both. Refer to chapter 6 on acute crisis intervention for a detailed discussion.

AFTERCARE

Defusings and CISD are useful following the critical incident or disaster. We believe that early cathartic intervention may impact some level of understanding or at least provide some normalization and may assist in re-establishing the viability of one's worldview following a trauma. CISD and defusings are designed to do just that. Early intervention tends to reduce subsequent arousal and the tendency to "concretize" the trauma, as will be discussed later in this book. In addition, basic stress management techniques can be effectively applied as emergency service personnel recover from a stressful shift or decompress from a disaster scene. Again the fundamentals of personal stress management will prove of great value.

These same techniques can be applied in the context of family support for all family members. Formal family support services can be very valuable. Both formal and informal family support groups may be considered. Some form of formal or informal follow ups are recommended for personnel if such a need is assessed. Referral to professional mental health services always remains an option. Table 3.4 provides a summary of a standard program that could be used for "psychological trauma immunization."

TABLE 3.4

BASIC OUTLINE FOR PSYCHOLOGICAL TRAUMA IMMUNIZATION

1. Pre-service orientation
   a. Prior to active duty
   b. Career in-service education
   c. Briefing prior to deployment at a specific incident

2. On-scene support
   a. Mental health support
   b. Peer support
   c. Rest, food, altering assignments and limiting exposure
   d. Brief support for individuals who are obviously distressed
   e. Advice to supervisors when necessary
   f. Limited support to actual victims, family members and bystanders as required

3. After care
   a. Defusings
   b. Debriefings
   c. Family interventions
   d. Follow up
   e. Referral options

SUMMARY

In this chapter, we have discussed the most severe variation of human stress, that is, post-traumatic stress. The term psychotraumatology was introduced and defined as the study of psychological factors antecedent to, concomitant with or subsequent to trauma. The chapter focused upon the official variations of post-traumatic stress, that is, Post-Traumatic Stress Disorder (PTSD) and acute stress disorder from the perspectives of the DSM-IV and the ICD-10. Recent advances in the nature, prevention and treatment of PTSD were briefly discussed in this chapter. These advances have the potential, we believe, to reduce the long-term adversity that this disorder may cause within the emergency service and disaster response professions.

It seems appropriate at this juncture to reiterate the point made early in chapter 2. CISM exists because of a generally perceived need. That need is recognized as the fact that emergency service personnel are at risk for the development of disorders of excessive stress, especially PTSD. As Leonardo da Vinci said "First study the science, then practice the art." In the final analysis, effective prevention and intervention programs are based upon an analysis of understanding of the problem being faced. Although admittedly not comprehensive, chapters 2 and 3 were designed to provide an initial lesson in "the science" of stress and trauma so as to allow a more potent "practice" of "the art" of CISM. These chapters should be seen as introductions, or overviews, rather than definitive reviews. Thus more exploration of "the science" may be desired before engaging in CISM interventions.

Chapter 4

HISTORY AND BACKGROUND OF CRITICAL INCIDENT STRESS MANAGEMENT SERVICES

INTRODUCTION

Few of life's most important pursuits are fully meaningful without an understanding of the historical roots which made them possible. There is great value in the theories and experiences of people who worked in both the distant and immediate past. Much can be learned from a review of the mistakes and successes of the past. In fact, the lessons from the past are vital in assuring competency in present day services in the relatively new field of Critical Incident Stress Management (CISM). Learning from the past can guide CISM teams in taking the right steps to help stressed emergency personnel. In addition, following the course of action of past experts can save us time and assure superior services by eliminating unnecessary guesswork. A thorough theoretical and historical foundation can serve as a protection against serious mistakes in the provision of CISM and CISD services.

The following chapter will review the basic historical and theoretical foundations of CISM as well as the more focused component of CISM which is Critical Incident Stress Debriefing (CISD).

MAJOR INFLUENCES IN CRITICAL INCIDENT STRESS MANAGEMENT

Without "critical incidents," (those significant turning point events, traumas, disasters, which have occurred throughout history), the field of Critical Incident Stress Management and its well-known intervention, "Critical Incident Stress Debriefing," would never have been developed. Human beings tend to be reactive to situations and not necessarily proactive in their approach to managing human problems. History is filled with instances of catastrophic events which have changed peoples' thinking and behaviors. When people suffered great disruption and pain in their lives, they frequently attempted to change the way they did things. Tragedies have frequently been the source of new ideas, discoveries and new technologies. The current knowledge base in the fields of traumatic stress, critical incident stress management and debriefings had its origins in the conflicts and turmoil of the past.

Four major influences, which set the foundation for Critical Incident Stress Management can be identified. They are:

- Warfare

- Disasters

- Law enforcement psychology

- Emergency medical, fire and hospital services

Each of these fields of human experience, over the course of thousands of years, gradually built a base on which the current concepts of traumatic stress as well as the present day support services could stand. From our past we draw understanding, a drive to make things better now and a hope for a healthier future.

THE INFLUENCE OF WARFARE

Stress has been part of the human experience since the very beginning of time. No one would survive without it. At best, it is a creative, driving force which can drive people to survive, to find great happiness and to achieve incredible accomplishments. At worst, it is a destructive force which can deprive people of joy, health, sanity, relationships with others and even life itself (Selye, 1980).

Among the many stressors which affect the human race, few can be imagined which are as destructive and psychologically debilitating as warfare. Few who have experienced its terror would disagree with General William T. Sherman's famous quote during the American Civil War - "All war is hell" (Holmes, 1985). War is a dramatic concentration of the most extremely powerful, destructive stressors known to humanity. With few exceptions virtually every generation has experienced the trauma of war. The victims of war are practically uncountable. War psychologically scars almost all who participate in it and even most who observe it from afar. The stress of war has the power to change individuals and entire communities forever.

Combat stress has been observed and recorded in military forces since about 603 B.C. Most armies are familiar with its harmful effects. During the American Civil War, for example, literally thousands of soldiers suffered from combat stress and many were seriously incapacitated by its effects. In the Napoleanic war, Lieutenant-General Sir Thomas Picton, once wrote to complain about his own combat stress to Lord Wellington, who commanded the British forces at Waterloo. He stated the following:

> "My lord, I must give up. I am grown so nervous that
> when there is any service to be done it works upon my
> mind so that it is impossible for me to sleep at nights.
> I cannot possibly stand it, and I shall be forced to retire."
> (Holmes, 1985).

Unfortunately, little was understood about traumatic stress and almost nothing was known about its treatment. In fact, in all wars prior to World War I, stress reactions were left untreated. Instead of treatment, many soldiers were ridiculed, imprisoned or even killed by their fellow warriors who believed that they were insane, lacking moral fiber, cowards or traitors (Holmes, 1985; Nakanomiya, 1975).

Warfare changed dramatically between the time of the American Civil War and World War I. Both the technology and tactics of waging war had changed. As a result, a widespread insidious enemy became more apparent in twentieth century warfare. For the first time in history, huge numbers of psychiatric casualties were encountered during battles. The Civil War experience of psychiatric casualties was between 2.34 and 3.3 per 1,000 troops. In World War I, the incidence of psychiatric casualties rose to 4.0 per 1,000 troops. Some combat units with sustained combat experience encountered even higher levels of psychiatric casualties (Holmes, 1985).

A successful army had to be kept up to relatively full strength to accomplish its mission. It was important to restore wounded and "shell shocked" soldiers to front line duties as soon as possible. In World War I, new techniques were being tested to assure a greater return of experienced soldiers to the front. This included better medical services as well as psychiatric interventions. "Shell shocked" (stressed) soldiers were being treated in field hospitals near the front lines instead of in remote hospitals far from the front. About 65 percent of those who received immediate treatment for stress were able to return to combat. If treatment for stress was delayed and given only when the soldiers reached a rear hospital, a smaller percentage of them were able to return to combat (approximately 40 percent) (Holmes, 1985; Brown and Williams, 1918; Salmon, 1919).

Most of the support services in the First World War were individual, one-on-one psychiatric based interventions. Little thought and no action was given to group interventions. There was no formal program of peer support. The same situation prevailed in the early to middle stages of World War II. Nearly 10 percent of all battle casualties in the Second World War were psychiatric in nature. Some units, such as the US 2nd Armored Division which experienced 44 days of sustained combat operations in Italy in 1944, sustained psychiatric casualty rates as high as 54 percent (Holmes, 1985; Appel, Beebe and Hilger, 1946).

By mid 1944, around the time of the D-Day invasion by the allies, the military had learned that the application of certain basic psychiatric intervention principles had an enormous impact on lowering the rate of combat stress casualties. Combat stress casualties dropped from a rate of 20 percent at the beginning of the invasion of Europe in June and July, 1944 to 8 percent in April and May of 1945 (Holmes, 1985; Appel, et al., 1946). Those principles still are applied in current military stress relief operations and are essential in today's "on-scene" support services and in certain aspects of defusings, demobilizations and debriefings with emergency personnel. The principles are:

- *Immediacy*

- *Proximity*

- *Expectancy*

Immediacy means, of course, that support services for the distressed should be applied as quickly as possible after the traumatic event. Proximity means that the intervention should take place as close to the scene as is safe and controlled. Removal to rear areas should only be utilized when the circumstances warrant it or when an individual's distress is so severe that effective intervention near the field of operations is not possible. Expectancy is defined as the expectations which are set up in the affected person's mind by the suggestions of the helper. When a person believes that they will recover and that they will be able to resume their normal duties and their usual life's activities when the stress reaction lessens, they are more likely to work toward those goals (Appel, et al., 1946; Noy, 1991).

The most rudimentary of debriefings were performed on the beaches of Normandy during the D-Day operations on June 6, 1944. These services were not named "debriefings" nor were they very structured. In fact, the neuropsychiatrist who provided "psychiatric first aid" on Utah beach, Dr. Glenn Srodes, mostly sat with groups of soldiers and let them talk about the traumatic experiences they had during the invasion. He found that those who were afforded this opportunity to ventilate were more alert and ready for battle the next day. The word quickly spread to other psychiatric aid stations during the remaining year and a half of the war and other psychiatrists tried these loose knit debriefings. Both those receiving the services and those supplying it felt that these unstructured sessions were quite helpful (staff, Pittsburgh Post Gazette, 1984). Units not receiving such help had many more combat stress casualties. The greater the delay of intervention, the less likely it was that soldiers would return to military duties (Appel, 1966).

Until the late 1980s little changed in the interventions applied by psychiatrists assigned to combat units. Psychological interventions, despite the apparent successes of small group processes which were utilized at the end of World War II and during the Korean conflict, remained essentially a one-on-one process. For example, in the late 1970s and early 1980s, the US Navy developed the "SPRINT" program. The initials stood for "Special Psychiatric Rapid Intervention Team." Several teams were established at naval hospitals and the teams would respond to special requests when traumatic events occurred which had a negative effect on naval personnel. The teams were led by psychiatrists and used psychiatric care workers to assist the psychiatrists. They were helpful, but they maintained a strong emphasis on one-on-one contact. It should be noted that during the last five years the teams have changed their name to *Special Personnel Rapid Intervention Teams* and have trained in the CISD model, which they now utilize to alleviate traumatic stress in groups of naval personnel.

Although some sporadic group interventions were used with US combat forces in Vietnam, group interventions were not formalized until after the Vietnam war. Even then, they were formalized in the non-military arena (Mitchell, 1983). The Israeli army, on the other hand, did employ a more structured form of group interventions with its troops. In addition, the use of peers to support other soldiers was initiated during the war in Lebanon in 1982. Of the 600 soldiers who were evacuated from the front with psychiatric distress problems, only 60 required further treatment and none required long term care. Overall, the use of support services for combat troops reduced the incidence of psychiatric disturbance in Israeli combat forces by 60 percent (Holmes, 1985; Breznitz, 1980; Solomon, 1986).

The Israeli military is also credited with the first serious research projects on the effects of psychological first aid and the use of group support interventions on combat personnel. Their well-managed studies and clearly documented results have laid a solid foundation on which to build the Critical Incident Stress Management movement and the CISD process which is such a major aspect of CISM (Pugliese, 1988).

DISASTERS' INFLUENCE ON CISM

Disasters have been occurring throughout recorded history. Their highly negative psychological impact on their victims had been assumed for centuries although no formal studies of disasters took place until the twentieth century. As was the case in warfare, before the twentieth century, psychological casualties were essentially left untreated. Little was known about the psychological impact of disasters on individuals or the community and psychiatry was still a relatively new science which had not, at the time, developed any effective means to intervene in a disaster (Raphael, 1986).

A catastrophic occurrence in 1943 set the stage for the development of practically all of the crisis intervention theory and practice which has evolved since that time. The Coconut Grove night club fire in Boston, Massachusetts killed over 400 people. It had the effect of significantly improving the fire protection codes in the United States and in many other countries throughout the world. The disaster also left major scars on the psyche of the American population as well as the survivors and the bereaved. Mental health professionals scrambled to make sense out of chaos and disorder. The work of Dr. Gerald Caplan and, most especially, Dr. Eric Lindemann with the survivors and the bereaved became a keystone to present day crisis intervention principles and it continues to serve as a core theoretical and practice component of Critical Incident Stress Management and Critical Incident Stress Debriefing (Caplan, 1964; Lindemann, 1944).

The emphasis of the crisis intervention work of Caplan, Lindemann and other theoreticians and practitioners was on the actual victims of disastrous events. Disaster literature and research reports are, in fact, filled with information on the plight of the victims (Cohen and Ahearn, 1980; Gist and Lubin, 1989). Little thought was given to the stress encountered by police officers, ambulance personnel, fire fighters, nurses, dispatchers, physicians and disaster workers. There was an assumption that training alone was sufficient to overcome the stress of the disaster. For example, in a 1954 document, *Psychological First Aid in Community Disaster*, which was prepared by the American Psychiatric Association's Committee on Civil Defense, disaster workers were warned that disasters could have some negative psychological effects upon them. The same warning was presented in the 1964 revised edition of that document. In the next paragraph, however, the text quickly dismissed or attempted to down play this possibility by stating, "The training you receive as a disaster worker will in itself protect you somewhat in time of stress." (American Psychiatric Association, 1964).

An extensive review of disaster literature between 1900 and 1975 revealed extremely little information on the effects of disasters on the workers. Beginning in 1975, a few hints about the potential negative impacts of disaster work on emergency personnel appear in the literature (Kliman, 1975). Dr. Beverly Raphael of Sydney, Australia was another rare exception to the significant lack of work in support of emergency personnel. She applied stress debriefing techniques in the late 1970s (Raphael, 1986).

Two very tragic and highly publicized disasters brought the reality of the negative psychological effects of disasters on both the victims and the emergency personnel into focus. The first event was the crash of a Pacific Southwest Airlines plane into a residential neighborhood in San Diego in 1978. The second event was another plane crash, American Airlines Flight 191, which crashed near Chicago in 1979. These two events accelerated the trend to recognize and attempt to intervene against the stress encountered by emergency personnel. In both events field personnel as well as hospital staff experienced significant stress reactions for as long as a year after the events (Graham, 1981a, 1981b; Mitchell, 1982; Duffy, 1979; Freeman, 1979).

It was yet another air crash disaster which motivated the finalization of the development of the CISD process. On January 13, 1982, Air Florida Flight 90 failed to achieve altitude after lifting off from National Airport in Washington, DC. The aircraft slammed into the Fourteenth Street bridge over the Potomac River and 76 people lost their lives. No immediate support was provided to the emergency personnel. Within three weeks, significant stress symptoms began to appear and personnel were asking for some help. A decision was made to provide a CISD. The debriefing process was still considered an experimental intervention. They had been applied on much less intense events for about eight years before the Air Florida incident (Mitchell, 1976, 1981). The Washington air crash was the first application of a formal CISD on a large scale incident. Emergency personnel in attendance included fire fighters, police officers, paramedics and disaster managers. The feedback from the personnel was quite positive. Personnel involved in the debriefing reported that the process was very helpful to them (Mitchell, 1982).

The CISD has been utilized on numerous disasters since the Air Florida crash. Some of the more notable disasters in which debriefings were provided include:

Barneveld, Wisconsin - Tornado, 1984

Mexico City - Earthquake, 1985

Cerritos, California - Air Disaster, 1986

El Salvador - Earthquake, 1986

Palm Bay, Florida - Mass Shooting, 1987

Bridgeport, Connecticut - Building Collapse, 1987

San Francisco, California - Earthquake, 1989

New York - Fire Bombing, 1990

Charleston, South Carolina - Hurricane Hugo, 1990

Persian Gulf - Desert Storm, 1991

Los Angeles, California - Civil Riots, 1992

Miami, Florida - Hurricane Andrew, 1992

Hawaii - Hurricane Iniki, 1992

Kuwait - Combat, 1992

Yugoslavia - Civil War, 1993

Rwanda - Mass Murder, 1994

Japan - Earthquake, 1995

Oklahoma City, Oklahoma - Terrorist Bombing, 1995

LAW ENFORCEMENT AND CISD

Although structured police services have been in operation in Europe for almost 2,000 years and in the United States for about 350, behavioral science applications to policing did not take place until the beginning of the twentieth century. The very first behavioral applications to police work came in the form of psychological evaluations of police recruits (Reese, 1987). This application was important because it laid the foundation for understanding the personality of emergency personnel, specifically the police officer.

It did not take long to recognize that police work was extremely stressful. In the mid 1930s, for example, the mayor of New York City, Fiorello H. La Guardia, ordered a study of police officer suicides. The suicide rate in police officers was found to be considerably higher than the rate for suicides in the average population (Heinman, 1975). Unfortunately, recognizing a stress problem is insufficient in and of itself to solve the problem. The absence of an easily applied intervention program to assist stressed law enforcement personnel only seemed to enhance the further neglect of the problem. In 1976 two police stress researchers stated, "There are few experts in the job stress field and even fewer in the area of stress in policing ...." (Kroes and Hurrell, 1976, p. iii). The majority of the research in the field of police stress was performed during the last two decades. The development of police stress intervention strategies came about only during the last few years (Reese, 1987).

Helping strategies for police officers including counseling services, spouse support programs, marriage and family counseling, stress inoculation training and other police stress education projects were pioneered in the late 1960s. Dr. Martin Reiser was the first full time law enforcement psychologist. He was hired in 1968 by the Los Angeles, California police department. San Jose, California soon hired Dr. Michael Roberts as their police psychologist. Other cities such as New York followed the lead of Los Angeles and San Jose. By the early 1980s the number of active police psychologists in the United States had climbed into the hundreds. In 1980, the FBI added a psychological services program to provide counseling to its employees (Reese, 1987).

The first "police stress" programs, which were developed in the mid 1970s, were offshoots of the earlier alcohol counseling programs of the 1950s and 1960s. Police stress programs, in fact, were modeled on the Alcohol Anonymous programs. They were often peer support type programs and can be credited with establishing the use of peers in support services for emergency personnel.

A form of debriefing was offered to police officers who had worked at the 1979 crash of American Airlines Flight 191 outside of Chicago. The process was described as helpful by the police officers who attended. Unfortunately, the literature available did not describe the process in sufficient detail (Wagner, 1979, a-b). It was not until 1983 that the debriefing process in use today was described in sufficient detail to serve as a model for the development of debriefing teams (Mitchell, 1983, 1991).

Today police departments are more frequently using the CISD process and many police officers are joining the CISD teams throughout the United States and in other nations. In addition, the work of many police psychologists and the leadership of the FBI's behavioral sciences services unit and has contributed to a wider acceptance of numerous support functions such as pre-incident stress education, family and marriage counseling, post shooting trauma teams and individual counseling (Reese, 1991).

HOSPITAL, EMERGENCY MEDICAL, AND FIRE INFLUENCES

The last major influence on the development of the CISD process and the many services which have developed into the Critical Incident Stress Management program was, in fact, not a single group but a combined set of influences. Stress management work in hospitals, emergency medical services programs and fire departments set the final segment of the CISD foundation. All of the influences were interdependent upon one another. In fact, the final stages of development of the process could never have been accomplished without the history which had preceded in the military, law enforcement and disaster fields.

The Shock Trauma Center in Baltimore was the first major medical trauma facility known to provide support services to its trauma staff. Marge Epperson-Sebour, a social worker in the family services section, was concerned with the turnover of experienced staff nurses. She developed a series of educational stress management and crisis intervention programs in the mid 1970s. There was a remarkable decrease in the turn over rate among the trauma nurses and other staff (Epperson, 1977; Epperson-Sebour, 1985). Some of the theory and applications developed at the Maryland Shock Trauma Center became a core for the eventual development of the CISD process in use today.

Nancy Graham's articles on stress and burnout in the emergency medical services field were some of the very first to describe the stress problems being encountered by emergency medical technicians and paramedics (Graham, 1981a,b). But the United States was not the only place in which there was interest in the field of stress effects on emergency workers. Dr. Tony Taylor of New Zealand was interested in the effects of body handling on disaster workers after an air crash in Antarctica (Taylor and Frazer, 1982). Dr. Robyn Robinson in Melbourne, Australia and Dr. Beverly Raphael in Sydney, Australia were working with fire, emergency medical and hospital staffs to reduce the negative impact of stress on staff members (Robinson, 1986). Dr. Robinson was responsible for the development of a sophisticated peer counseling debriefing unit which serves Melbourne, Australia's fire and emergency medical services. Dr. Atle Dyregrov, a Norwegian psychologist who specialized in pediatric traumatic stress also was very interested in work place trauma among hospital workers, military police, fire fighters and industrial employees (Dyregrov and Thyhodt, 1988). He has published extensively in European psychological journals and is credited with the spread of CISD throughout Europe.

The first article which specifically addressed the details of the Critical Incident Stress Debriefing was written by Dr. Jeffrey T. Mitchell and published by the *Journal of Emergency Medical Services* in January, 1983. It was this article which described the debriefing process and stimulated the development of CISD teams throughout the world (Mitchell, 1983, 1988).

Although the 1983 article is the most frequently cited CISD article, it is not the most up to date as these concepts were updated in 1984 and again in 1988. The CISD model has remained essentially intact since it was first described in 1983, however, a few changes have been made. What has occurred is the natural refinement process of the concepts and procedures which would occur in any new stress intervention process. Originally the CISD had only six phases. Articles written shortly after the 1983 article show seven phases. A "Thought" phase, which was assumed under the "Fact" phase in the original article, was added as a transition between the "Fact" and "Reaction" phases. The "Reaction" phase was originally named the "Feeling" phase. The name was changed from "Feeling" to "Reaction" for several reasons. First, the word feeling was found to be somewhat uncomfortable for emergency operations personnel who resisted any efforts to discuss feelings. Secondly, it was recognized that people have many ways to react to a traumatic situation; feelings are only one of those ways. The differences between the original CISD process and the one in use today are outlined in Table 4.1 for the convenience of the reader.

Several other developments are important to note before concluding this chapter. The descriptions of the various types of debriefings have changed during the last decade as debriefers learned more about the CISD process. Today there is a greater emphasis on the role of peer support personnel. This does not lessen the importance of the mental health professional. The importance of that role remains consistent. But there is an expanded and

TABLE 4.1

COMPARISON OF CISD PHASES

1983 to 1984	*1984 to date*
1. Introduction	1. Introduction
2. Fact	2. Fact
3. Feeling	3. Thought
4. Symptom	4. Reaction
5. Teaching	5. Symptom
6. Re-Entry	6. Teaching
	7. Re-Entry

(Mitchell, 1983, 1988, 1993)

enhanced role for the peer support personnel. The on-scene support functions are no longer considered a type of debriefing. Instead, they are one-on-one services provided mostly by well-trained peer support personnel and only rarely, under the most extreme circumstances, by mental health professionals. They are always individual interventions and never a group process.

The name "initial defusing" has been dropped and only the name defusing remains. Additionally, the services of the defusing are more often provided by peers. Debriefings, defusings or any group process for that matter, are never provided at the scene. They are reserved for when the incident is complete and personnel are no longer at the scene. Significant changes to the follow up services have been made and they will be described in a later chapter in this book.

Finally, CISD and CISM are no longer seen as being reserved for emergency service workers. CISD and CISM are now seen as viable interventions for the prevention of traumatic stress among all high risk professions (Everly and Mitchell, 1992).

SUMMARY

This chapter has described the major influences which have enhanced the development of the CISD and CISM. The contributions of several notable researchers, mental health professionals and emergency personnel to the field have been briefly described. Those whose works were mentioned are indeed luminaries in the field.

There were, of course, many others who contributed to the development of the CISD model and CISM. It would be impossible to list every one of those contributors because of the limitations of space and time. But it should be recognized that no single person can be credited with the development of a major movement in the field of CISM. Many dedicated experts contributed a piece to its history. Many more continue to make contributions of their talents and energies as they provide debriefing services to their communities. Those who benefit from CISD and CISM program owe their gratitude to the many who suffered stress in their lives and especially to the stress management pioneers in the military, disaster, law enforcement, hospital, fire service and emergency medical services fields.

Chapter 5

COMPREHENSIVE CRITICAL INCIDENT STRESS MANAGEMENT

INTRODUCTION

Despite the fact that Critical Incident Stress Management has been written about and practiced for almost 20 years there are some people who still believe that it is either not needed or that only those who are weak or otherwise badly suited for their jobs are in need of support services. This false belief has caused some administrators and supervisors to actively fight the development of traumatic stress management or, for that matter, any stress management programs within their organizations. The cost of this short sighted and badly thought out management strategy may never be adequately measured. Since many people suffer through the painful situations they encounter in silence, no one may ever know just how many people have prematurely left their jobs, suffered deterioration in their health, endured negative changes in their relationships or personalities or lost the joy of living and working in their chosen careers as a result of unresolved work place stress.

What all of us have to realize is that good management means good stress management and good stress management is, in fact, good management. The two concepts are blended together, not separate and mutually exclusive. Carefully managing the human resources in our organizations is the single most important management task in any business or organization. Mismanagement of those resources reduces the efficiency and effectiveness of any human system regardless of its mission. Mismanagement of the impact of traumatic stress on the personnel within an organization is indicative of poor management of the entire organization. A well-developed, comprehensive general stress management program which includes a CISM component is vital for the health of members of an organization. It will offer a great deal to the maintenance of the integrity of the organization itself.

This chapter will explore the Comprehensive Critical Incident Stress Management aspects of an overall organizational stress management program.

WHAT IS CRITICAL INCIDENT STRESS MANAGEMENT?

CISM is an integrated system of services and procedures designed to achieve several important goals. They are:

- Prevention of traumatic stress
- Mitigation of traumatic stress
- Intervention to assist in recovery from traumatic stress
- Acceleration of recovery whenever possible
- Restoration to function
- Maintenance of worker health and welfare

CISM requires a well-trained staff as well as the acceptance, encouragement, participation and support of the organization's management at all levels. CISM is not just the job of the well-trained team. Those people will offer the leadership and education for CISM activities within an organization. But good CISM is really the responsibility of everyone in the organization.

CISM TEAM

The CISM team may be configured differently for different types of organizations. It utilizes peer support personnel when the team serves an emergency services organization such as a police department, a fire service, a hospital or the military. Any front line emergency oriented organization would be unwise to operate a CISM team without peers.

When teams serve school systems the teams usually consist of professional mental health providers. In some situations, teachers or school staff may be given special training to participate on a team. It is unwise to use students as peers because they do not handle traumatic events well. Service on a trauma intervention team could be potentially harmful to youngsters through the process of vicarious traumatization. It is best that such delicate and important work be left to mental health professionals perhaps with the assistance of some carefully selected school based adults.

In commercial and industrial settings, the use of peers who are drawn from the various professions is more of an option. It can have some major advantages accompanied by some significant disadvantages. Much will depend on the size and structure of the organization.

In a large company with a stable work force, a well-trained and skilled peer team may be essential. In smaller companies, in which everyone knows everyone else very well, it may be very difficult to utilize peers effectively. Some companies experience traumatic events so infrequently that peers would almost never get the opportunities necessary to provide services and gain experience. Under those circumstances, mental health professionals would most likely provide the CISM services.

In traumatized community groups and after large scale disasters, the use of community based peers to provide support services has been found to be quite helpful for those affected by the trauma event. The National Organization for Victim Assistance has used this method for many years and has been given positive feedback from those they served. Again, there are disadvantages and advantages to using peers under these circumstances. Training, experience and appropriate supervision may pose the most formidable problems to be encountered.

Carefully selected and well-trained peers from the emergency services have been very instrumental in assisting mental health professionals in helping distressed community groups and disaster victims. This particular approach has been utilized on many large disasters such as hurricane Andrew.

Depending on the circumstances, a community based CISM team may be made up of any one of the following sets of helpers:

1. Mental health professionals only

2. Mental health professionals with commercial or industrial peers

3. Mental health professionals with emergency services peers

4. Mental health professionals with specially selected community based peer support personnel

COMPONENTS OF CISM

EDUCATION

No other CISM component can match education for its importance. It is the central focus of practically any other service provided by the CISM team.

Every person in the organization deserves some stress education and traumatic stress information. Stress education programs do not have to be expensive or excessively time consuming to be effective. A few hours with a trained CISM team member can do much to achieve the goals of CISM outlined above. Stress education courses should be instituted early when new recruits are in their academies or orientation programs. Then, periodically throughout the length of one's career, in-service education sessions should be provided to keep workers abreast of new knowledge in the field of stress.

Comprehensive critical incident stress management programs are generally better accepted and utilized when administrative and supervisory personnel have been familiarized with the key elements of the program. If they understand that the program is helpful to the organization and that its use will assure greater productivity, they will encourage their personnel to use the CISM services.

People who are forewarned about traumatic stress are generally able to manage it better. They tend to recognize the signs and symptoms of traumatic stress earlier. Some information which has been provided in the stress education program may help them to handle elements of the stress on their own or with the help of others in their own group. When people recognize that the stressful situation is greater than what they can manage with their own resources, they may then utilize the stress management resources of the organization. In other words, they call for help earlier and obtain that help faster and thus have a more rapid recovery.

There are several levels and types of stress management training which should be provided in work settings. The table below (table 5.1) describes these stress programs.

The best stress education is that which takes place before a person or group is exposed to a traumatic event. This type of stress education is often called pre-exposure or pre-incident stress education. Unfortunately, it is not always possible to provide education before people are traumatized. But stress management education, even after the fact, can be helpful in providing useful information which can help reduce chaos and restore a person to function. Crisis events can be useful learning experiences which a person can use as a springboard to greater growth (see Table 5.1).

PEER COUNSELORS

In the early 1980s, when the first CISM teams were just beginning to develop, there was considerable mistrust of the concept that "peer support personnel," who had very limited training and skills, could eventually be trained to be peer counselors. Mental health professionals were unsure of the capabilities of peers. Administrators, supervisors and agency leaders feared that training peer counselors would divert these personnel from normal duties in a manner which might prove harmful to the organization.

TABLE 5.1

SUMMARY OF STRESS EDUCATION PROGRAMS	
Stress program	*Intended audience*
General stress management (including cumulative stress)	Entire work force
Supervisors guide for stress control	Administrators / supervisors
Critical Incident Stress	Anyone likely to be exposed to traumatic events
CISD	Critical Incident Stress team members

There was also considerable fear that peer counselors might cause legal jeopardy for their organizations. So intense was the fear of using peer counselors that the name, "peer counselor" was shunned by most emergency organizations.

The last dozen years have demonstrated that these concerns have been unfounded. Peer counselors have been trained and they have repeatedly proven their value. This is especially so in the emergency services professions. Peer counselors are generally conservative in their approach to stressed fellow workers. They function only within the limitations of their training. They have been successful in intervening in some very complex situations. Considerable anecdotal reports exist which indicate that peer counselors have guided numerous distressed people through troubled times and may have been quite instrumental in preventing suicides, premature retirements, mitigating marital discord, job dissatisfaction and other painful situations.

A model peer counseling program is the Victoria, Australia ambulance peer counseling program based in Melbourne. The program was established in the mid-1980s and has received consistent positive evaluations by the many emergency personnel who have had occasion to use it.

A key to the success of the Melbourne program and, in fact, any peer counselor program, is the mental health supervision which is provided by dedicated mental health clinicians. Proper mental health professional supervision keeps the program on track, limits mistakes and potential legal consequences and assure the highest quality services by the peer counselors.

SIGNIFICANT OTHER SUPPORT

Providing support to the members of an organization is, of course, very important, but without also supporting the environment in which the personnel live, the organization cannot adequately support the members. Family life is very important to people. When one's family members are cared for by the organization, personnel are more content and morale stays high. Stress is easier to tolerate if there is a supportive climate around the people in an organization. That climate can best be created by a program of significant other support.

Significant other support includes not only social activities, but more importantly special stress education programs for the spouses and significant others. On some occasions debriefings and other support services such as crisis intervention counseling must be provided to significant others and family members. Children should not be forgotten when services are provided to significant others.

Programs to assist significant others in managing stress are extremely important in emergency services organizations. In fact, they are more frequently used in those organizations than in any other. It is up to the CISM team to provide significant other services. If the team does not take up the responsibility, it is likely to be forgotten. The result could be devastating for the personnel and for their significant others.

CRITICAL INCIDENT STRESS MANAGEMENT TEAM

A trained team to provide the right services at the right time is a prerequisite to the prevention and mitigation of traumatic stress reactions and the recovery of those who have been traumatized. CISM teams are a partnership between mental health professionals, clergy personnel and peer support personnel.

Team members provide the actual day to day services of the team. Teams which do not pay attention to a comprehensive approach to critical incident stress management and, instead, think that one process such as the debriefing (CISD) is enough to support the people they serve are making a significant error. No one service can be equally applicable to all people in all circumstances at all times. Quality teams provide a variety of services to suit the needs of the people they serve.

The following are the most common services provided by a CISM team:

- Pre-incident education
- On-scene support services
- Defusings
- Demobilizations after disaster
- Debriefings (CISD)
- Specialty debriefings (community outreach programs)
- Informal discussions
- Significant other support services
- Individual consults (one-on-one)
- Follow up services

Detailed information on these services is provided in other chapters throughout this book.

The CISM team is the first line of defense against traumatic stress in many organizations. Team members provide extensive stress education programs. They can also be called upon quickly after a traumatic incident. They can provide advice, defusings or debriefings, peer counseling, organization of the administrative response to stress and other support services after a crisis event. CISM team members also make referrals for additional services for those who may need more support than can be provided by a debriefing alone.

PROFESSIONAL REFERRAL SYSTEM

Traumatic stress is a complex process which affects each individual in a different manner. Some may recover from it on their own or with only limited assistance from family and friends. Many benefit from the services of a CISM team. A few may need professional assistance to make a full recovery. In any case, the majority of traumatized people do achieve satisfactory levels of recovery after psychotrauma. They are able to learn and grow from the experience and they can continue happy and productive lives even in the aftermath of threat, shock, loss and grief.

Some traumatic events are so horrific and so overwhelming that some who have experienced them will need professional assistance to assure maximal recovery. This is not a negative reflection on their competency, mental health or any other abilities. Remember, a traumatic stress reaction is generally considered a normal reaction of normal people to an overwhelming experience. Only in relatively rare circumstances is a traumatic stress reaction considered psycho-pathological. Obtaining appropriate assistance can make the difference between a fairly short, painful reaction and a prolonged, complex one. Mental health professionals, who are trained in the treatment of post-traumatic stress can guide and accelerate the healing process which people must pass through after they have been traumatized.

There are many methods of treating post-traumatic stress reactions. This book will not attempt to completely list or describe those processes since adequate coverage of such topics is well beyond its scope. The focus of this book is on comprehensive critical incident stress management, which is a health enhancement and stress prevention, program. CISM is not a treatment program. Let it suffice to say that the knowledge and skills to treat post-traumatic stress reactions has expanded enormously during the last 30 years. Neuro-cognitive therapies, Eye Movement Desensitization and Reprocessing and pharmacological interventions, to name a few, are some of the most recent promising developments in the field. Referrals for the treatment of traumatic stress should be made only to mental health professionals who are properly educated and skilled in the treatment of post-traumatic stress.

Some people may not need therapy for traumatic stress reactions, but they may be having difficulty with some questions of a spiritual nature such as, "Why did God allow this to happen?" Many clergy personnel have taken training in pastoral counseling with traumatized people. It is not unusual to find clergy serving on CISM teams. When the questions are beyond the capabilities of CISM team members, individuals in need of spiritual guidance should be directed to clergy who are familiar with post-traumatic stress reactions.

COMMUNITY OUTREACH

During the last decade there has been an increasing recognition of the need to provide crisis intervention services to the general community after traumatic events. The severe impact of disasters, violent crime and other tragic accidents on individuals and whole communities has been well documented. Without appropriate intervention in such events, human suffering can expand dramatically.

Initially, in the early 1980s, CISM teams were formed to serve emergency services organizations. On occasion, emergency services CISM teams were called in to assist communities in crisis. But as the needs of communities have become more apparent, several important developments have occurred. First, organizations such as the National Organization for Victim's Assistance took on an expanded role of direct interventions in communities after crisis events. Second, the Red Cross has taken on the responsibility to assist communities in managing the psychological after- shocks of disaster. Community Response Teams (CRT) have been established in many communities throughout the country.

Finally, the demands from community groups on emergency services CISM teams have been intensifying. In some areas it is common for CISM teams to respond regularly to non-emergency services organizations and community groups when requested by community organizations and local community mental health centers.

Emergency services CISM teams should be prepared to assist their communities in major situations even if they ordinarily do not serve organizations outside of the boundaries of their own. It would be wise to discuss and practice responses for situations in which community needs far exceed the available resources.

RESEARCH AND DEVELOPMENT

The field of crisis intervention is now over fifty years old. Accepted and proven intervention strategies have been practiced in many formats throughout the world. CISM has developed as a direct offshoot of the crisis intervention field. The number of peer support, clergy and mental health professionals entering the field make CISM one of the fastest growing psychological support programs in the world. Its growth, to date, has been remarkable and is likely to continue into the next century.

It is difficult for programs like CISM to maintain growth, expand its services and continue to be accepted by the individuals and organizations which benefit from the services unless there is a solid research and development component in place. The CISM movement is a dynamic one which has developed a wide range of individual and group post-traumatic stress management processes over two decades. Improvements have been made in the interventions over time. A solid literature base has been developed.

Today there is a need to research the effectiveness of the CISM interventions to assure that the very best services are maintained. Everyone who functions in the CISM field requires an expanded knowledge base which explores the effectiveness of CISM processes. In addition, the exact mechanisms which make CISD and CISM processes effective need to be explained in greater detail.

The future of CISM looks bright and further research should set the stage for the current and future interventions to provide the most effective assistance to people suffering from workplace or community psychotrauma.

FIGURE 5.1

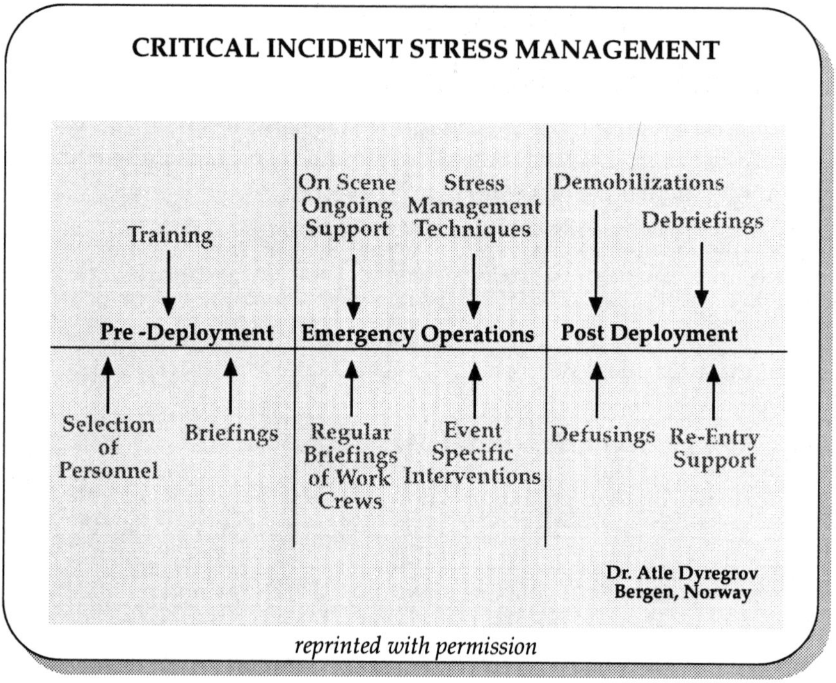

CRITICAL INCIDENT STRESS MANAGEMENT

| | On Scene Stress | Demobilizations |
| Training | Ongoing Management
Support Techniques | Debriefings |

| Pre -Deployment | Emergency Operations | Post Deployment |

| Selection
of
Personnel | Briefings | Regular
Briefings
of Work
Crews | Event
Specific
Interventions | Defusings | Re-Entry
Support |

Dr. Atle Dyregrov
Bergen, Norway

reprinted with permission

SUMMARY

This chapter has presented an overview of the field of Critical Incident Stress Management. It defined CISM and addressed several important areas such as the team approach to CISM and the key components of CISM. This chapter provides a jumping off point for the details of CISM to be presented in the chapters to follow.

Chapter 6

CRISIS INTERVENTION:
THE SAFE-R MODEL

It was noted earlier in this volume that critical incident stress management (CISM) consists of far more than simply the CISD intervention. Comprehensive CISM provides for on-scene support services for emergency personnel, as well. Such on-scene critical incident support services include one-on-one crisis intervention capabilities. One-on-one crisis intervention services may be provided by either peer counselors or by mental health professionals in the role of crisis interventionists. Greenstone (1993) attests to this point in his description of "Litman's Law." Simply stated, Litman's Law postulates that the more severe the crisis, the less the need for a highly trained professional to handle its acute manifestations. The main goal of this chapter is to introduce a model for crisis intervention expressly developed for utilization with emergency services and disaster response professionals who are in crisis. The model may be implemented by either trained emergency services peer counselors or by mental health professionals.

Let us begin by briefly reviewing some basic concepts concerning crisis intervention. In chapter 11, we shall significantly expand this discussion of the basic concepts of crisis intervention, but for now let us examine crisis intervention as the foundation for one-on-one intervention.

DEFINING CRISIS

What is a crisis? From a psychological perspective, a crisis results when an individual finds him/herself unable to cope with a challenging or aversive situation. Psychological homeostasis is destroyed at that point and a dysfunctional spiral of distress and decompensation is initiated in response to this failure of usual defenses and coping mechanisms. Caplan (1961) defines a crisis as a condition wherein an individual meets an obstacle or challenge that proves insurmountable through the use of usual coping or problem-solving mechanisms. This condition results in a subsequent state of emotional discord and decompensation.

Reactions to a crisis may commonly include cognitive, affective and physiological symptoms. The emergence of maladaptive coping behaviors may occur, as well. Common cognitive symptoms may include cognitive distortions or a decrease in decision making capabilities. Affective symptoms could include panic, anxiety and / or depression. Physiological symptoms could include a myriad of stress-related physical complaints. Finally, common behavioral symptoms of crisis include irritability, hostility, interpersonal withdrawal and self-medication (alcohol, nicotine, caffeine, antihistamines for their sedative effect and various illicit drugs).

GOALS OF CRISIS INTERVENTION

Most simply, crisis intervention is the provision of "emotional first aid." Crisis intervention is an exercise in psychological "damage control." Whether a mild crisis or an acute trauma situation, the concept of emotional first aid remains applicable.

Specific goals of crisis intervention may be thought of as follows:

1. Stopping the acute process of psychological deterioration/decompensation that typifies a crisis condition.

2. Stabilization of cognitive and affective processes.

3. Management of acute symptoms of psychological distress/dysfunction.

4. Restoration of independent adaptive functioning or providing assistance in receiving continued acute care.

Crisis intervention is <u>NOT</u> psychotherapy. Therefore, the use of traditional psychotherapy techniques designed to promote abreaction, the uncovering of repressed information and the explicit discouragement of transference reactions are usually contraindicated.

HISTORICAL PERSPECTIVES

The concept of crisis intervention is by no means a new concept. According to Greenstone (1993), crisis intervention centers first emerged in the United States within the first decade of the Twentieth Century and were seen primarily as suicide prevention centers. Greenstone goes on to note that crisis intervention, as we know it today, emerged largely form the work of two individuals Gerald Caplan and Eric Lindemann.

Lindemann (1944) studied grief reactions among those who lost loved ones in the Coconut Grove Club fire in Boston in 1943. Lindemann was joined by Gerald Caplan in the creation of a community mental health program affiliated with Harvard University where they refined their approach to patients in crisis.

The field of crisis intervention grew dramatically during the late 1960s and through the 1970s. Crisis intervention centers and telephone hotlines could be found in virtually every major urban setting. Law enforcement agencies began developing special crisis units as did hospitals (Greenstone 1993). The crisis intervention movement grew largely because of the influx of para professional and non-professional volunteer workers in response to dramatic economic, political and sociocultural changes that typified those turbulent years. In chapter 11, we shall continue and expand our discussion of the process of crisis intervention.

Crisis intervention is now viewed as an integral part of any system of psychological support services for high risk as well as general citizens groups.

Let us now examine the actual processes of crisis intervention.

THE SAFE-R MODEL OF CRISIS INTERVENTION

As noted earlier, the concept of crisis intervention is not new, however, experience in working with emergency services and disaster response professionals has taught that some alterations in otherwise accepted notions and mental health protocols may be of value when dealing with these task-directed, action-oriented individuals. The SAFE-R model represents a model of crisis intervention developed over a five year period which is directed specifically for use with emergency services personnel and may be used by peer counselors as well as mental health professionals. This model is summarized in Table 6.1 provided below. Let us take a closer look at this crisis intervention protocol.

STIMULATION REDUCTION

The initial step in the SAFE-R model urges the crisis interventionist to reduce the level of stimulation affecting the person in crisis. Most commonly, this involves removing the individual in crisis from the acute crisis situation. This may be achieved by taking a walk, getting a cup of coffee, or any other diversionary process that provides the individual with some "psychological distance" away from the source of the acute crisis or any other cues that appear to fuel the crisis situation. Prior to any such intervention, however, the crisis interventionist must always introduce him/herself and describe the role that is being served or performed.

TABLE 6.1

THE SAFE-R MODEL:

Crisis Intervention with Emergency Services and Disaster Response Personnel

Step One - **S**timulation reduction

Step Two - **A**cknowledgment of the crisis

1. "What happened?"

2. "How are you doing?"

Step Three -**F**acilitation of understanding and normalization of symptoms /reactions

Step Four - **E**ncourage effective coping techniques

Step Five - **R**estoration of independent functioning or provision of assistance in obtaining acute care.

ACKNOWLEDGEMENT OF THE CRISIS

The second step in the SAFE-R intervention is the acknowledgment of the crisis itself. This step is fostered by a skillful use of basic helping communication techniques. In this step, the crisis interventionist most typically asks the person to describe "what happened" to create the crisis situation. As a crisis is often punctuated by escalating emotions, this question gives the person in a crisis a cue and reason to return to the cognitive thinking domain, at least temporarily. Yet it is not usually advisable to completely discourage cathartic ventilation, therefore, after having described the nature of the crisis situation, the person in crisis is asked to describe his / her current state of psychological functioning. A simple prompt such as, "How are you doing now?" allows the first re-sponder who is in crisis to return to the cathartic ventilation, but now in a somewhat more structured and secure manner. Thus, we see within this step, the crisis interventionist has superimposed cognitive oriented com-munications over the potentially labile emotional foundation. Later, how-ever, having listened to the nature of the crisis, the interventionist encour-ages emotional ventilation in a safer, more structured communication environment.

FACILITATION OF UNDERSTANDING

The third step in the present model involves a transition back to the cognitive psychological domain for the person in crisis. In this third step, the crisis interventionist begins to <u>actively</u> respond to the information revealed by the person in crisis during the previous step. Here the person in crisis is encouraged to view his/her reactions to the crisis as generally "normal," expected reactions being experienced by a "normal" individual, in response to an abnormally challenging situation, that is, a crisis situation. The primary goals of this step of the SAFE-R model are: 1) to assist the person in crisis in returning to the cognitive domain of psychological processing and 2) to encourage the person in crisis to see his/her symptoms as basically "normal" reactions to an extraordinarily stressful event.

ENCOURAGE EFECTIVE COPING

The fourth step of the model represents what is usually the most overtly active step with regard to the behavior of the crisis interventionist. Here the interventionist engages in teaching of basic concepts in 1) crisis, 2) stress and 3) stress management. As with the previous step, it takes place largely within the cognitive domain of psychological processing. Basic stress management techniques may be discussed and a <u>plan</u> for coping with the acute crisis situation is conjointly developed by the crisis interventionist and the person in crisis.

RESTORATION OF INDEPENDENT FUNCTIONING

The goal of the previous four steps is always to assist the person in reestablishing independent psychological and behavioral functioning. In the vast majority of cases, this will have been achieved by this point in the process. In some instances, however, it will be evident that the person in crisis remains in a highly unstable condition. If such is the case, the crisis interventionist's goal becomes that of providing assistance in obtaining continued acute care. Resources for such continued care might be family members, other departmental resources, or in extreme cases where no other resources seem suitable, an emergency room at a local hospital.

To review, the SAFE-R model is designed for use by either emergency services peer counselors or by mental health trained professionals working with emergency services and disaster response personnel who are in crisis. The model has five basic step with a final resolution determination step. The model processes several key elements within each step: 1) a content structure, 2) a process domain, 3) an action, and 4) a goal. These are presented in Table 6.2.

TABLE 6.2

A SUMMARY OF THE SAFE-R MODEL

Steps	Content	Process	Action	Goals
One	Stimulation Reduction	Behavioral	To remove the person in crisis from provocative cues.	To mitigate affective escalation. Mental status assessment
Two	Acknowledgement of Crisis	Cognitive - Affective	To have the person in crisis describe "what happened" and current reactions	To encourage cathartic ventilation. Reduce arousal and rumination. Establish rapport and sense of safety
Three	Facilitation of Understanding	Affective - Cogitive	To explain symptoms	To have the person in crisis view symptoms as "normal" reactions albeit protentially problematic
Four	Encourage Effective Coping	Cognitive-Behavioral	To teach basic stress management	To improve immediate and short term crisis coping
Five	Restoration of Functioning	Behavioral	Assessment of current adaptive functioning as adequate or seek further assistance	Re-establish psychological homeostasis or provision of continued acute care

In the next section, we shall examine the most fundamental of all crisis intervention skills, the ability to communicate.

COMMUNICATIONS

BASIC COMMUNICATION TECHNIQUES

As the scalpel is to the surgeon, words are to the crisis interventionist. Verbal techniques may be categorized, much the same as surgical techniques, with regard to their nature and expected effect. Thus, it may be of some value to briefly review some of the basic communication techniques that may be employed in crisis intervention.

It is important to keep in mind the goals of one-on-one crisis intervention when reviewing the communication techniques listed below. The goals of crisis intervention, it will be recalled, are to:

1. Stop the acute process of psychological deterioration / decompensation.

2. Stabilize psychological functioning.

3. Manage any acute symptoms of psychological dysfunction.

4. Restore independent functioning or assist in obtaining continued acute care.

In reference to the SAFE-R model described earlier, these basic communication techniques will be useful in facilitating rapport, promoting catharsis and in the understanding/normalization of symptoms.

DIRECTIVE VERSUS NONDIRECTIVE COMMUNICATION TECHNIQUES

Communication techniques may be classified on a continuum reaching from extremely nondirective techniques to the extremely directive techniques.

Nondirective techniques provide the person in crisis with the greatest amount of communication flexibility. They tend not to restrict nor direct the responses of the person in crisis. Directive techniques, on the other hand, tend to be far more task oriented, selective and targeted in their context. They tend to restrict the communication options available to the person in crisis. Such techniques appear more structured when compared to nondirective communication techniques.

Figure 6.1 depicts a continuum of communication techniques. Let us examine these techniques in greater detail.

FIGURE 6.1

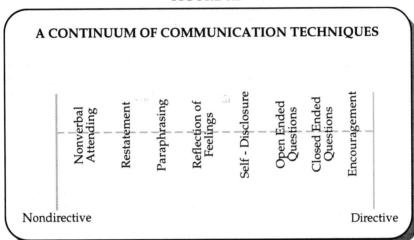

NONVERBAL ATTENDING - refers to the process of attending to and monitoring the nonverbal behavior, also known as "body language" exhibited by the person in crisis. There are no hard and fast rules pertaining to just what certain postures or gestures actually mean. Rather, the crisis interventionist should monitor for obvious changes and whether these changes facilitate or inhibit communication.

RESTATEMENT - the support person literally restates a key phrase or important point that has been made by the person in crisis. In this technique, the support person uses the same key words as did the person in crisis. This technique is used to check for listening accuracy and to clarify semantically ambiguous terms.

PARAPHRASING - is the term used to denote when the support person uses his /her own words to summarize the main points or theme of what the person in crisis has just said. This technique is more conversational than is restatement. It can be used to check for listening accuracy, to clarify ambiguities, to allow the speaker to "hear" what he/she has just said, or simply probe for further clarification /elaboration.

REFLECTION OF FEELINGS - refers to the technique by which the support person "mirrors" or reflects back to the person in crisis the nature of the emotions that have just been observed. For example, "You look like you're angry." This technique is useful for helping individuals talk about emotions that they might be otherwise hesitant to disclose.

SELF-DISCLOSURE - is a technique designed to facilitate the disclosure of information by the person in crisis by first having the support person disclose some minimal personal information about him / herself.

OPEN ENDED QUESTION - are questions that tend to provide maximum response flexibility for the respondent. Open ended questions typically begin with words such as: what, why, and how. Open ended probes typically begin with:

- "Describe for me ..."
- "Tell me about ..."

CLOSED ENDED QUESTIONS - are questions that tend to restrict the response options available to the respondent. Closed ended questions typically begin with words such as:

Is	Who	Shall	Do	Did
Have	When	Would	Are	Which
Could	Where	Can	Should	

ENCOURAGEMENT - refers to a technique of communication by which the support person "encourages" or endorses a particular course of action or perspective for the person in crisis. While not typically used in traditional psychotherapy, encouragement can be a useful crisis intervention tool to reduce confusion or dissonance on the part of the person in crisis.

Although seemingly quite simple, the aforementioned techniques of communication can be the "life blood" of the crisis intervention process. Skillful utilization requires practice and appropriate training. The biological abilities to speak and hear are no guarantee that we can effectively communicate or listen.

In the final analysis, the most powerful tool of persuasion is the ability to ask a thoughtful question. As the famous Harvard psychiatrist Henry Murray noted, "There is nothing so powerful as the well-phrased question." Change ultimately comes from within the individual, that is, it is the individual who decides to make a change in behavior. People do not change a behavior unless they feel it is a good idea. By posing a question, the impetus for change comes from within the person, not from some external directive.

PRECAUTIONS IN CRISIS INTERVENTION

In this last section, we shall briefly review a few basic precautions that the crisis interventionist should be sensitive to:

1. Don't probe or confront a person in crisis so that ego defenses are further jeopardized.

2. Never probe or question beyond the point where "closure" can be attained.

3. Don't become overly analytical so as to try to interpret the "hidden" motivations for one's behavior.

4. Don't probe, question or confront so as to lose rapport with the person in crisis.

5. Try to avoid anything that puts the person in crisis on the defensive.

6. Don't moralize or "preach" to the person in crisis.

7. Don't progress too quickly in the crisis intervention process.

8. Don't dismiss discussions of suicide or homicide as merely verbal gestures or "posturing." Failure to take even a veiled threat seriously could lead to escalations.

9. Don't use "reverse psychology" by encouraging someone to do something that you actually don't want them to do.

10. Don't take personal risks with your own well-being!

SUMMARY

In this chapter we've been introduced to the concept of one-on-one crisis intervention as an integral part of critical incident stress management. Crisis intervention may be operationalized by trained peer support personnel or by mental health professionals.

This chapter has proposed the use of a special model, the SAFE-R model, developed especially for use among the emergency services professions.

Chapter 7

THE CRITICAL INCIDENT STRESS DEBRIEFING FROM START TO FINISH

INTRODUCTION

The Critical Incident Stress Debriefing (CISD) is the most complex of all of the Critical Incident Stress Management (CISM) interventions. This is so whether the process is employed by CISM teams in their work with emergency personnel, or Community Response Teams (CRT) which work with the citizens of various communities, schools and other organizations after traumatic events. The Critical Incident Stress Debriefing was originally designed to reduce stress in emergency personnel after extremely traumatic experiences. More recently it has found application in schools, industries, commercial operations and community groups.

The debriefing was not designed to be applied in the so called "routine" cases. CISD is a useful tool for stress mitigation when applied properly. The overuse of the procedure on relatively minor events is not a proper application of the process. Nor is it a proper application for organizations to make too broad of a use of the procedure for events that are not truly critical incidents in nature, such as mediating management - employee conflicts or investigating employee behaviors. Other procedures would be more applicable in those situations.

The basic concepts of CISD are easy to understand and are clear on paper. The complexities enter the picture when a debriefer is faced with the problem of applying those concepts. When a group of people in distress is before the CISD team, there are many variables which can present a challenge to the team. This chapter will help experienced and newly trained CISM or CRT members provide a most valuable service to the emergency personnel or to the community in an efficient and effective manner.

DEBRIEFING DEFINED

A CISD is a group process. It can best be defined as a group meeting or discussion, employing both crisis intervention and educational processes, targeted toward mitigating or resolving the psychological distress associated with a critical incident or traumatic event. The debriefing team consists of one mental health professional and one, two or three peer support personnel when a CISD is applied to emergency services personnel or disaster workers. The structure of the team often is modified when a debriefing is applied to community groups, schools, industries or other populations. In the "Community Response Team" (CRT) mode, a debriefing team may be made up of only mental health professionals. In any event, traumatic stress interventions should only be applied by trained individuals who are familiar with traumatic stress and its effects on people.

The CISD has seven phases. The structure allows participants in the groups to discuss a traumatic incident in a controlled manner which does not leave them feeling out of control of themselves. The CISD uses some techniques common to counseling, but it is not counseling nor psychotherapy nor a substitute for psychotherapy. One of the main components, which makes a debriefing different than psychotherapy, is the fact that a substantial portion of the debriefing process is dedicated to teaching the participants about their stress reactions. Stress survival techniques to manage traumatic stress are also taught.

In its applications to emergency personnel, a debriefing is a peer managed and peer driven process which uses mental health professionals for oversight and guidance. In its general community (CRT) applications, a team of traumatic stress trained mental health professionals runs the debriefing without the assistance of peer support personnel unless they request assistance from trained CISD peers from the fire, police, nursing or emergency medical services agencies. When a debriefing is applied to non-emergency group populations, certain structural and process modifications may be necessary to accommodate ethnic, cultural and traditional issues within those groups. It is also important that all CISD related interventions be appropriate to the age of the participants. In sum, it is important that team members have expertise in dealing with the special needs of the populations they serve. If this is not the case, the ability of the CISD team to achieve the primary goals of the debriefing will be severely jeopardized.

Generally the process of the debriefing and its goals and objectives are essentially the same whether it is being applied to emergency services groups or to citizen groups from the community.

GOALS AND OBJECTIVES OF DEBRIEFING

There are two main goals of a Critical Incident Stress Debriefing. The process has been designed to:

1. Mitigate the impact of the critical incident on those who were victims of the event, be they:
    a. primary victims, (those directly traumatized by the event)
    b. secondary victims, (emergency services personnel) who witnessed or managed the traumatic event)
    c. tertiary victims, (family, friends, and those to whom the traumatic event may be indirectly communicated)

2. Accelerate recovery processes in people who are experiencing normal stress reactions to abnormal traumatic events.

As described earlier, the CISD process is considered one of the most important mechanisms to reduce the potential of Post-Traumatic Stress Disorder (PTSD). It allows people to verbalize their distress and form appropriate concepts about stress reaction before false interpretations of the experience are fixed in their minds.

The core focus of CISD is the relief of stress in normal, emotionally healthy people who have experienced traumatic events. The debriefing has not been developed to resolve degenerative stress, psychopathologies or personal problems which existed before the disaster or traumatic event which is the subject of the debriefing.

There are some sporadic anecdotal records in which clinicians have reported some success in using the debriefing process with clinical subjects. We are happy to hear of those reported successes, but they are beyond the original design of the debriefing process and formal studies of those unusual applications of CISD are encouraged.

There are several secondary goals and objectives of a CISD. They may not always be achieved in every CISD but they should always be goals. It makes no difference whether the debriefing is provided to emergency personnel by a CISM team or to community groups by a CRT team. The objectives of the CISD are identical. Secondary objectives of the process are:

- Education about stress, stress reactions and survival techniques

- Emotional ventilation

- Reassurance that the stress response is controllable and that recovery is likely

- Forewarning people about signs and symptoms which might show up in the near future

- Reduction of the fallacy of uniqueness (or the feeling that one has been singled out to be a victim)

- Reduction of the fallacy of abnormality

- Establishment of a positive contact with mental health professionals

- Enhancement of group cohesiveness

- Enhancement of interagency cooperation

- Prevention or mitigation of post trauma syndromes and PTSD

- Screening for people who need additional assessment or therapy

- Referral for counseling or other services as necessary

CRITICAL INCIDENTS

A critical incident is defined as any event with sufficient impact to produce significant emotional reactions in people now or later. It is an event which is considered generally extremely unusual in the range of ordinary human experiences. The incident may be the foundation for Post Traumatic Stress Disorder if it is not resolved effectively and quickly.

The CISD has been developed to help people cope with the most stressful of events. It was never designed with the routine in mind. CISD should be applied only to those events which are extraordinary. Overuse of the process will dilute its potency and cause it to be far less helpful on more serious events. If mildly distressing events occur, other types of interventions should be applied by the CISM team or the Community Response Team.

TABLE 7.1

CRITICAL INCIDENTS FOR EMERGENCY SERVICE PERSONNEL

- Line of duty death
- Suicide of an emergency worker
- Multi-casualty incident / disaster
- Significant event involving children
- Knowing the victim of the event

- Serious line of duty injury
- Police shooting
- Excessive media interest
- Prolonged incident with loss
- Any significant event

GENERAL ORGANIZATION OF A CISD TEAM

A brief description of the organization of a CISM team will be helpful in understanding the procedures and functions of the CISM team once it is called into action to provide a CISD.

The typical CISM team is made up of 20 to 40 people from a large jurisdiction or a region made up of smaller jurisdictions. Roughly one third of the membership of a CISM team is made up of mental health professionals and two thirds are peer support personnel. Peer support personnel are law enforcement, nursing, fire suppression, emergency medical services personnel as well as those from corrections, search and rescue groups, life guard services, dispatch centers and other specialty "first response groups."

Each team has a basic organizational structure which includes at least the following roles:

CLINICAL DIRECTOR - A mental health professional who provides oversight and consultation to other team members on matters relating to mental health.

SENIOR TEAM COORDINATOR - A peer who serves as the day to day manager of the team. The senior team coordinator deploys the three or four team members to provide the debriefing. The senior team coordinator also arranges team meetings and maintains any team related records. The senior coordinator guides the efforts of the assistant coordinators and other team members and provides stress education programs to emergency personnel.

ASSISTANT TEAM COORDINATORS - There may be more than one assistant coordinator depending on the size and activity level of the CISM team. Assistant coordinators take over the responsibilities of the senior coordinator when he or she is away or occupied with other functions.

MENTAL HEALTH PROFESSIONALS - These people lead the three or four member team assigned to provide a formal debriefing. Mental health professionals on the team also provide brief consultation to individuals who have been identified during a debriefing as people who may need additional support services. The mental health professionals provide advice and back up to peers who are doing the bulk of the day to day work of the CISM team. Mental health professionals also assist in providing stress education programs to the various organizations the team serves.

PEER SUPPORT PERSONNEL - The majority of team members on a CISM team which serves emergency personnel are emergency workers themselves. They provide stress education to their fellow emergency workers. They handle most of the one-on-one contacts as well as defusings and follow up contacts. Peer support team members work actively in concert with the mental health team leader in a formal debriefing.

COMMUNITY RESPONSE TEAMS

These team members may be part of a CISM team or they may function separate from the CISM team. The basic structure of a CRT may be quite different from a CISM which is designed to serve emergency personnel. Those teams which serve school systems, the general community or industrial settings may or may not need peer support personnel. They may solely utilize the services of mental health professionals or they may incorporate the services of the medical team which serves the organization. The CISM services for the community do not change substantially. Only the team organization needs to be altered.

CALL OUT PROCEDURES: ACTIVATING THE CISD TEAM

A debriefing is a time and labor intensive function which requires a team of between two and four team members. It takes approximately two to three hours to complete a CISD, so debriefings should only be provided when they are necessary. There are other techniques such as defusings and individual consultations which might be more applicable and more effective than the debriefing under certain circumstances. CISM teams should carefully evaluate the true need for a debriefing before setting one up.

Once an incident occurs a set of procedures will be initiated. Someone makes the first call for help. The caller may be a CISM team member or one of the emergency personnel or a representative of the Red Cross or a community official who recognizes the need for assistance for the affected group. Typically the first call comes from someone who is somewhat familiar with the CISM Process and the need to apply it. Sometimes the request for assistance is made while the incident is in progress. At other times the call may not come in for several days because there is no apparent perceived need, or in some instances it is not known that help is available.

FIGURE 7.1

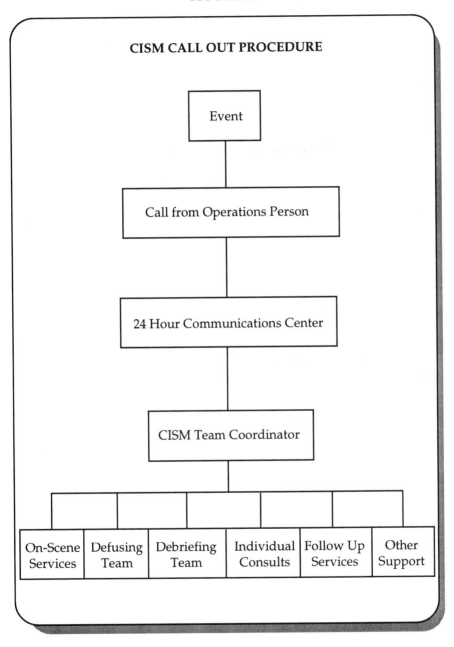

CISM CALL OUT PROCEDURE

Event

Call from Operations Person

24 Hour Communications Center

CISM Team Coordinator

| On-Scene Services | Defusing Team | Debriefing Team | Individual Consults | Follow Up Services | Other Support |

Regardless of when the call is made, the call out process begins when the first contact is made for help. Some calls are made directly to the team coordinator. This practice is to be discouraged, however, because the coordinator is frequently not in the office when a call comes in through the routine phone system. A far better way for the system to work is to educate all potential callers to contact a 24 hour communications center where a trained communications operator or dispatcher answers the call. The dispatcher attempts to gather pertinent information which will be handed off to a team coordinator:

- What is the nature of the call?
- Is the situation considered an emergency or is the caller asking for information of a routine nature?
- Is there a need for an immediate deployment of a CISM team or Community Response Team?
- Is the incident complete or ongoing?
- Where is the caller now?
- What are the call back numbers?
- Is there someone else to call if the caller is unavailable for the call from the team coordinator?

When preliminary information is collected the dispatcher calls or pages the team coordinator or a backup coordinator. The dispatcher advises the coordinator that the services of the CISM team or community response team are being requested. The information the dispatcher has been able to gather is passed off to the team coordinator.

At that point, the dispatcher drops out of the system unless further assistance is needed with communications. The coordinator must then make an immediate call to the original caller to determine what CISM or CRT services, if any, are necessary. The coordinator has the responsibility to assess the need for a debriefing or any other type of service. When the coordinator completes the assessment task and a determination has been made that one form of service or another is necessary, the coordinator then begins the team assignment procedures. Calls are made to team members on the call down list which every team coordinator has readily available. Mental health professionals, chaplains, clergy and peers are chosen according to the needs identified by the requesting party and the coordinator.

ASSESSING THE NEED FOR CISD

Since CISM and CRT teams want to do debriefings only when they are necessary, they should be careful to properly assess the need for doing a debriefing when a traumatic incident occurs. The following questions and comments should be helpful in determining if a debriefing is necessary or if some other form of intervention would be more appropriate. The team coordinator should use these questions as a guideline for assessment of the situation which needs either a CISM or a CRT response. Some of the questions will be asked directly of those requesting a debriefing service. The answers to other questions may be self-evident or may be determined through other means.

Here are the questions which can help a team coordinator assess the need for a CISD:

1. What is the nature of the critical incident?
2. How long ago did it occur? Is the event ongoing?
3. Is the event of sufficient magnitude as to cause significant emotional distress among those involved?
4. Does the event fit within the definition of a critical incident?
5. How many individuals are involved in the incident?
6. If more than three, think CISD! If less, perhaps a defusing or a individual consult would suffice.
7. Are there several distinct groups of people involved or is there only one? For example, are the targets of CISD operations personnel, victims, witnesses or community members? If so, more than one CISD will be required.
8. What is the status of the involved individuals? Where are they and how are they reacting? Some incidents may need a more immediate defusing rather than waiting for a debriefing.
9. What signs and symptoms of distress are being displayed by the participants or the witnesses of the incident?
10. How long have the reactions or signs and symptoms of distress been going on? Significant symptoms which have continued longer than a few days are a good sign that a debriefing may be necessary. If symptoms of distress are going on longer than one week after the incident, a debriefing is definitely necessary.
11. Are symptoms growing worse as time passes? Worsening symptoms in a group may indicate a need for debriefing.
12. Is the distressed group unusually fearful or anxious?
13. Is the distressed group suffering sleep disturbance?
14. Are members of the group avoiding certain activities?
15. Has the behavior of the group changed significantly?
16. Is the group preoccupied with death or fear of death?
17. Are members of the group suffering from mental confusion?
18. Is there anyone who seems so distressed that they may be contemplating suicide?

19. Are any of the following key indicators of a need for a debriefing present :
    - behavioral change
    - continued symptoms
    - new symptoms arising
    - regression
    - intensifying symptoms
    - group symptoms
20. Is the formal debriefing process necessary or are group members requesting information on stress and stress management?
21. Is the group willing to come to the debriefing or are they being ordered to come?
22. Are there other concurrent stressors going on?
23. Has the place and time of the debriefing been chosen?
24. Are there any other issues which should be discussed?

The questioning process goes along like a conversation. Remember, these questions are only a guide. Other questions could be asked by the coordinator and other bits of information can be offered by the people requesting the debriefing.

Based on the answers given to the above questions, the coordinator makes a decision to deploy a team for on-scene support services, a demobilization (in the event of a major disaster), a defusing, a debriefing, an individual consultation or an educational program. Operational procedures for debriefings will be discussed in the paragraphs to follow. Other interventions will be given special attention in other chapters of this book.

If, after asking these and other questions, the coordinator is still unsure if a debriefing is necessary, one should be provided anyway. If the team arrives to provide the debriefing and realizes, by circulating around and talking to the participants before the debriefing starts, that the event is really not all that bad and the people only wanted a stress education program, the CISD can always resort to teaching an extemporaneous stress education class. Nothing has been lost under those circumstances and the group may benefit form the stress education. Be cautious never to substitute an education process if there is any chance that a debriefing is really necessary.

PREPARING FOR A CISD

When the decision to hold a debriefing is made, a series of important preparations must be made to enhance the potential that the debriefing will run smoothly and be beneficial to the participants.

The coordinator stays busy making phone calls to confirm each aspect of the preparations to be made.

DATE AND TIME

The ideal debriefing in response to acute, well-defined critical incidents, takes place between 24 and 72 hours after the incident. It is only in a rare case that everything will work out so well that it can actually be held within the 24 to 72 hour time frame, but that is the ideal target time. There are a few important points which need to be made here regarding the time of the debriefing from the conclusion of the incident.

Emergency personnel are so cognitively defended that it often takes about 24 hours for them to be ready to discuss the details of their reactions to the event. There are certainly exceptions such as line of duty death or a mass disaster, where the shock, numbing or denial mechanisms may last for days or weeks. The CISD will not realize its full potential unless the recipients are psychologically receptive, or ready, for the intervention. In some circumstances, therefore, the CISD may be applied literally weeks after the traumatic event.

The average non-emergency trained individual tends to be less well-cognitively defended. They are ready earlier to let their emotions and other reactions come to the surface. Debriefings with the average citizens (non-emergency trained) may be held earlier than 24 hours after the event. In fact, there is something to be said for doing debriefings with the non-emergency groups as soon as possible after the traumatic event.

If a debriefing is necessary before a CISD team can be organized, a defusing will be helpful initially and a debriefing can be done later if it is still required. No one should "throw" a debriefing together without a full team of trained CISM personnel. Under those circumstances the CISD has substantial potential to fail.

While intervening too soon can be a problem, waiting more than several months to do a CISD can be potentially harmful to the participants. Victims' defense systems are often reintegrated by that time. The debriefing may break up some natural defenses and re-traumatize the group or individuals within the group if done after too long a passage of time.

If too much time has passed since the incident (3 to 4 months) one might consider not holding a debriefing, but seeing people on an individual basis and seeing if they have left over reactions to the incident. In some cases, referrals to mental health professionals may be required. In other cases, an educational program on critical incident (or traumatic) stress may be helpful.

There has been no evidence developed to date which indicates that one time of the day is better for a debriefing than another. Debriefings have been held successfully at any time of the day or night. Of course, what is of importance is to have the debriefing at a time which is mutually convenient to the CISD team and the participants in the debriefing. Most importantly, debriefings should be held at a time when the participants are emotionally "ready" to accept and benefit from the debriefing. The right kind of help at the right place will not be useful if the recipients of the help are not ready to accept it. Psychological readiness in response to acute critical incidents often occurs within the 24 to 72 hour "window" previously mentioned, but some critical incidents, especially disasters, require a far longer waiting period.

PLACE

Debriefings can take place in practically any private, quiet location. They have been provided with the group gathered under a tree. This is certainly not the most ideal setting, but it emphasizes the point that a debriefing is not limited to one site or another. Debriefings have been held in living rooms of homes, libraries, meeting halls, hotel conference rooms, union halls and many other facilities.

It is usually not possible to obtain a perfect facility, but if an ideal debriefing room did exist, it could be described as follows:

- Private
- Quiet
- Movable furniture
- Well-lighted but with adjustable lights
- Comfortable seats
- Suitable for the size of the group, not too large or small
- A single door
- Air conditioned or heated
- Well-ventilated
- No windows which allow a view in from the outside
- Available for the full length of the debriefing
- With one or more small private rooms for individual consultations

DEBRIEFING ROOM ARRANGEMENT

Having an ideal room will not be helpful to the CISD team if the room is not arranged properly. If the group is small (4 - 12 people) the debriefing can be carried out in a living room of a home or in a small conference room. It does not matter if the group participants are seated around a table or if a coffee table is in the middle of the group. In some countries the local culture prefers this arrangement. Local customs and cultural differences should be adhered to whenever possible. If the group is larger than twelve, this arrangement may not be possible. Choose a larger room and arrange the chairs in a circle large enough to accommodate the group. Tables and other furniture may have to be moved to the side of the room to assure that each person in the group has a good view of most of the others.

Avoid placing the chairs so close that the participants grow uncomfortable with the close proximity to one another. Enough chairs should be in the circle to accommodate the CISD team as well as the participants. Sometimes, people arrive late for the debriefing and a few extra chairs should be placed into the circle before the debriefing starts. Having the chairs in place produces less disruption if someone does come in late. The CISD team is spaced more or less equally among the group members. The CISD team does not sit all together on one side of the circle. The following diagrams provide samples of the typical debriefing seating arrangements. Figure 7.2 shows a typical two-member team debriefing team placement. Figures 7.3 and 7.4 show typical three-member CISD team placements. Figures 7.5 and 7.6 show four-member placements.

The door to the debriefing room should be closed, but not locked. A sign may be placed on the door which notifies anyone who would come to the door that a debriefing is in progress and personnel from the emergency organizations who were involved in the event are welcome to enter. Late arrivals should be instructed to enter without knocking. If there is fear that news media representatives or other people who are not to be involved in the debriefing might show up, an extra peer support person is brought to debriefing and stationed outside of the door. If unwanted people show up, that peer does not permit them to enter the room.

In cases in which only one or two mental health professionals are working as part of a Community Response Team with non-emergency groups, it would probably be better to lock the door to maintain better control of the group without fear of interruption (as long as the locked door causes none of the participants to become distressed). The team leader might simply inquire among participants as to whether the door should be locked to keep uninvited people out of the room. Late arrivals in such a group would have to knock to gain entry into the debriefing. They should be instructed by means of a sign to knock in order to get into the room.

The team leader should be positioned in such a manner that the door is not behind him or her. The management of the door is the responsibility of one of the peers (see "door keeper" role below), not the mental health person who is the team leader. A position as far away from the door as possible is usually best for the mental health professional who holds the team leader role. (See the section below entitled, "Team member debriefing roles").

FIGURE 7.2

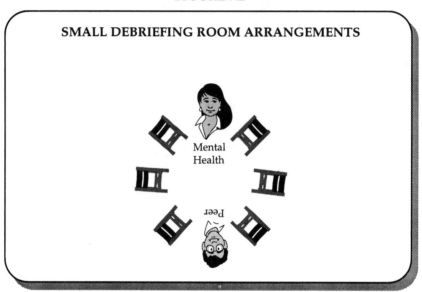

SMALL DEBRIEFING ROOM ARRANGEMENTS

FIGURE 7.3

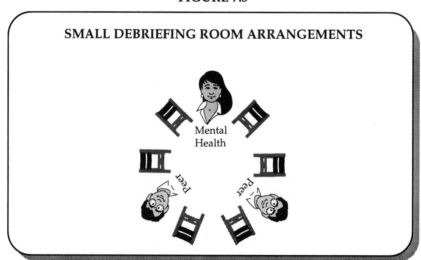

SMALL DEBRIEFING ROOM ARRANGEMENTS

FIGURE 7.4

LARGE DEBRIEFING ROOM ARRANGEMENTS

FIGURE 7.5

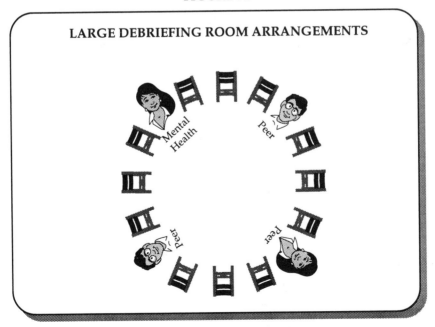

LARGE DEBRIEFING ROOM ARRANGEMENTS

FIGURE 7.6

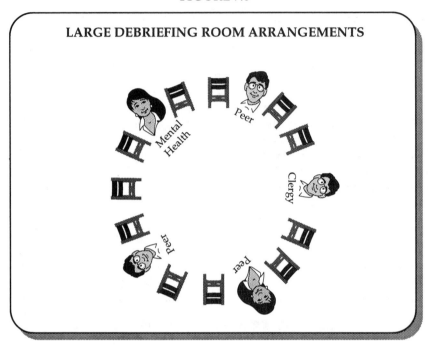

LARGE DEBRIEFING ROOM ARRANGEMENTS

Sometimes, the team leaders may use eyes or very slight hand motions to communicate with one or more of the peers. So it is important that the leader be able to see the peers who are serving on the debriefing team.

FOOD

Whenever possible, refreshments should be served after the debriefing. It helps to keep those who attended the debriefing together a little longer. This allows the CISD team members the opportunity to contact every person on an individual basis. Words of support, encouragement and understanding can be offered by the CISD team members to those who participated in the debriefing. Some people like to speak to a team member personally and privately rather than to talk about their reactions to an event in the group setting.

The best types of food are those which are not likely to enhance stress such as fresh fruits, fruit juices and alike. The practical realities are that what people like to eat may not be the very best for them. Having some refreshments available is better than not having any at all. Sometimes a CISD team needs to arrange for cookies or cake to "entice" the participants to stay nearby for a brief period of time after the debriefing. All food arrangements must be made in advance of the debriefing.

INSTRUCTIONS TO THE PARTICIPANTS' SUPERVISORS

Many supervisors want to know what to tell their personnel before the debriefing team arrives. If the CISD team is cognizant of the fact that the supervisor is in the position to either enhance the debriefing or destroy its potential benefit, the question will be taken seriously and answered appropriately.

Supervisors need to have an explanation of what a debriefing is and what it is not. They need to know that it is not psychotherapy, nor is it investigative. The supervisor should know that it is his or her job to encourage the personnel to attend the debriefing session for the good of the entire organization as well as the individuals in the group. Supervisors should be told about the team and the fact that peer support personnel have a major role to play should be emphasized. The supervisor also needs to assure the personnel that no one has to speak if they choose not to. The fact that no notes are taken and that the information is strictly confidential is of significant importance. The supervisor should be advised to tell the personnel that their attendance and participation is very important because each of them experienced the incident from a different perspective and each has a part of the event to add during the debriefing to help all of the others have the same information. Supervisors can serve as useful role models when they are honest and candid about their own reactions to the critical incident.

Supervisors should be informed as to the CISD team requirements, for example, requirements for the size of the room and what is needed in the room; that the chairs are set in a circle; that personnel should have their pagers and radios turned off during the debriefing; and that the food should be provided after the debriefing.

The supervisors have another responsibility which can directly affect the CISD team's performance. For a team to work well during a debriefing they need to be well aware of the incident. They need to see the pictures and diagrams of the incident and listen to tapes of the call. The supervisor should make sure that the CISD team gets the opportunity to review the incident report or at least that some member of the department give the team a brief overview of the incident which is to be debriefed.

HELPING THE ORGANIZATION PREPARE FOR THE DEBRIEFING

Besides the instructions given to the supervisors, which are described in the previous section, the organization hosting the CISD should be helped to prepare for the debriefing in several other ways. The command staff should invite every member who was involved in the incident. Field command personnel should be part of the debriefing. Only in very unusual cases are the commanders split out from the rank and file personnel for debriefings. For example, when a commander is the target of extreme anger or resentment by rank and file personnel, or when the rank and file feel they can't trust the command staff. In those cases, a separate debriefing is probably necessary. It may be helpful, somewhat later, to bring both groups together for a discussion of the event in an effort to resolve outstanding difficulties.

Sometimes it is necessary for the CISD team to hold an additional meeting with the commanders who may have special needs which they would like to discuss with the CISD team members without having their personnel listening in.

The organization should be advised to keep a low profile with the media regarding the debriefing. If the media representatives are asking questions about the debriefing, they should be referred to the local CISD team or to the International Critical Incident Stress Foundation to obtain further information about the debriefing process.

The team members should listen carefully to the questions and concerns of the organization and attempt to alleviate those concerns. The team coordinator usually has numerous telephone contacts with the organization before the debriefing actually occurs. Communications with the organization is of paramount importance during the crisis period. Sometimes the coordinator is able to help the organization find some local resources before the CISD can be deployed. Sometimes a trained CISD peer lives nearby the organization and can be sent in as an advance stabilizing force before the full team arrives.

INCIDENT REVIEW

CISD teams arrive at the site of the debriefing about an hour before the debriefing starts. One of the first tasks they have is to perform an incident review to familiarize themselves with the event they are going to be addressing in the debriefing.

The more a CISD team knows about the incident before starting the debriefing, the better they will be able to do their job. Significant surprises during the debriefing usually cause discomfort in the team members and possibly in the debriefing participants as well. Surprises also cause disruption in the flow of the CISD process.

Most CISD teams like to review the written information on the event. They like to read the newspaper clippings and the incident report. If a preliminary report has been worked up by the time of the debriefing, it too is read by the CISD team. The team members also listen to the audio tapes of the incident, view slides or video tapes, look at charts and diagrams and review any other materials which can give them a good working knowledge of the incident.

Sometimes the reports or newspaper accounts of the incident are incomplete or inaccurate. CISD teams should then ask pertinent operational questions of training officers, commanders, supervisors and or some members of the organization. It is important to avoid questions which lead people into discussions of their reactions to the event. Those will be brought out in the debriefing. What is important during the review is that the CISD team become familiar with the operational aspects of the case.

CIRCULATION WITH THE GROUP

The incident review is seldom sufficient to fully prepare the team to process the debriefing. There are two other steps which may be taken before the debriefing begins. Once the incident review is complete, the CISD team splits up and each member begins to circulate among the group members and meet the participants who are coming into the debriefing room. Conversations are a mix of questions with a serious purpose and casual conversation designed to take the edge off the tension and let the participants know a little about the CISD team members. The minimal familiarity between the CISD team and the debriefing's participants usually helps the introduction to the debriefing to progress smoothly. It helps the group relax a little and begin to trust the CISD team members.

The questions which are more task oriented are listed below. Other questions can easily be added to the list and some can be modified or eliminated if the team member decides that they are not important or need to be revamped. The CISD team must use an enormous amount of sensitivity as they ask these questions. They should also be ready to drop any question which would not be handled well by the participants for any reason. It is also important the CISD team not have a memorized set of questions. They should have a free flowing question pattern which gives them some good information but does not come across as artificial or contrived. It is important that people use there own words when working with a distressed group. The words printed in the questions below are only a guide and not to be taken as some unchangeable absolute. Common sense needs to be the guide of CISD team members.

1. How well do the people in this organization work together?
2. How well do you get along with the boss?
3. What is the relationship between the staff and the supervisors?
4. Is there anything about the situation that you folks believe might not come out during the debriefing, but which you think we ought to be aware of?
5. Is there anything really unusual or bizarre about this situation which the CISD team should know before we start the debriefing?
6. Are there any relationships going on between people in this organization which either affected the situation or are now being affected by the situation?
7. Anything else which we might be interested in?
8. Has anything similar to this critical incident ever occurred before?
9. Any other pertinent information.

Once the team has had sufficient time to circulate around with participants, (10 - 45 minutes) it excuses itself from the group and holds a brief meeting in a separate room. They should encourage the debriefing participants to take care of their personal needs by utilizing the rest rooms before the debriefing begins. The CISD strategy meeting is the last opportunity for the team to make a plan for the debriefing intervention before it actually begins. When possible, the CISD should start on time to reduce anticipatory anxiety.

STRATEGY MEETING WITH CISD TEAM MEMBERS

During the strategy meeting the CISD team privately discusses its approach to the debriefing. Team members are assigned to specific roles - door keeper, co-leader, teaching team and so forth (see below for details). The mental health professional encourages the peer support personnel to actively participate in the debriefing by making statements or introducing questions as necessary for the good of the group. The exact seating position of the team is discussed and agreed upon. The CISD team briefly discusses the event and any points which are considered unusual are brought out so that each of the team members has a good idea of what to expect in the debriefing. If more than the ordinary group resistance is expected, the team members are forewarned about it and a decision to have a slightly longer and more carefully worded introduction is made. Special teaching topics are assigned to the CISD team. If team members have any clarifications or questions, they are handled during the strategy meeting. Special instructions for this particular debriefing are given by the team leader. When every member of the team feels that he or she has been well informed about the incident and the strategy to be followed in the debriefing, the team ends its brief strategy meeting and goes into the debriefing room.

TEAM MEMBER DEBRIEFING ROLES

The CISD team has to perform numerous functions during and after the debriefing. No person can do all of the functions single-handedly and expect to do an excellent job with all of them. The tasks of the debriefing must be divided up among the team members. Peer support and mental health professionals need to blend their talents and abilities together for the benefit of the entire group.

TEAM LEADER

The team leader is the mental health professional assigned to the debriefing. The team leader's role is to use his or her communication skills to tactfully invite and encourage the group participants to discuss the traumatic event. The team leader also keeps a careful eye on the overall psychological well-being of the group and especially on any one in the group who may be experiencing more distress than the others.

The team leader is very involved in the teaching aspects of the debriefing and attempts to help people clarify their own perspectives of the incident. The team leader frequently has to weave the various aspects of the group experience into a coordinated pattern so that people can recognize their own part of the experience as a part of a bigger picture. The team leader asks occasional questions, or makes occasional comments when it is appropriate, and listens intently throughout the debriefing. If the discussion becomes too intense for the other team members to manage effectively, the team leader may need to enter the discussion to balance it, to explain certain issues or to help people see their own parts of the experience more clearly. The team leader attempts to bring the group out of the debriefing on as positive a level as possible in light of the tragedy they have experienced.

Good team leaders develop their skills over time and with a variety of experiences. They would be far more effective if they were to come to the debriefing with a background of exposure to the emergency services professions. The more they have cross familiarized themselves with the emergency services before the debriefing, the better. Ride along programs, visits to the emergency room or the communications center and spending time at the fire, police and emergency medical service stations is crucial to developing a proper understanding of the emergency services personality and their jobs. In fact, we urge all mental health professionals to become familiar with the emergency services "culture" before providing any service to those personnel.

Team leaders who are solely working on Community Response Teams with non-emergency populations in the community do not require such exposure to emergency services personnel. A point to be emphasized is that team leadership is actually shared among all of the CISD team members. Running an effective debriefing requires a very interactive leadership style which recognizes the abilities of each team member.

CO-LEADER

If the debriefing is with the emergency services professions, the co-leader is one of the peers. The peer who is chosen for this role typically has the most experience as a peer debriefer. If the debriefing is for a community group not associated with the emergency services, the co-leader is usually another mental health professional.

The co-leader's main role is to share the leadership of the group with the team leader. The co-leader will bring up any items in the introductory remarks which the team leader did not say and will add several important comments of his or her own. The co-leader watches the group members for signs of distress and questions, clarifies and makes statements whenever they are appropriate. The co-leader plays a significant role in the teaching phase of the debriefing. The co-leader helps the leader to summarize the debriefing and remains available to the participants after the debriefing to make contacts with those who need a few extra words of support or perhaps a referral.

The co-leader usually has a considerable role in providing for follow up contacts. In many cases, especially with emergency personnel, it is the peer support personnel more than the mental health professionals who have the primary responsibility for the initial contacts within a few days of the debriefing. The peers usually encourage emergency workers who need more help to contact mental health professionals.

The co-leader assigns specific follow up tasks to appropriate CISD team members, for example one peer may be assigned the task of advising the unit supervisor. Another may be given the task of calling two people in the debriefing who are more troubled than the others.

DOOR KEEPER

The door keeper has a key role in debriefings. The door keeper will prevent any unauthorized or inappropriate individuals from entering the room where the debriefing is taking place. This includes people in the organization who were not involved at the scene, family members of participants in the debriefing who are not part of the organization, spectators, media personnel and citizens who just happened to be at the scene of the incident. The door keeper allows in any appropriate person who is a member of one of the organizations being debriefed and who was involved in the incident and arrives late.

The door keeper has another vital role. If someone leaves the debriefing, it is the door keeper's job to go out after that person and encourage that person to return. This task is easy if the person is only going to the men's or ladies' room to take care of personal needs. The door keeper simply has to remind the person to come back into the debriefing as soon as possible. If, however, the person is distressed and is leaving the debriefing because of that distress, then it is important for the door keeper to gently question, listen intently, and give as much support as possible to the distressed person. It is very important to encourage the person to return to the debriefing as soon as possible. Sometimes the person needs reassurance that they will not be called upon nor will they have to speak if they do not want to. Occasionally, they need to be told that they are needed by the other participants inside the debriefing and that they can be of great help to some of the people in the debriefing room but they have to be inside the room to be helpful. Almost everyone will return to the debriefing.

Only in rare instances do people leave the debriefing and refuse to return to it. In those cases, it is important that the door keeper try to engage the person on a one-on-one basis. If the person refuses any effort to assist them, then an attempt is made to get the person's name and phone number or at least to give them one's card and a verbal invitation to call if they would like to go back over something related to the incident.

CLERGY

If clergy, who are trained in the CISD process, are part of the CISD team they play a significant role as a listener and guide. Preaching and praying are generally discouraged during the actual debriefing process in that not all participants may share similar religious beliefs.

The clergy, then, may make appropriate comments or ask questions during the debriefing. They may also listen and try to see which people might need a little extra support after the debriefing is concluded. They are very active in checking with people after the debriefing to see that people are coping adequately or if they need help with any aspects of the event or their return to normal functions (especially from a spiritual perspective). Spiritual interventions such as praying or preaching are generally best implemented after the debriefing, usually on a one-to-one basis.

PEERS

Community Response Teams can work without peers. They may utilize only mental health professionals. But CISM teams doing debriefings with emergency personnel absolutely need peer support personnel. The keys to success in working with emergency personnel appear to be:

1. Familiarity with the nature and culture of emergency services

2. Rapid intervention

3. An emphasis on the pragmatic, for example, stress management techniques

4. Emergency service "peer" personnel are the embodiment of these characteristics and are therefore an integral pact of the CISD team

During the debriefing, the peer support personnel who are not assigned to specific tasks such as co-leader and door keeper do not just sit back during the debriefing. They have important roles to fulfill. They must listen carefully to the discussion, observe the participants, pick out those who they think might need additional help and teach some of the stress reduction suggestions during the teaching phase. There is no room in a debriefing for someone to just watch. There are too many things which must be done. All of the peers on a CISD team are part of the process.

The peer support personnel help to make the introductory remarks, ask questions and make statements when it is appropriate and they help to bring the debriefing to a close by participating actively in the summary remarks. When one of the participants is talking, the team leader might be listening intently to that person and looking at the person as he or she speaks. In that case, the peer support personnel should be looking at the other group members in an effort to read their facial expression and their body language. If the team leader or co-leader is ready to move ahead into another phase in the debriefing, but one of the peers recognizes that a participant wants to say something else, the peer gives the person the opportunity to speak.

The peers and mental health professionals work together during the entire debriefing. Each has an important job to do and assists the others in doing their jobs. The debriefing process is a team effort.

THE CRITICAL INCIDENT STRESS DEBRIEFING

All of the preparations which have been made before the debriefing help to assure its success. Teams should take the time necessary to set up the debriefing properly because the debriefing is the most difficult of the CISM interventions to apply. Efforts made to arrange it properly and to choose the right team members increase the potential that the debriefing will be a success. Since the objective of the debriefing is to mitigate the impact of stress and restore the personnel to normal functions as quickly as possible, a carefully planned approach to the distressed individuals is essential.

It is very tempting for the person who is untrained in the CISD process to read the sections below and believe they are fully trained and ready to manage debriefings. That, of course, is a false belief. Reading about debriefings is not considered training. There are many subtle issues and techniques which cannot be adequately described here. Only appropriate training by qualified and experienced CISD trainers will provide adequate preparation for conducting debriefings. Anything less would be unprofessional and could prove to be dangerous to distressed people expecting quality trained services from debriefing team members. It is easy to negatively affect distressed individuals by attempting CISD services without the proper training.

The formal CISD intervention has seven phases. Figure 7.7 below will be of assistance as the reader goes through the sections to follow.

We will now examine the CISD process step by step.

The overall strategy for a CISD team during a debriefing is to start at the point which is easiest to discuss and then move gradually into more emotionally intense discussions. After handling the intense materials the group is gradually brought back out of the intense discussions to the less intense until the discussion finally concludes.

1. INTRODUCTION

The introduction to the CISD is crucial. It sets the stage for all of the other phases of the debriefing. If the introduction is not handled well, it is likely that the remainder of the debriefing will be difficult. When debriefing teams have examined debriefings which they believe did not run as smoothly as they would have liked, they can almost always trace the problems to the introduction. This section of the debriefing should help a debriefing team to set a good base for the remainder of the debriefing process.

There are several objectives to be achieved during the introduction. The CISD team must:

- Point out the team members
- Introduce the team leader
- Establish the leadership of the team
- Explain the purpose of the meeting
- Explain the process
- Motivate the participants

FIGURE 7.7

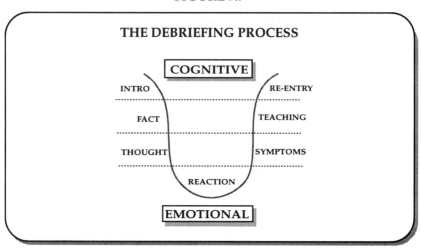

- Reduce resistance

- Explain the guidelines of the CISD

- Gain the cooperation of the participants

- Answer primary concerns and limit anxiety

- Announce the first set of questions to come

- Encourage mutual help

Although the peer team members are pointed out in the introductory phase, their actual introductions are held off until the fact phase. Peer introductions can be used to help the group get past the discomfort which can occur if there is any significant display of powerful emotions early on in the debriefing process. More information will be presented on peer introductions in the section to follow on the "Fact" phase.

The entire CISD team must show itself to be confident, and as relaxed as the horrible circumstances of an event will allow. They will need to demonstrate by their mood and words that they are sympathetic and concerned with the plight of the distressed personnel. The team needs to believe that they have the proper training and experience to help. They do not however, want to appear over confident or arrogant. Arrogance can be avoided when the team realizes that they can easily be in the same position of turmoil as the participants in the debriefing if the incident had happened to themselves instead of the distressed group before them. It also helps to recognize that a debriefing team is in the very privileged position of hearing the thoughts and emotions of emergency personnel, a position which few other people will have in their lives.

The rules or guidelines for a debriefing which must be discussed in the introduction are:

- Participants are asked to look around the room and point out anyone, who for any reason might not belong in the group. A few minutes might be spent confirming people's suitability for participation in the debriefing session. (Remember, in a line of duty death situation, the entire organization is affected and all members are invited to a debriefing, not only those at the scene).

- Strict confidentiality. Whatever is stated in the room should stay in the room. This rule applies to the team as well as to the participants. After a debriefing, people may discuss their own feelings and reactions or the things that the team taught, but they may not discuss what they have heard from another person in the debriefing.

- The participants should speak for themselves. People may describe others reactions as they saw them ("I saw John running"), but they may not interpret those observations ("He was afraid"). Each person has the right to speak for themselves ("I was afraid") and not have someone else do that for them.

- Participants in the debriefing do not have to speak if they do not want to. Everyone has a right to refuse to speak. It may not be in their best interests, but they do have that right. Participants are told that they merely have to shake their heads in a "no" pattern and the team will leave them alone.

- Participants are asked not to leave the room and not return. It is important that they complete the entire process. The participants should be forewarned leaving the debriefing may actually cause them to feel worse later. If they must leave to utilize a rest room, they should be instructed to return immediately.

- No cameras, recorders or note taking of any type is ever permitted in a debriefing. There is never a reason for taking notes in a debriefing. If a team member is concerned about following up on an individual they can get their name and phone number after the debriefing is over.

- CISD is not psychotherapy nor is it a substitute for psychotherapy. It is simply a discussion of a traumatic event which is led by a team of specially trained people who are attempting to mitigate the impact of a traumatic event and restore people to normal function as soon as possible.

- CISD is not an investigation. Participants are instructed not to disclose any information which would jeopardize an investigation, or would constitute an admission of criminal activity or deliberate violations of any usual policies and procedures. Participants are given permission to filter out any information which they feel is inappropriate to discuss in a large group. They are urged to save such information for the investigative team.

- Participants are urged to temporarily forget their rank or station in life and just be a person who is affected by a tragedy.

- Participants are urged to turn off pagers, radios and other distracting devices.

- Participants are informed that the CISD team is there for them and that the team will be available after the debriefing is complete.

- Participants are urged to help one another by participating actively in the debriefing. They are instructed that even if they do not feel that they need a debriefing, others in the group might benefit from it. They can be helpful to those people by discussing their role in the incident.

- CISD is not a critique of the operational aspects of the incident.

- The participants are told that the only reason the debriefing is held is to help people to recover as quickly as possible and return to normal aspects of their lives. Experience shows that people who talk about traumatic events sleep and eat better and generally resume normal aspects of their lives faster.

- People in the debriefing need to be informed that reports are not made about the individuals in the debriefing to their supervisors.

- Participants are informed that within a few minutes the team will be asking them to state who they are, what their role in the incident was and what happened from their own perspective.

- No breaks will be taken during the debriefing. If participants need to take care of personal needs, they may leave, but they are requested to return immediately.

- Participants are informed that the team has many important pieces of information to teach to the group. The teaching aspects of the session will occur toward the end of the debriefing.

- Reminders of the need for confidentiality are made several times during the introductory remarks.

- Participants are urged to ask questions any time they need to.

The items in the introductory remarks phase of a debriefing may change somewhat from debriefing to debriefing. At times, it is necessary to elaborate on many of the guidelines. This is especially so when a debriefing is being provided to a new group which has never had one before. In a group which has a number of experiences with debriefings, the participants usually know the rules and only need a reminder.

Throughout the introductory remarks the team should be speaking with confidence and concern. The CISD team members need to be relaxed as they speak so that they do not raise unnecessary anxieties in the group of participants. The team members need to be very alert to the verbal and non-verbal emotional cues which will be displayed by the participants in the debriefing. They must likewise be prepared to manage the resistance expressed by individuals in the group. If they ignore the resistance during the introductory remarks phase, it will not go away. It will show up again later in the debriefing. Unresolved resistance usually damages the debriefing when it shows up in more delicate phases of the process.

2. FACT

The easiest thing for emergency service personnel to discuss is usually a description of the facts of an incident. Facts are a collection of items outside of oneself. Facts are impersonal. Discussions of facts are not as distressing as attempting to talk about how one feels, which is a very personal discussion. This is especially so for emergency personnel who are highly cognitively defended and cautiously avoid almost any discussions of emotions. They sometimes fear that they will be overcome and incapacitated by those emotions and, therefore, unable to perform their jobs adequately. They are often comfortable when someone asks them to describe what happened. They understand facts; they use facts all the time in their work. They almost cling to facts during discussions about a situation. The fact phase is the most logical place to begin a discussion about a tragic event.

To get people talking about a situation in the fact phase, the team leader simply needs to state something like this: "The CISD team wasn't present during the incident. We only know some bits and pieces of the incident. It would be very helpful if we could get some understanding of what happened by having you tell us about the incident. So, we would like you to tell us who you are, what your role was during the incident and, briefly, what happened from your perspective. It doesn't matter if what you experienced is different from what everyone else experienced. You all had an important part to play in the situation and it would help everyone to have a big picture built by putting all your pieces of the incident together. If you choose not to speak that is okay. Just shake your head and we will pass right over you. For the sake of organization we are going to start over here on my left (right) and go around the room. Again, what we need to know is:

1. Who are you?

2. What was your job or role during the incident?

3. What happened from your point of view?"

The participants in the group will begin to tell their stories. The exact order of the telling does not really matter. The last to arrive at the scene might be the first to speak. All of the pieces will come together as everyone gets their chance to speak. The sorting out of the story comes naturally to an alert CISD team which has done its homework before the debriefing.

If the group is larger than about twenty people, or if there is some unavoidable and arbitrarily mandated short time frame, it may be too time consuming for each person in the group to tell their part of the incident. An alternative fact phase is then employed. The questions differ a bit from the ones outlined above, but they still cause the group to discuss the facts. The alternate fact phase questions are:

1. Who arrived first on scene?

2. Which units came in after them?

3. What happened as additional units arrived?

Usually a "spokesperson" from each unit will describe their unit's role in the operation in a shortened version. Perhaps only six or seven people will speak. That is perfectly fine. There is no need to be alarmed if some people do not get an opportunity to speak during a debriefing. It is a mistake to think that people derive no benefit from a debriefing unless they speak. Many people choose only to listen during a debriefing, even when they have ample opportunities to speak. Yet they report that simply listening to others was beneficial. Often during the fact phase, participants will spontaneously begin to show emotions.

When participants in a debriefing are asked to describe the *facts* of the situation and they begin to express their *emotions*, it is a sign of how badly they have been affected by the incident. But it does not signal an invitation for the debriefing team to probe further. Personnel who have been probed feel angry. They feel that they may be expressing far more than they had intended. They usually feel surprised by their own emotional reaction to the situation. They prefer to be left alone and not encouraged to let more of their emotions show. The CISD team needs to remember that emergency personnel in particular have a great deal of difficulty losing control in the presence of their fellow workers. They are very embarrassed by an unexpected show of their own emotions. They will have to face their fellow workers long after the debriefing team has left. The very best actions which can be taken by the CISD team are to:

- Acknowledge the emotion.

- Validate that the emotion is appropriate.

- Reassure the individual and the group that the emotion is expected and that any person in a similar circumstance would have the same emotional reaction.

- Move off the person and onto someone else unless that person signals that they wish to continue talking.

In addition, the other participants may become very unnerved by this early show of emotion. They do not know what to do. They begin to fear that the CISD team is losing control of the debriefing. It is usually this kind of a circumstance which causes a great deal of anxiety for the other participants in the debriefing. The next few participants to talk will hold back much of what they would have said had they not seen the emotional reaction in their fellow worker, or they may not speak at all. This is where the peers, who have not yet had the chance to introduce themselves will be very helpful.

As each participant completes his or her answer to the fact phase questions, the team listens carefully and notices the change in the discussion which has occurred from the beginning of the fact phase until the emotions have shown up. If a strong emotion has been expressed and the group has become anxious, the next *peer* to speak will introduce him- or herself. The introduction of that particular peer is a bit longer (by perhaps a few sentences) than usual. The extra time it takes the peer to make this introduction is usually all the time it takes to calm the entire group. The peer's introduction, coming as it does in the middle of the fact phase, adds a degree of control to the debriefing. The introduction allows a little breathing space before the next participant begins to discuss their answers to the fact phase questions. When the discussion of who they are, their roles and what happened continues, the discussion lacks much of the uncomfortable anxiety which had been stirred by the emotions brought up by one of the previous participants.

The fact phase may take between five and twenty five minutes depending on how many people are present and the depth of information they bring up. Team members may have to clarify certain responses. They do so whenever it appears appropriate. Sometimes the participants bring up elements of the thoughts or reactions phases even though those questions were not yet presented to them. The team members listen carefully to those items but do not usually react to them in the fact phase. They may use those comments from the participants as material to be presented later in the debriefing during the teaching or re-entry phases.

When the fact phase is complete, the thought phase begins immediately.

3. THOUGHT

The thought phase begins when the team leader asks the participants to state what their first thought or most prominent thought was once they got off an auto pilot mode of operating. Since many emergency personnel are predominantly cognitive in their defense system, most of their answers will orient somewhat toward the operational aspects of the incident. Many say things like, "I thought the suspect wouldn't jump out the window" or "My first thought was, 'God, don't let this one be a kid.'" But the emotional aspects of the case cannot be eliminated or blocked altogether. Some will say things like this: "I was afraid that we would lose the whole street," "I was really angry that one human being could do something like this to another."

The thought phase is a transitional phase between the factual world and the world that is close and personal. The facts are outside of a person; the thoughts are internal and part of the person. It is impossible to respond to the questions about thoughts without some leakage of feelings into the discussion. CISD teams should expect this leakage as a part of the CISD process. *The thought phase represents a transitional phase from the cognitive domain to the affective (emotional) domain.* The CISD team should welcome the emotion-related comments of the thought phase as a sign that the process is working and on schedule.

If, however, the emotional content becomes too intense too quickly, the group being debriefed may experience more anxiety and a desire to resist any efforts to bring them any closer to their own emotions. Sometimes the participants express diffuse anger at the team members by claiming that the process is bad. Sometimes, they try to stick only to further discussions of facts and operational procedures. Occasionally they show powerful emotions and look for immediate rescue from the team. Sometimes they will walk out of the debriefing.

No one can predict all of the possible responses from the participants in a debriefing during the transition phase. The participants are testing themselves as well as the CISD team. The team has to be ready for anything. If someone leaves, the "door keeper" team member goes after them and attempts to bring them back. If the emotions grow intense, acknowledgment, validation and /or reassurance may be required by the team members. If defuse anger is expressed, some of it may need to be absorbed. Some of it may need to be redirected. The CISD team must stay very alert during this phase. Their reactions will be made after only a few seconds of thought. They usually make the right choices because they are calm and thinking more rationally than the people in the debriefing who are distressed.

4. REACTION

The reaction phase is typically the most emotionally powerful of all. If the introduction, fact phase and the thought phase have been managed carefully by the CISD team, the reaction phase will flow relatively easily from the thought phase. The CISD team will find that its interactions in the group will quiet substantially during the reaction phase. In fact, most of the talking is done by the participants, not by the CISD team. This is how it should be. The CISD team should commit itself only to speak if their remarks are truly necessary and only if they will not interfere with the flow of discussion from the participants.

The question which triggers most of the discussion in the reaction phase is:

- What was the worse thing about this situation for you personally?

There are numerous variations on the question which will bring about a discussion of the emotions associated with the event. They are:

- What part of this event bothers you the most?

- If you could erase one part of the situation, what part would you choose to erase?

- What aspect of the situation causes you the most pain?

The discussion at this point is freelance. The team no longer goes around the room with the discussion. Whoever wants to speak may speak. Those who choose to be silent are silent. There is no order in the discussion. Going around the room is only done in the fact phase and in the thought phase. Now the whole group is given the opportunity to speak if and when they choose.

Initially the discussion may be slow. The participants are wrestling with the emotions that they have begun to connect to the incident. One participant will eventually say something and admit a feeling. Another will typically acknowledge fear, anger or grief. After a short period of time, most of the participants have said something.

Some of the comments may cause the entire group to go momentarily silent as another emotion crashes into their consciousness. Some comments will trigger a strong verbal group response. There may be shifting in the chairs, wringing of hands and many other nonverbal signals. Eyes may drop to the floor. Sometimes there are blank stares, sometimes tears or a voice that trembles with every painful word.

There are also many debriefings in which the emotions are very subtle. Tears may not be shown. There may be no significant observable emotions displayed. The words, however, may carry a great deal of emotional content. Every debriefing has its own character which depends on the magnitude of the event, the trust established in the group and the group's willingness to openly discuss their experiences and their reactions to it. Another factor which ties into how a group functions in the debriefing is the skill of the CISD team and how well they have established rapport with the group.

The reactions phase may last between 10 and 40 minutes (sometimes a bit longer) depending on the size of the group and the intensity of the incident. When the discussion drops off and several attempts by the team members to bring out more discussion from the group end with little or no response, it is a signal that the reaction phase has come to an end. The team should now move the group into the next phase of the debriefing, the symptom phase.

5. SYMPTOMS

The symptom phase is another transitional phase. The objective in this phase is to begin a movement of the group back from the emotionally laden content of the reaction phase toward more cognitively oriented material. The symptom phase is a natural part of the overall process from the cognitive domain to the emotional and then back to the cognitive domain. Stopping the debriefing at this point in the process would leave people in a charged emotional state which could possibly be detrimental. The debriefing is always continued to the end to complete the process and to restore people to the cognitive level so that they can resume the normal responsibilities of their lives armed with their customary set of psychological defenses intact.

The symptom phase is initiated when the team asks the participants to describe any cognitive, physical, emotional or behavioral experiences they may have encountered while they were working at the scene of the incident. The debriefing team may need to give several examples of stress related symptoms such as trembling hands, inability to make a decision, excessive silence or feelings of anger. Then the group spends several minutes talking about the various ways in which they experienced symptoms of distress while working at the scene.

The CISD team then asks the group what it was like for them during the next few days after the incident but before the debriefing. Again the participants begin to discuss the symptoms or signals of distress they encountered over the next few days.

Finally the CISD team asks the group if they have any leftover symptoms of distress from the time of the incident right up to and during the debriefing. The group may describe a variety of symptoms which they have carried into the debriefing.

On occasion, the participants are reluctant to bring up their symptoms because they fear that they are the only ones and that their symptoms may be abnormal. If the CISD team suspects that the group is reluctant to open up because of such a fear, the team may approach the question in a different manner. For example, the team may ask the entire group to answer by a show of hands how many had one type of symptom or another. Usually the team member asking the question picks a very common stress reaction and presents that symptom to the group and asks for a show of hands. Since it is more than likely that several members of the group would have experienced that very reaction, several hands typically go up. A few questions in a similar manner leaves the group feeling more relaxed and then the CISD team can generally ask the participants to add more information without a show of hands.

The symptoms phase is typically five to ten minutes long. Once the number of people pointing out symptoms decreases dramatically, the team makes a decision to move into the next phase of the debriefing, the teaching phase.

6. TEACHING

The teaching phase comes naturally after the symptoms phase. One connects very well with the other. It is easy to begin the teaching phase by pointing out several of the symptoms just described in the symptoms phase and letting the group know that those symptoms are normal, typical or to be expected after the type of critical incident they experienced. A skillful and experienced team can make the transition so smoothly that the participants in the debriefing do not even know that a new phase has begun.

All of the team members are very active in teaching the group. Some of the team members describe the typical symptoms of distress that are usually encountered. Other team members forewarn the group about symptoms which might not have shown up yet but might in the future. Other points made by the team members include comments that the group could not have done anything different during the operation because they had been trained to perform the operation in the manner in which they did. The team spends a good deal of time teaching the group a variety of stress survival strategies. Instructions are given on diet, exercise, rest, talking to one's family, working with the supervisors to initiate necessary procedural changes and a wide range of topics.

The teaching phase is very cognitive in approach. It is designed to bring the participants further away from the emotional content they had worked through in the reaction phase. Some of the information presented in this phase may be "earmarked" for specific participants, but the message is delivered to the group as a whole.

The teaching phase continues until the topics which are most important for this particular group of participants in a debriefing are exhausted. It is important not to drag this phase on to an extreme, however. The group being debriefed is likely to be quite tired by this phase and so will the CISD team. Teaching more than is really necessary will only infuriate the group and cause them to miss some of the most important messages from the team.

It is also important for the team to recognize that there are serious limitations to what can be taught in the teaching phase of a debriefing. Teaching somewhat complex techniques like meditation, progressive muscle relaxation and academically oriented cognitive restructuring strategies can be inappropriate at this point. It takes about five exposures to most stress management skills before they can be learned adequately. This type of teaching and learning cannot take place during a debriefing. Those learning experiences should be saved for other stress education opportunities. The teaching of less complex stress management techniques is encouraged, however.

Many times, at the end of the teaching phase, one of the CISD team members asks the group if there is anything which happened during the incident which makes them feel just a bit positive even if the overall event was one of the worst things they could have encountered. The question, if it is to be asked, must be asked with a great deal of sensitivity and concern. People may have a hard time seeing anything positive about the situation.

The question may be asked in the following manner.

- "Was there any small thing that happened during this incident that makes it just a little less chaotic or painful? Is there anything which gives you a little hope in the midst of all this pain?"

The teaching phase leads quite naturally into the re-entry phase.

7. RE-ENTRY

The last phase of the formal debriefing, the re-entry phase is the final opportunity to clarify issues, answer questions, make summary statements and return the group to their normal functions. This phase puts closure on the discussions which have just occurred in the debriefing. Like most things which are human, debriefings have a beginning, a middle and an ending. No part stands alone without the others. Only when an experience has an ending can the beginning and middle make any sense.

The re-entry which ends the debriefing has several segments and several tasks which need to be performed. The participants in the debriefing have several tasks which they need to work through and the CISD team also has several tasks which it must work through. The *participants* in a debriefing will need to:

1. Introduce any new material they wish to discuss.

2. Review old material already discussed.

3. Ask any questions they might have.

4. Discuss anything they wish which would help them to bring closure to the debriefing.

The *debriefing team* will need to:

1. Answer any questions posed to it.

2. Reassure and inform as needed.

3. State any feelings which are suspected to be there, but which have not been brought up by the participant.

4. Provide appropriate handouts.

5. Make summary comments.

The summary comment made by the CISD team members are drawn from their hearts. They are usually words of respect, encouragement, appreciation, support, gratefulness and direction. Every CISD team member must make a summary comment in the last few minutes of the debriefing. The participants are welcome to comment if they wish, but they are not called upon to do so.

As soon as the debriefing draws to a close the team begins its post debriefing activities. The team comes to its feet and begins to make contact with those people who seem to need something more than what the debriefing was able to do for them.

POST DEBRIEFING ACTIVITIES

ONE-ON-ONE

It was stated earlier in this chapter that one of the most common mistakes for a debriefing team was to believe that all of the work which needed to be done could be done in the debriefing. The debriefing is used more as a preventative than a cure. It is more of an assessment or screening tool than a treatment. There is much more which is left undone at the end of a debriefing. Teams which are not alert to that fact will make the mistake of thinking that the work is complete once the debriefing is finished.

As the group breaks up the debriefing team may begin to shake hands with the participants in the group and to move toward those who showed significant signs of distress during the debriefing. Another target will be those individuals who were too silent during the debriefing. The objective is to reach out to those who seem to need more. The debriefing may only have served as an opportunity for screening. They may only need a few supportive words from peers. For some that will be enough. For others, however, they will need a referral for individual therapy. (Referrals for individual psychotherapy are rare. A good guess would be 1 to 3% need referrals. Slightly more under extraordinary circumstances).

Frequently peer support personnel can manage the distressed person by a brief supportive visit or phone call. If a CISD team member believes that such a contact will be helpful to one of the personnel, arrangements are made between the distressed person and the peer support person and phone numbers or addresses are exchanged.

Refreshments are usually served immediately after the debriefing. The refreshments facilitate the interactions between the CISD team and the participants in the debriefing. The refreshments make it easier to keep the group together in one place and makes the contacts between team members and the participants much more natural.

The mental health professional is frequently called upon to see one or another of the participants in a one-on-one session in another room. The extra session may be enough for most people, but others may need a referral for therapy.

The contacts continue until the participants in the debriefing begin to drift away. When it becomes clear that no one is left to make a personal contact with, the CISD team prepares to leave. The team needs to hold its post debriefing meeting before leaving or it might decide to hold its post debriefing meeting right in the car on the way home or at some stop off point before returning home.

POST DEBRIEFING MEETING

The post debriefing meeting is a must.

The post debriefing meeting is one of the most important protections for the team against distressing the team members. There are several important tasks which will be accomplished during the post debriefing meeting. They include:

- Explore what was done during the debriefing so that the team members can learn more about the process and why certain decisions were made at one point or another, or why certain questions were asked.

- Assign specific follow up tasks to individual debriefing team members. There should be no confusion as to who is going to do follow up services for whom.

- Make sure the team members are "okay." This is a time to "debrief" the debriefers. If this is not done after every debriefing, people may return home distressed. Allow that to happen too often and a CISD team will lose good members.

The most important element of the post debriefing meeting, then, is the debriefing of the debriefers.

POST ACTION REPORT

The post action report is *optional*. It is kept as a mechanism by which the incident can be discussed at the next team meeting during the case review segment. The post action report should not contain any information which can be used to identify an individual who was in the debriefing. It is recommended that the post action report be simple and short. If one is written, it should consist of a single page with three paragraphs. Each paragraph has a specific function. They are:

- Brief description of the incident

- General themes discussed in the debriefing

- Summary of the instruction given to the participants of the debrieifing by the CISD team

The names of the CISD team, date of the debriefing and overall number of people debriefed may be useful information if the CISM team is trying to keep statistics on each of its team members. Those same statistics can be kept in a much more efficient manner if all the names of CISM team members are listed in one column and the types of CISM services are listed across the tops of other columns. When a team member provides a type of service the date of the intervention is recorded on the tally sheet. There is no need then to put this type of information on the post action report.

OTHER IMPORTANT CONSIDERATIONS IN DEBRIEFING

GROUP SIZE

- The ideal debriefing group size is between 4 and 20 people.

- A group of between 20 and 30 is okay, but it does take more time and certain other adjustments must be made in the debriefing.

- A group larger than 30 is obviously more difficult to work with.

- A larger group requires that the debriefing team utilize the alternative fact phase format (Which units arrived first? Who came in after them? What happened?) and allow less people to speak. It is also a good idea in the thought phase to ask, "What did you think when you got involved in the incident? Anyone who wants to speak feel free."

- Any group larger than 40 should cause the team to consider breaking the group into smaller subgroups if that is possible.

TARGETING GROUPS

When there are many people who need a debriefing, logical groups have to be targeted. Those most affected by an incident are the primary targets of a debriefing. Those directly involved are the next most logical target. Then the supervisory staff. Then those only involved in an indirect sense. Finally those who are affected but who were not involved.

Groups can be broken down according to several logical categories such as:

- Geographical location of the groups

- Time of arrival

- Specialty function

- Usual working group

- Common profession (law enforcement, fire, EMS)

PARTICIPANTS

Any emergency personnel who were involved in the incident should be invited to attend the debriefing. This includes supervisory staff. To exclude them produces an "us and them" atmosphere within the organization.

Bystanders, media personnel and other non-emergency people who might need support services should be handled separately from the emergency personnel. Mixing the groups is seldom wise since the non-emergency service workers might hear information that may be stressful in and of itself.

Family members of emergency personnel should also be handled separately. They may be distressed by hearing too much detail from their emergency services loved ones and the emergency services personnel may then shut down their discussions to protect their families.

BREAKS

No breaks are taken during a debriefing. Breaks in the flow of the debriefing disrupt the entire process and destroy the emotional momentum in the group.

NOT ON DUTY

Personnel in a debriefing must be relieved of all response duties. It is harmful for them to leave a debriefing in the middle to handle emergency calls. They are brought out of their cognitive defense system during a debriefing and having them respond on an emergency call could jeopardize their safety because they will be functioning more at the emotional level than at the cognitive level.

NOT A CRITIQUE

The CISD is not an operations critique. Ideally the operation critique would follow the CISD. But since that is frequently not possible, it would be a good second choice to have the operations critique complete when the debriefing is set up. It is never a good idea to mix the operations critique and the debriefing together.

CONFIDENTIALITY

Confidentiality is a must. When confidentiality is destroyed, the CISD team's effectiveness can be destroyed. CISD team members must take this commitment seriously.

FOLLOW UP SERVICES

Follow up services are crucial to completing the work begun in the debriefing. No one should assume that simply because the debriefing was provided the entire work of supporting the personnel has been accomplished. There is much more left to do. Without follow up services, the symptoms may return to some of the participants even more forcefully than they had before. People without follow up may feel abandoned and uncared for. They often feel that the help was incomplete.

Follow up services begin with the contacts made with the participants of the debriefing immediately after the debriefing is complete. Within 24 hours, follow up services will intensify for those who have been identified as needing it most.

There are many types of follow up services which can be provided: they include but are not limited to:

- Station visits
- Telephone calls
- Chaplain visits
- Individual consultations
- Referrals for therapy
- Additional meeting with a subgroup
- Ride along programs
- Family sessions

- Follow up meeting with whole group one week after the debriefing

- Others as required

SUMMARY

This chapter has described the debriefing process in detail. It should be seen as the most complex of intervention strategies for CISM teams. In fact CISM teams are urged to assess carefully the real need for a debriefing and determine if there are other interventions which might be more suitable before committing the team to a CISD.

The chapter includes numerous specific guidelines which have been developed by many teams throughout the world over a ten year period of time and many thousands of experiences with debriefings.

The reader is again cautioned that the debriefing process cannot be learned adequately by simply reading about the process. One who expects to do debriefings well should have appropriate training to assure excellence in the provision of services.

Chapter 8

DEFUSINGS

INTRODUCTION

The previous chapter discussed the debriefing process in great detail. The debriefing was described as the most complex of all of the interventions by CISM teams. It was also pointed out in that chapter that since debriefings were time and labor intensive and also somewhat difficult to organize, a CISM team should perform a careful assessment of the need for a debriefing. It was suggested that there are other interventions which could be used to assist emergency personnel. These other interventions might eliminate the need to do a debriefing. In some cases, they may actually be more suitable than the debriefing. This chapter will discuss the defusing process which has been widely used by CISM teams in several countries. It is frequently a replacement for the debriefing. In many cases, the defusing is equally effective as a debriefing if it applied within certain time limitations. Even in situations in which a debriefing was still necessary because the event was so powerful, the defusing was an effective intervention. It calmed the reactions of the emergency personnel sufficiently to allow the necessary time to properly set up a full debriefing.

DEFUSING DEFINED

The word defusing means to render something harmless before it can do damage. That is the essence of the support service which a CISM team provides when it deploys a defusing team after an incident. The overall objective is to render the situation harmless to those who were exposed to it. If the situation cannot be made totally harmless, then at least every effort is made to reduce its potential for harm.

A defusing is a small group process which is instituted after any traumatic event (critical incident) powerful enough to overwhelm the coping mechanisms of the people exposed to it. The events which necessitate a defusing have the same or very close to the same intensity as events which would trigger a debriefing. The difference is not to be found in the type of incident, but in the timing of the response and the type of response to the incident.

The defusing is a shortened version of the debriefing, but it is more immediate in its application. The defusing team does not have to wait out the first twenty four hours to intervene. Instead, they attempt to intervene as early as possible after the critical incident. Because it is provided so early, it does not go as deep into the emotional material as a debriefing does. It offers an opportunity for people involved in a horrible event to talk briefly about that experience before they have time to rethink the experience and possibly misinterpret its true meaning. There is at least some evidence which suggests that an immediate intervention is more beneficial than waiting until the usual twenty four hours has passed before the debriefing is set up for emergency personnel.

Although the defusing has some structure, it is much less organized than the formal debriefing. Its structure will be described in the sections to follow. The defusing is less complex than the debriefing. It is easier to organize and manage. It has the advantage of being less costly to provide since it takes people out of service for shorter time frames. The defusing is more immediate than the debriefing and it does not require the services of a full team of debriefers.

There is another significant difference between the debriefing and the defusing. The debriefing is usually applied to larger groups of participants. It can bring people together from different emergency professions. The defusing, on the other hand, is generally aimed at much smaller groups. The focus, in the defusing, is on small teams of people which ordinarily work together. The defusing team may have to provide three or four defusings. For example, one may be provided to the nurses, another to the paramedics or emergency medical technicians and another to the police officers who handled a case.

A defusing is certainly not applicable in all situations. It is limited by considerable time constraints which will be explained later in this chapter. But the defusing does have many applications and CISM teams need to look at it seriously. It is a primary intervention technique after traumatic stress and it has been successfully utilized not only with emergency personnel, but also with industrial programs, commercial ventures, schools systems and the general public.

GOALS OF DEFUSING

There are four main goals of the group process called the defusing:

1. A rapid reduction in the intense reactions to a traumatic event.

2. A "normalizing" of the experience so that people can return to their routine duties as quickly as possible.

3. A re-establishment of the social network of the group so that people do not isolate themselves from each other, but instead see that their reactions are similar to one another. In recognizing similarities to others, people are often more willing to help each other in troubled times.

4. An assessment of the personnel to determine if a full debriefing is necessary.

There are several other objectives which are also of importance in the provision of a defusing. The defusing team is attempting to accomplish:

- Equalization of the information about the incident available to all of the personnel.

- Restoration of cognitive processes which have been disrupted by the incident.

- Provision of practical information for stress survival.

- Affirmation of the value of the personnel.

- Establishment of linkages for additional support.

- Development of expectancies about recovery.

USUAL EFFECTS OF DEFUSING

There are two desirable effects of a defusing which are typical in most cases. The effects depend upon the proper application of the defusing within the time frames described below. A carefully applied and well-managed defusing will usually:

- Eliminate the need to do a debriefing, or

- It will enhance a debriefing if the debriefing is still necessary.

TARGET GROUPS

A defusing is aimed at the core working group that was most seriously affected by the event. Typically, six to eight people from an engine or truck company, an ambulance service, an emergency room staff, a police tactical unit or some specialty team are brought together for a defusing after a particularly bad incident. The defusing team provides as many defusings as necessary for the different groups which have been affected by the incident. That is, separate defusings are provided for each of the groups.

In some rare instances, all of the various groups are together in the same area. It is then easier to bring them all together and provide one defusing. The defusing team makes that decision only if it appears that a joint defusing is in the best interests of the entire group. Of course, if a joint defusing is held, it is a much more difficult task for the defusing team. It will certainly take them longer to handle a large group defusing. It should be pointed out here that the large group defusing is possible and sometimes beneficial, but it is not the generally recommended course of action.

PROVIDERS

Only people properly trained in CISM should provide defusings. Those who have experienced a highly distressing event are quite vulnerable to further psychological damage if they are being managed in the crisis state by untrained people.

Defusings may be provided by CISM trained peer support personnel, members of the clergy or chaplains, or mental health professionals. Some times the defusing is led by a combined team of peer support and professional support personnel. Even if only peer support personnel or only mental health professionals are leading a defusing, it is best that a defusing team be made up of at least two people because it eases the burden a person working alone would face. But in some circumstances, only one CISM team member is available. Since the defusing is dependent for success on its relatively immediate application, the single trained team member might then have to proceed with the defusing.

It should be noted that, although it is a desirable course of action, it is not necessary for mental health professionals to be present at the defusing. The defusing is so close in time to the incident that people have not had sufficient time to process the experience and they have not yet formed deep emotional reactions to it. They are often in a state of shock or denial and they postpone their processing of their emotions until later. Most of what they are experiencing after the incident, at the time of the defusing, can be managed relatively easily by a team of well trained peer support personnel.

Although mental health professionals may not be present at a defusing, it would be foolish for peer support personnel to provide defusings without contacting one of the mental health professionals later to obtain supervision and additional instructions regarding their intervention. In some CISM teams, peer support personnel have the authority to provide defusing services, but they also have the obligation to contact one of the mental health professionals on the team within 8 to 12 hours after the defusing. The mental health professional goes over the defusing with the peer support person(s) and offers praise for a job well-done and advice on how to make even more effective interventions in the future.

TIMING

It has been mentioned several times so far in this chapter that a defusing must be provided within certain time limitations to be maximally effective. Defusings are designed to be given within 8 hours of the conclusion of an incident. The first 3 hours after an incident is the ideal time frame. Some exceptions to the 8 hour rule do apply in certain circumstances. For instance, in a line of duty death situation or after a catastrophic incident, the shock of the event may allow the defusing to be effective for 12 and perhaps up to 16 hours after the incident.

The reason for such a tight time frame is the whole process of traumatization after traumatic events. During the incident those exposed to it are in a state of shock. They are very vulnerable to further damage. Coincidentally, they are also very open to help. But over the next few hours, people try to reestablish their defense systems. They shut down their connections with the world around them. They begin to "put their guards up." Even though help is waiting outside to assist them, the shock of the incident causes traumatized people to defend themselves from friend and foe alike. They seem to seek no stimuli at all. Traumatized people, within a few hours of the traumatic event, shut off most outside influences without distinguishing between friend or enemy. All influences are interpreted as dangerous until they can stabilize themselves.

It is during the early hours after the trauma, when people are more open to help and before they have begun their "shut down" that the defusing is most helpful. Once the "shut down" has occurred, the defusing is relatively ineffective. After about 24 hours, the person has been able to stabilize and reorient themselves. They have also begun to emotionally process the experience. They may misinterpret aspects of the situation and blame themselves for a failed mission. They also gradually open up and are again more ready to accept help. This is when the debriefing is the intervention of choice rather than the defusing. By the time the first 24 hours has passed, the defusing is not a powerful enough intervention to make much of an impact. The debriefing is a more powerful tool and therefore more appropriate after the first day.

If the defusing is delayed beyond the 8 to 12 hour time frame, it is usually best for the CISM team to not provide the defusing. Instead they should rely on one-on-one interventions until a debriefing can be organized.

DISASTER: A SPECIAL CASE

A defusing may be used as an immediate support service after a disaster. It has been used effectively on several disasters. There is, in addition, another intervention called a demobilization. The only time a demobilization is ever used is in a large scale incident such as a disaster. In a disaster, a demobilization may be provided instead of a defusing, but not in addition to the defusing. One substitutes for the other in a disaster. They both have advantages and disadvantages. Sometimes one is easier to apply than the other. There is no harm to using one technique over the other. The choice to use a defusing or a demobilization depends on the circumstances of the event, the support of the supervisors and administrators of the involved organizations, the CISM staffing and the logistics associated with the situation. A defusing is choosen for selected groups who have encountered severe trauma during the disaster. The demobilization will be described in the next chapter. For now, it is important to recognize the existence of an alternate intervention to the defusing for disasters.

DEFUSING PROCESS

LOCATION

The defusing is held in a neutral environment, free of distractions. A defusing is never held at the scene of an incident. The room in which the defusing is held should be adequate to accommodate the small group. It should be comfortable, well-lit, and air conditioned or heated as necessary for the weather. The seats should be as comfortable as possible and arranged in a circle or around a conference table or a coffee table. Defusings have been held in meeting rooms, living rooms of homes, church basements, classrooms and hotel meeting rooms. As long as the requirements of quiet and privacy are fulfilled, there are very few places in which a defusing could not be held.

MOST USEFUL TIMES

When a particularly bad incident occurs at the very beginning of a shift and the personnel must work through the remainder of that shift, it is very helpful to bring the group together and provide a defusing. This enables them to talk about the bad incident, lower their level of distress and return to their normal duties without the distractions which go along with distress over a disruptive event.

Likewise, when a bad incident occurs at the very end of a shift, it is better to provide a defusing before the group goes home. In this way, they will not be carrying the distress associated with the incident to their homes and families.

TIME COMMITMENT

The defusing usually takes between twenty minutes and one hour to complete. Sometimes they go on for slightly over one hour. If they are going much longer than an hour, it is a signal that either the group is highly traumatized or the defusing team leadership is not in control of the defusing. It is generally best to keep the time of the defusing to within twenty minutes and one hour. If it appears that much longer time periods will be necessary, consideration should be given to only providing minimal stabilization immediately and then to setting up a full debriefing in the days to follow.

PREPARATION

Since the notice for the defusing is short, it is rare that a defusing team will have very much time in which to prepare for the defusing. A brief description of the incident is often all the defusing team has to go on. They will have to do their best with the information available. There is also no time to arrange for refreshments after the defusing, so the defusing team does not have the luxury of an anchor to hold the group together for any length of time after the defusing.

OVERVIEW

The defusing has three main segments which are linked to each other in a free flowing conversation about the traumatic event. The segments are:

- INTRODUCTION
- EXPLORATION
- INFORMATION

The introduction usually takes about five to seven minutes. Then the defusing team guides the participants into the exploration segment. Exploration goes on for ten to thirty minutes before the final segment, the information segment is initiated. The information segment lasts from between five to fifteen minutes.

INTRODUCTION

The defusing begins as soon as the group sits down with the defusing team. Team members provide a very brief introduction of themselves and then begin to accomplish several tasks which are necessary in the introduction to the defusing. The defusing team is attempting to do many of the same tasks which are required in a debriefing. One of the main differences between the debriefing and the defusing usually shows up at this time. The defusing is much shorter in time so the defusing team does not have very much leeway in accomplishing the introductory tasks. The defusing team:

- Introduces itself

- Tells the group why they have gathered

- Describes the defusing

- Motivates the participants

- Summarizes the main guidelines of a defusing

- Encourages mutual support

- Encourages their participation

- Instills the need for confidentiality

- Accepts any questions before beginning

- Alleviates group anxiety about the defusing process

- Assures the group that the defusing is not investigative

- Offers additional support if it should be needed after the defusing

Many of the introductory remarks for the defusing are very similar or identical to those made in the debriefing. It is a good idea to read over the "introduction" portion of the "Debriefing Process" in the previous chapter before conducting a defusing especially if it has been a long time since the last defusing or debriefing.

EXPLORATION

In the second phase of the defusing the participants are asked to discuss the experience they just had. This segment of the defusing would equate to a combination of the fact, thought, reaction and symptom phases of the debriefing. The tone set by the defusing team is conversational, not investigative. Anyone in the group who wishes to speak is invited to speak. There is no order in the defusing process. Anyone wishing to remain silent can do so, although that is not in his / her best interest. Throughout the defusing process the team members make several gentle efforts to involve everyone in the group by inviting them to speak. The participants are not accompanied by any sense of pressure, just concern for the members of the group.

There is a broad range of questions which team members can ask during a defusing. They start off by asking the group to tell the team what happened. Then there are many clarifying questions which can be asked about the incident and their roles in it. The range of questions goes from asking for additional detail to asking about interactions with people who are not even present at the defusing. Sometimes the defusing teams asks about signs and symptoms of distress which are already being experienced by the group members.

It is impossible to list the questions which are asked by the team members during the defusing. They vary from defusing to defusing. They can be fairly straight forward or complex. Sometimes the group does a good deal of the talking and there is very little need for the team to ask questions. As a group relaxes and begins to trust the defusing team, they tend to talk in more detail about the traumatic experience.

When the conversation about the incident begins to lag or when the side topics begin to take on more importance than the main issues, the team should start wrapping things up so that they can move into the final phase of the defusing. Remember, the entire defusing is only between twenty minutes and one hour long in most cases so there is little time in which to finish the process.

INFORMATION

The information phase of the defusing is equivalent to a combination of the teaching and re-entry phases in the debriefing. There is a considerable amount of information to cover and it must be covered quickly. In this phase the defusing team is trying to provide as much useful information as possible to assure that the group members are prepared to manage their stress. The defusing team will need to:

- Accept and summarize the information provided by the group in the exploration phase.

- Answer any questions the group members may bring up.

- Normalize the experiences and reactions of the group.

- Teach practical stress survival skills to the group.

- Organize a debriefing if it appears that one is necessary.

- Make summary comments which will send the group on their way.

- Make themselves available to the group once the defusing is complete.

AVERAGE LENGTH OF A DEFUSING

When a defusing team is listening to the defusing participants, it is easy to get caught up in the discussion and forget that the defusing needs to be limited to one hour or less. Anything significantly beyond the hour limit indicates that the group probably would benefit from a full debriefing which should only be provided by a trained debriefing team. In 20 to 45 minutes the average defusing team has completed its work and is ready to release the group.

CONTRAINDICATIONS

Any tool which is designed for a specific purpose can usually do that specific job, but over use or inappropriate uses of the tool can be ineffective and might possibly be harmful. The same is true for use of CISM interventions which were developed with specific purposes in mind. Overuse or inappropriate uses can be ineffective at best and damaging at worst.

The defusing was designed as a small group, rapid intervention for distressed people which is applied within eight hours, in most cases, of a traumatic incident. Using the defusing after many days have passed is an abuse of the technique. Using the defusing process at the end of every twelve hour shift is another misuse of the defusing which will dilute its power and cause it to become ineffective. Attempting to substitute a defusing for a referral for psychotherapy is a dangerous abuse of the technique. That type of abuse of a technique has a great deal of potential to cause permanent, possibly life threatening, harm to people who need serious help from skilled professionals.

The defusing should only be used by CISM trained individuals and in the manner in which it was designed to be used. Violations of the basic principles of defusing, or any CISM intervention for that matter, should not be tolerated by CISM teams. Allowing team members to use any of the

CISM techniques when they are contraindicated, as in the descriptions above, is a dangerous and unprofessional behavior.

FOLLOW UP SERVICES

As in debriefings, the follow up for defusings begin immediately after the session is complete. The team members attempt to contact each of the group members to make sure that they are okay. If there are some particular concerns about one person or another, the team members will attempt to obtain that person's phone number so that a call can be made in the next 24 hours or so to determine if the person needs any additional assistance.

One-on-one consultations are very common after a defusing. Many people have questions which they did not wish to discuss in the presence of other group members. Many of the people who seek an individual consultation have very private concerns which they would be embarrassed to discuss openly.

A full debriefing is the most desirable follow up service if it appears that the defusing was ineffective in resolving the main issues for the majority of the group. It is also the most logical step for an entire group which is seriously affected by the power of a extremely traumatic event.

Other types of follow up services may be identified during the defusing and these should be applied as necessary.

SUMMARY

This chapter explored the defusing process which is one of the main intervention strategies utilized by a CISM team immediately after a traumatic stress. It was described as a small group process which is very effective in either eliminating the need for a full debriefing or enhancing the debriefing if one is necessary. The steps involved in providing a defusing was discussed in detail.

Chapter 9 will describe the demobilization process. This intervention is limited in use. It is only applied to disaster situations.

Even though limited in applications, the demobilization process can be very helpful in the aftermath of a disaster and it "buys time" in which a debriefing can be properly arranged.

Chapter 9

DEMOBILIZATION

INTRODUCTION

In previous chapters, different CISM interventions designed for rapid stabilization and accelerated recovery from stress were presented. Defusings will be helpful when the CISM team is able to intervene in a traumatic situation within hours of the incident. They are aimed at small core groups which have been traumatized by their exposure to an incident. The Critical Incident Stress Debriefing (CISD) is most helpful when the first window of opportunity has been missed or when the incident is so intense that a more powerful form of intervention is required. In both cases, the size of the groups to be managed in the interventions is generally small. Most defusings have six to eight people and debriefings generally have ten to thirty participants.

When an incident draws a great many emergency personnel, who may need some immediate support after the incident, it will be very difficult to manage those people with a defusing. Defusings are designed for small groups and they take more time than is available in a disaster. The task of working through defusings with hundreds of emergency personnel would be a monumental one. The defusing team would be quickly drained and there would be a backup of people waiting for a defusing.

Debriefings were not developed with immediate applications in mind. Most emergency personnel need about twenty four hours before they begin to react to the emotions associated with the incident. Again, hundreds of personnel in need of something more immediate could not be processed through debriefings.

This chapter contains information on a CISM technique which has immediate applicability for the large scale incident.

DEMOBILIZATION DEFINED

The demobilization is a primary stress prevention and intervention technique which is applied immediately after the personnel are released from a large scale scene and before they return to normal duties. The demobilization consists of two main segments. The first is a 10 to 15 minute period in which personnel are given information which might be helpful to them in understanding and managing their stress reactions. 10 minutes of lecture is all that is necessary for emergency personnel. Non-emergency populations may need 15 minutes or more. The second segment of the demobilization is a 20 minute period of time to rest and eat before they return to the routines in their lives.

USES

The demobilization has only two uses. It has been developed for use when emergency personnel have encountered either:

1. A disaster

2. A large scale traumatic event

Demobilizations have already been successfully applied to several major disasters in the United States. They may be difficult to organize, however, so CISM teams should be very familiar with the process before they attempt to provide demobilizations.

CAUTION

Demobilizations are usually only applied during the first two or three shifts of work at a disaster. If the disaster is going to be a prolonged operation lasting several days or even weeks, the demobilization process is no longer applied after the first two or three shifts. That is, demobilizations are provided after personnel have completed their first exposure to the disaster scene. Then they are not used again for the same personnel. To continue to use a group process such as demobilization would be dangerous because the demobilization process raises the consciousness of a stress reaction in the disaster worker and they must work harder to surpress their emotions to do their jobs. When a disaster is prolonged, group processes beyond the first few shifts should be avoided and only one-on-ones should be utilized with obviously distraught individuals.

If a severe trauma occurs to a small group during the disaster, a defusing might be applied for that small group of traumatized workers. It is especially important to avoid multiple applications of the demobilization or defusing to same groups during a prolonged disaster. Each additional group process makes the rescue workers more vulnerable to significant stress reactions. Disaster workers should be allowed to complete their daily assignment with a minimum of support by CISM teams.

The sections below will help any CISM team which is trying to plan a demobilization program for a disaster or other large scale event.

GOALS AND OBJECTIVES

The goals and objectives of a demobilization are very similar to the goals and objectives of a defusing. There are some modifications because the two techniques are different. In a demobilization the CISM team members are aiming at:

- Providing a transition from the traumatic event to the routine

- Reduction in the intensity of immediate stress reactions

- Preliminary assessment of group needs for additional support services

- Forewarning of participants about potential reactions

- Provision of information about the incident and the reactions of the personnel involved

- Provision of practical information for stress management and the establishment of linkages for additional support

- Establishment of positive expectations about outcome

PROVIDERS

The demobilization should be provided only by people trained in CISM. The actual demobilization is handled by a team of CISM personnel. It usually takes one or two demobilization center managers and six to eight team members who make the presentations at the demobilization center. Presenters are CISM trained mental health professionals, clergy personnel and peers either from other jurisdictions or who are off duty and not directly affected by the disaster. Presenters should not be involved in the actual operations at the scene of the incident.

DEMOBILIZATION REQUIREMENTS

The arrangement of the demobilization center can be a challenge to the CISM team members. There are many things which need to be brought together to assure the success of the demobilization. This list should be helpful to the organizers on a CISM team. It can be used like a check sheet.

- Several pre-designated centers in a jurisdiction

- Two large rooms in each center

- Moveable furniture

- Adequate supplies of chairs, tables to handle the group

- Ample supplies of food, juices and so forth

- Resources from which to obtain food if it is not at the center chosen for the demobilization

- At least one demobilization manager

- Six to eight CISM team members to present the information

- A check-in desk

- Staff to keep the food stocked

- Parking to accommodate several emergency vehicles at a time

- Several people to control or deny access to the media and other interested parties

ORGANIZATION

Having the right facilities, staff and materials is only a part of the establishment of a demobilization center. There are many other considerations which must be addressed or the demobilization will fail. Success in a demobilization can be achieved only when there has been considerable planning and practice before the large scale incident occurs. If a demobilization is arranged successfully during a disaster without a plan, the success is most likely fortuitous and not likely to be repeated in the future. Demobilizations demand thought, organization, practice, and planning. Here are some of the most important considerations for the development of a demobilization pre-plan:

- Presenting the idea to administration and command

- Authorization of the administration and command

- Cooperation of administration and command

- Instructions for use to administration and command

- Pre-designation of sites

- Pre-incident arrangements for food

- Pre-printed handouts for the demobilization

- Additional training to CISM team members

- Written plan

- Agreements with all neighboring jurisdictions

- Development of brief (ten minute) stress presentation

- Practice sessions for the CISM team in classrooms

- Practice with emergency operations people at disaster drills

- Written authorizations from the pre-designated sites

- Emergency numbers of officials who control the sites

- Education sessions to the rank and file personnel so that they know what to expect

- Pre-incident briefings to the media so that they know that the demobilization is simply a method to rest crews and give them information before they are returned to their normal duties. Letting the media know in advance will generally prevent the disruptive condition of trying to explain demobilizations when a real event is actually occurring

DIFFICULTIES

It should be clear from the preceding sections that the organization and management of a demobilization can be a difficult process. No CISM team should go into it blindly. A demobilization can be a marvelous success or an abysmal failure. Much will depend on the organization which took place before the disaster or other large scale incident occurred. Some of the difficulties which must be overcome by CISM teams who are trying to organize a demobilization are presented here as a forewarning to teams. These are the practical realities which will make a demobilization difficult. They are most common (and most destructive) when there has been no pre-planning for the demobilization. Good pre-planning could eliminate most of these problems:

- Supervisors or commanders unfamiliar with the process or the need for it.

- Poor communications at the scene from upper level to lower level supervisors.

- The overwhelming nature of the incident makes the demobilization a very low priority in the minds of the leaders.

- Notification of the team is delayed.

- The CISM team is slow to open the demobilization center.

- Insufficient CISM team members are available.

- Personnel are kept at the incident for too long a period of time and they are extremely exhausted.

- There is insufficient food and fluids.

- The distance from the scene to the center is considerable.

- Personnel have been told they are going home and then they are informed that they have to go through the demobilization.

- The demobilization center is not easy to find.

- There is no communication system between the demobilization center and the command post.

- CISM members try to help too much or too often.

- CISM members attempting to provide debriefings or defusings when only the demobilization should be provided.

OVERVIEW

The demobilization is more difficult to set up than it is to run. The simplest thing is to think TWO. There are two key segments to a demobilization and each takes place in a separate room. So there are two segments and two rooms. This may sound a little silly when it is written out like this but it can help the pressured CISM team to pull the demobilization together when it is necessary. The diagram, Figure 9.1, will help to conceptualize the overall structure of the demobilization center.

In this diagram the presentation room is on the left and the food room is on the right. Personnel receive the ten minute presentation first and then they move to the food room where they have twenty minutes to one half hour of rest and food.

Once the demobilization center has been arranged, the supervisors are advised that, when they are ready, they can begin to move people to the center after they have completed their work. It is very important to note that a demobilization is a group process and it is never provided at the scene of an incident. The demobilization only occurs away from the scene. The only people sent to the demobilization center are those who have completed their work at the scene and are being released from the scene by their supervisors. They will NOT be returning to the scene to continue to work. Once a

FIGURE 9.1

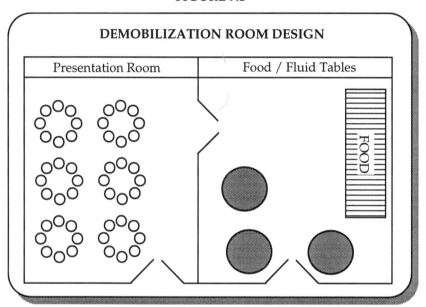

supervisor makes the decision to send his or her personnel to the demobilization center, they no longer need those people and are releasing them from any further activity at the same scene for the remainder of the shift or until the next day. The personnel may work elsewhere but not at the disaster or large scale incident scene from which they have just been released. Returning people to the scene of a stressful incident after they have had the demobilization process may make them more vulnerable to intense stress reactions at the scene. They should not have that problem if they work at different scenes. They usually see a different scene as not associated with the disaster and they can handle it without problems.

The next step in the demobilization process is the transport of the personnel from the scene to the demobilization center. This is usually accomplished by having the personnel go to the center on the same piece of apparatus or unit that they used to get to the scene. The equipment from that unit will be collected and placed in its proper places on the unit before it is released from the scene. Equipment still in use may be left at the scene. If that unit is hopelessly caught at the scene and blocked by other emergency vehicles, arrangements may be made to move the personnel by means of utility vehicles. The drivers are ordered to take the unit and its personnel to the demobilization center (which should be close by if proper pre-planning has been accomplished).

The personnel enter the center and go into the presentation room. They are assigned to a set of seats which are arranged in a circle. It is best to keep units together. People who work together on the same operations units sit with their own group. It is also important to keep law enforcement personnel with law enforcement personnel from their own units. Likewise, fire personnel stay with fire personnel and emergency medical services stay with their own. If the demobilization is being provided for disaster workers such as Red Cross personnel, they are handled as a "unit" in the demobilization. Avoid mixing the groups up. They need to be with their own people because they derive support from their fellow workers.

When the personnel from a particular unit are settled into their seats in their unit's assigned circle, one of the presenters from the CISM team will come to their group and begin the demobilization. The remarks presented by the team member will be described in more detail in the section to follow, "The Process." The comments made by the presenter are the same for each group. Usually each presenter has the same outline from which to work. The presenter spends ten to fifteen minutes (maximum time) giving information to the group. They are then asked if they have any questions of if they would like to say anything. It is very rare that they have either comments or questions. Once the questions have been handled and the statements accepted, the demobilization leader disengages from the group and sends them to the food room.

In the food room the personnel will have twenty minutes or so to eat and rest and prepare to return to routine functions. At the end of their twenty minutes the personnel are given instructions about their functions or about their release to go home. Many times, at the end of the rest phase, a supervisor will come into the room where they are resting and will give information and instructions to the crew(s) who are preparing to leave the demobilization center.

More than one group is handled in a demobilization at one time. While the first group of emergency personnel is being given its ten minute presentation, a second, third or fourth group of emergency personnel might be released from the scene and arrive at the demobilization center. Each group is assigned to its own circle of chairs in the presentation room. A different CISM team member will go over to one of the new groups and begin the same presentation which is already going on for the first group which arrived earlier.

At the conclusion of the presentation the group which has just finished its presentation from the CISM team member will go to the food room. The groups which are in progress will continue until the presentation is complete. They, in turn, will depart the presentation room for the food room when their presentation session is complete. New groups just released from the scene will come to the presentation room and the cycle begins again.

THE PROCESS

During the demobilization the following topics are usually covered in this predominantly didactic presentation:

- Introduction of the presenter

- Brief description of the demobilization

- A statement that the presentation portion of the demobilization will only take ten minutes and that the information is important and it may prevent stress or help the personnel to cope with it faster and better

- A statement that some may already have stress symptoms, some may develop them later and that some may escape them altogether

- Assurance that stress symptoms are normal under the circumstances

- A warning that stress symptoms could become more severe or disruptive to the personnel if they are ignored

- Descriptions of common cognitive, physical, emotional and behavioral signs and symptoms of stress

- Specific advice on eating, resting, avoiding alcohol and drugs, conversing with loved ones, coping with the media and other helpful hints to recover from stress

- An announcement of the debriefings to follow in a week or so after the demobilization

- A brief statement to encourage the participants to ask questions or make any comments they might wish

- A summary and distribution of handouts

Unlike the defusing or the debriefing, participants in a demobilization rarely ever talk unless they really want to. The CISM presenter does NOT try to question the participants to get them to speak. The main objective of the demobilization is to give information. If participants wish to discuss their experiences they are invited to do so either at the end of the demobilization or privately afterwards.

MILITARY ADAPTATIONS

In enormous operations, such as a military operation, where thousands of personnel are involved, the demobilization changes its structure to conform to the special needs of the group. With thousands of people to serve it would be impossible to provide formal debriefings for all of the personnel. The aim would be to debrief only those groups which saw the most action and provide an adaptation of the demobilization process to all of the others.

In emergency service operations, there are usually groups of six to eight demobilized as a unit immediately after their work at the scene is complete. In military operations there may be one hundred in a unit being demobilized and the demobilization may be given several days to several weeks later when the personnel are returning home from the operation. The delay is caused by the fact that their operations were prolonged over several days or weeks and a demobilization given earlier would have interfered with their ability to perform their duties.

Under the circumstances described in this section, the demobilization begins to look more like a lecture in a large classroom rather than a small group of people gathered in a circle. It is important to make sure that each person in a unit demobilization were involved in the same event or performed the same type of service or were part of a team dealing with a specific objective or task. The ten minute information giving session may need to be expanded to twenty to thirty minutes because the demobilization may be the only type of group support service which will be offered to the many thousands involved in the incident. More information is given and a larger handout packet is developed and distributed for this special type of operation. In the handouts, a great deal more emphasis is placed on providing information about many other types of resources which may be available to the service personnel.

CONTRAINDICATIONS

The demobilization was designed to provide minimal stress control information to large numbers of people in a very short period of time. The technique is inappropriate when there is a small event with only a few emergency service personnel involved and adequate time to provide other types of services such as defusings or debriefings. Other types of interventions would then be preferable.

It was mentioned earlier that a demobilization is easy to perform as far as the actual delivery of the service is concerned. It does not take much energy for trained CISM team members to give a ten minute talk on critical incident stress management and then tell people to go and eat and rest in the next room. What is very difficult to manage is the logistics behind this type of support service. If food is unavailable for the hundreds of personnel in the operation, about one half of the demobilization service has just been disrupted. If operations people have not been educated about the demobilization process they will resist it. If the CISM team has not arranged in advance for the demobilization service with the different emergency organizations involved in operation, it may become an impossibility to carry out in the chaotic atmosphere of a disaster. If the supervisors have not learned about the process in advance and agreed to it, the demobilization is doomed from the very start. Instead of cooperation, the demobilization team will encounter resentment and resistance.

Pushing the concept of a demobilization without the necessary support, cooperation and logistics from the organizations involved can be a self destructive endeavor for the CISM team. There is a fall back position for the CISM team when it becomes obvious that the demobilization, although a generally good idea, is not going to work in this particular disaster. The team must quickly modify its approach and do defusings for selected groups which were exposed to the worst parts of the incident. A defusing is a direct substitute for the demobilization. Either one or the other are provided, not both. They may also provide on-scene support services on a one-on-one basis to individuals involved in the incident who are showing obvious signs of distress.

Multiple demobilizations of the same personnel during the disaster should be avoided since they may stir up more symptoms then they resolve.

The demobilization process is simply one step in a whole series of steps to render support to emergency personnel after a large scale event or a disaster. It should never be looked at as a one time process which will help everyone. The demobilization is quite limited. It is only a tool with which a CISM team can address the needs of many hundreds of personnel after a chaotic situation. It may not be the best intervention overall, but it is the best under very strenuous circumstances.

FOLLOW UP SERVICES

The demobilization is *always* followed up with a debriefing several days or weeks after the end of the disaster work. The large scale event is generally so distressing to emergency personnel that debriefings will be required anyway. Numerous debriefings may need to be set up in the weeks following the incident. It is best to start with the groups which were most seriously affected by an incident such as the first arrivals or those who had to deal with the dead or dying. Once debriefings have been provided to those groups, the CISM team organizes CISDs for groups which received less impact until there are no other groups which need support.

Individual sessions with single emergency service personnel are always indicated when the personnel are requesting them. In a disaster, it is not uncommon to find about ten percent of the personnel who seek out individual support through the CISM team or in private therapy.

SUMMARY

This chapter describes a process which has been developed to provide support services to many hundreds of personnel who may be involved in a disaster or other large scale incident. The advantages and disadvantages of the process were described. It was noted that the demobilization process is easy to apply but very difficult to manage because of the needs for logistical support and the pre-incident agreements which are necessary.

Chapter 12 will provide more information on disasters and the functions of CISM or Community Response Teams with non emergency service populations.

Chapter 10

ON-SCENE SUPPORT SERVICES

INTRODUCTION

Distress in people who function on the front lines is unpredictable. Most events have a routine about them and cause little noticeable stress. Every once in a while, something happens or a circumstance exists which turns the routine into a significant stress for one or two people or perhaps for an entire group. When that happens it is a good idea to have trained CISM personnel on the scene to help manage the personnel having stress reactions. This chapter will present some guidelines to assist organizations and CISM teams in responding to a call for on-scene support services.

THE SCENE DEFINED

A "scene" is where the action takes place; where people work. For law enforcement personnel it is the patrol sector. For emergency medical services, a scene is the ambulance or the place where the accident or sick person happens to be. For a communications officer, it is the operations center. For a nurse, the scene is the emergency room or other in-hospital facilities.

Whenever a distressing situation occurs in any place where people work (the scene) and support services are initiated at or very near that location those services are called "on-scene support services." Services provided under "on-scene" conditions are brief, practical crisis intervention functions to limit the level of distress encountered by the workers.

METHODS OF APPROACH

There are two main approaches to on scene support services. The first approach is a haphazard method in which services are provided if a trained person just happens to be on the scene during the incident. If that person is not too busy with other duties, they may be able to put a little attention on distressed fellow workers. Obviously, the services provided with a haphazard approach are limited.

The second approach to on-scene support services is a planned and organized approach. With this method, trained CISM personnel are organized in advance of an incident. They may have regular duties, but be assigned to a specialty team which is released from normal duties to provide on-scene support services. Or they may volunteer to be on call a few days or nights per month. If something happens they can be called to the scene to provide support services. In some jurisdictions, members of CISM teams are automatically dispatched on certain events to standby in case they might be needed at the scene. There are clearly many advantages to an organized approach.

Chapter 6 discussed a formal on-scene intervention called the SAFE-R crisis intervention model. On-scene interventions certainly include models such as the SAFE-R model but are not limited to them.

GOALS OF ON SCENE SUPPORT

The goals of on scene support are identical to or similar to the goals for crisis intervention. They are:

- Stabilize the situation and protect from additional stress.

- Mobilize a wide range of resources to assist the distressed person.

- Normalize the experience and reduce the feelings of uniqueness and abnormality.

- Restore to function as quickly as possible.
(see chapter 6 for on-scene crisis intervention suggestions)

USUAL EFFECTS OF ON-SCENE SUPPORT

The early intervention achieved by on scene support services disrupts the person's movement toward "freezing up" or dysfunction. Early recognition of distress allows for a low profile and inexpensive intervention which encourages a rapid return to normal. On-scene support services may lessen the impact of a traumatic event and block further deterioration of the individual so that there is less need for time off or prolonged physical and emotional distress. People who are given the brief breaks provided by on-scene support services feel cared for and respond quickly with a movement away from being emotionally overwhelmed. They return to the normal cognitive defenses which help them to perform their jobs.

TARGET GROUPS

There are only three groups who are targeted for field interventions. They are:

- Individuals with obvious signs of distress

- Command and supervisory personnel to provide only advice and consultation

- Distressed primary victims, their families and witnesses or by-standers involved in the actual incident

Most on-scene support services are provided during prolonged field incidents or during incidents which have become large scale incidents. Any incident of any magnitude, however, may contain distressing conditions which might cause an individual to become temporarily overwhelmed and in need of quick support.

PROVIDERS

On-scene support services are provided by peer support personnel who have been trained in Critical Incident Stress Management processes and who have some working knowledge of crisis intervention. Chaplains and clergy personnel who have been trained in crisis intervention and CISM are often called upon to assist people at the scenes of tragedies. Likewise, CISM trained mental health professionals are called upon when the situation is so huge or so overwhelming that the peer members of the CISM team are too busy to do support services or are overwhelmed by the incident themselves. Well-intentioned but untrained people can inadvertently make a situation worse by choosing the wrong techniques to attempt to help others. So, trained CISM team members provide the very best services.

TIMING

There is only one word to describe the time frame of on-scene support services and that word is *immediate*. On-scene support services are provided immediately while an incident is in progress. The services are provided as close as possible to the actual situation although it can only be done in a relatively secure area in which people are not endangered. One key to successful intervention is that the support is very short in duration.

CORE RULES

The intensity of field operations and the defense systems of people who work in such conditions do not allow for complex interventions at the scene. Everything the CISM team members do must be short and simple. There are three core rules to follow:

- Provide support services only to obviously distressed individuals. Those who are functioning fine should be left to do their jobs without any interference. Do not interrupt those who are functioning well to check on their emotional status. Just let them work.

- Interventions should be very brief. Sometimes only a few seconds are necessary. A five minute intervention is considered long and fifteen minutes is extremely long. In fact, if a person at a scene does not show marked improvement by the end of fifteen minutes it is unlikely that the person will recover sufficiently to go back to work at that scene.

- Focus on immediate concerns. There is no need to explore old history. Support personnel should stick to "here and now" issues.

GUIDELINES FOR EFFECTIVE ON-SCENE SUPPORT SERVICES

- Be safety conscious both for yourself and for the personnel working in the situation.

- Do not get physically involved in the situation if your assigned job is CISM support. You cannot do both jobs adequately at the same time.

- On-scene support services is a common sense approach. Think first before intervening. Anticipate the reaction the "help" you are contemplating is going to have on the person.

- If your only duties are CISM services stay outside of the internal perimeter.

- Never criticize the performance of the personnel involved in the incident.

- Avoid drawing unnecessary attention to the distressed individual.

- Look for signs of obvious distress:
  * wandering about aimlessly
  * unjustified angry outbursts
  * overall loss of emotional control
  * shock like state
  * crying
  * "thousand mile" stare
  * unusual behaviors
  * inappropriate behaviors
  * exaggerated behaviors
  * isolation from the group
  * others
- Limit advice giving to only what is required at the scene.
- Reinforce any activity they perform which seems to help in the situation.
- Fulfill first request if possible.
- Avoid asking "feeling loaded" questions. Ask about what happened and let the affected individual tell the story in his or her own words.
- Listen carefully. Use the best listening skills.
- Dispel feelings of uniqueness and abnormality.
- Let the individuals know that the reactions they are having are normal and temporary and that they can return to work as soon possible after the reactions subside.
- If the stress subsides, restore people to function as quickly as possible after a brief break.
- Sometimes an alternate duty station at the scene is required to reduce the possibility that the same duty will stir up the distress again.
- If necessary, encourage the distressed person to make contact later or to go to a defusing or a debriefing if one is to be provided.

MENTAL HEALTH AND CLERGY AT SCENES

On occasion, mental health and clergy personnel are requested to assist at the scene of a tragedy. There are several things they should keep in mind to assure that their services are accepted and helpful.

First they should not go to a scene unless they are called upon to do so or they are part of pre-arranged and normal response system. To show up at scenes without being called in or part of a normal response team can generate anger and resentment in the personnel at the scene. Many fear that these "uninvited guests" at the scene will take some personnel out of action unnecessarily and cause embarrassment and interference with their jobs and possibly with their advancement in the system.

If requested at a scene, the clergy personnel and mental health professionals should report into the command center. They should never wander about the scene without checking in first. Additionally, they should keep a low profile which means they must be discrete as they check out a person who shows obvious signs of distress. They should always avoid any unnecessary attention on an individual. Neither should they wear clothing which attracts unusual attention from the personnel at the scene. Blending in at an emergency is very important. Keeping a low profile also entails avoiding the media unless they have been requested to render assistance to the organization by making a specified and approved statement to the media.

Again, they should approach only those demonstrating obvious signs of distress. Everyone else should be left to do their work. Mental health professionals and clergy should avoid getting physically involved in the work. It will distract them from their primary duties of rendering support. When they are not needed immediately, they should stay near the command post or some other designated area. They usually are assigned to the safety officer at the scene.

Staying out of the internal perimeter is very important because there are inherent dangers at scenes and one could get easily injured. An injury would complicate an already complex situation and cause more work for the overburdened operations personnel.

Mental health professionals and clergy do their best work when they provide consultations to command staff and supervisors. They are, of course, helpful in their brief contacts with obviously distressed individuals. They are providing a support service, not psychotherapy or a religious service. Mental health and clergy are at their best at a scene when they are displaying good listening skills and care and concern. They should also be ready to point out appropriate resources which might be helpful after the incident concludes. These resources might include defusings, debriefings and other CISM services.

One requirement for participation at the scene of a major incident should be a special orientation program to the emergency services. Mental health professionals and clergy should go on ride-alongs and tour facilities and talk to operations personnel so that they can learn as much as possible about the personnel and the jobs they perform. The more a CISM trained mental health professional or clergy person knows about the services they are supporting the better able they will be to render the best possible services.

FOLLOW UP SERVICES

With on-scene support services there is a need to draw a careful balance between providing inadequate services and too much service. Too limited an approach to distressed personnel leaves them hurting and uncomfortable. To avoid under-serving people involved in a significant event, it is necessary to contact people when they are resting. The approach should be a friendly, casual, conversational one which occurs when they are on rest breaks. If they see that the members of the CISM team have interest in them and are friendly, they may make approaches later on their own.

Constant checking and rechecking, on the other hand, will eventually annoy people and cause them to reject the help which is being offered. Likewise, following people around with a clipboard with a check list of signs and symptoms of distress will cause the operations personnel to go into a rage. This actually happened in a recent plane crash situation. People who were not trained in CISM procedures tried to be helpful by "assessing" the signs and symptoms of distress in the emergency personnel at the scene. The emergency personnel found the procedure to be intrusive and they freely vented their anger on those who were holding the checklists.

The key rule of thumb for on-scene support services is to do only that which is absolutely necessary and no more. The scene is simply not the place to try to fix everything. Many things must be left alone. Remember, the personnel at a major incident know their jobs, do them well and are generally quite healthy and normal in their reactions to a situation. There is virtually no need to "fix" them, especially at the scene of a major incident. Leave people alone to perform their jobs. If there is any need to provide brief support services, that will become clearly evident.

SUMMARY

This chapter covered the topic of "on-scene" support services. It defined the processes and discussed the scope of the interventions. The targets, timing and providers (CISM trained peers, mental health professionals and clergy) of on-scene support services were addressed. The core rules of on-scene support services were also presented. Many cautions designed to make the process run smoothly and effectively were discussed. Specific instructions were provided for the peer support personnel and the mental health professionals and clergy members.

The overall emphasis of on-scene support services is to provide only as much support as is actually necessary and to assure that help is provided by trained people who avoid the extremes of too little or too much.

On-scene support services include, but are not limitied to crisis intervention models such as the SAFE-R model discussed in chapter 6. On-scene support services need to be flexible.

Chapter 11

CISM SERVICES: MECHANISMS OF ACTION AND A RATIONALE FOR CONSIDERATION

In previous chapters the CISD and post-trauma defusings, as well as other CISM services, were operationally defined and a step-by-step analysis was provided for each. As noted, the CISM "field" has been engendered and has proliferated despite an absence of well-controlled experimental research. The CISD and defusing interventions have become widely adopted (over 400 CISM teams worldwide) and have been generally accepted based upon what may be considered by some a far more rigorous, grueling, and adversarial mechanism of appraisal (i.e., over a decade of empirical field testing performed by and upon a population which was professionally, and perhaps at times personally, inclined to disprove any need whatsoever for CISM or CISD). Despite this gauntlet of administrative, professional and personal resistance, the use of CISD has grown dramatically to the point that psychological debriefing has emerged as a virtual field, or subspecialty, of its own. Upon what factors can this success be based? Let us first look at the mechanisms at work in the defusing and debriefing processes, then we will turn to a discussion of why one should consider establishing any form of CISM program.

CISM IN THE CONTEXT OF CRISIS INTERVENTION

In chapter 6, we briefly reviewed the concept of crisis intervention as it may be used as an acute "one-on-one" or individual intervention. In this chapter, we shall significantly expand our discussion of crisis intervention as a foundation for all of CISM to be put in context.

To properly understand the mechanisms of action which make debriefings, defusings and other Critical Incident Stress Management processes work effectively, it is necessary to understand the theoretical foundations upon which CISM was built. Contrary to the beliefs of some people, CISM services have a long history imbedded in the fifty-two year old field of crisis intervention. The CISM field is not an independent, self standing one which has no roots. In fact, CISM is best thought of as a subcategory of the broader field of crisis intervention. It developed directly out of crisis intervention theory and utilizes basic crisis intervention principles. The very same factors which are known to make crisis intervention work effectively and efficiently also make Critical Incident Stress Management and its most well known tactic, Critical Incident Stress Debriefing (CISD), work effectively.

The literature on crisis intervention is filled with a broad range of reports or studies which indicate the successes of crisis intervention procedures and the mechanisms which are believed to be most important in making crisis intervention effective. Since CISM and CISD are subcategories of crisis intervention, there is then over a half century of studies which provide a solid foundation for the provision of these services to people who have been traumatized by crisis events. Some of those studies will be referred to in this chapter. For additional information on crisis intervention, the reader is referred to the numerous books, articles and studies on crisis intervention which fill library shelves. In addition the reader might also refer to chapter 4 in this text, in which a fairly comprehensive history of CISM is presented and the major influences behind CISM are described.

A crisis is described as a temporary state of emotional turmoil and disorganization which is characterized by lowered individual or group ability to cope and which has an elevated potential for negative or positive outcomes (Parad, 1965; Rapoport, 1965; Slaikeu, 1984). A crisis is time limited and usually resolves within hours or days and may, in some unusual circumstances, last as long as 4 to 6 weeks. Crises tend to be an opportunity for positive growth. They may, however, leave permanent damage if they are not managed quickly and appropriately. Recovery from a crisis event, or critical incident, depends heavily upon several important factors including the severity of the event, the personal resources available to manage the event and the resources available to provide assistance from significant others in the person's environment (Slaikeu, 1984).

There are two types of crises, maturational and situational. Maturational crises include such issues as entering puberty, turning 21 and retiring from one's profession. Situational crises include illnesses, injuries, threatening circumstances such as fires or floods, destruction, being exposed to grotesque experiences, viewing deaths and dismemberment and other situations well-outside the normal range of human experience (Slaikeu, 1984). It should be obvious from these descriptions that the majority of the work of critical incident stress management teams is associated with traumatic events which are, of course, situational crises.

The mere existence of a crisis event is not sufficient to produce a state of emotional turmoil in most people. There is another factor which is essential to the development of a stress reaction to the crisis situation. That factor is human cognition. It is largely the person or group's perceptions of the event which cause the distress. If what is being experienced is far different than one's expectations or if the experience overwhelms the ability to process it adequately, a person may then suffer painful reactions (Taplin, 1971).

Obviously once a person perceives an event as disturbing, the emotions quickly become involved. Crisis reactions are characterized by severe emotional upset or by a state of emotional disorganization and disequilibrium. Subsequently, coping behaviors become somewhat impaired as the full impact of the situation becomes apparent to the individuals or to the groups involved in the crisis situation (Slaikeu, 1984).

Crises tend to follow a relatively standard set of crisis phases. They are:

1. Outcry

2. Denial

3. Intrusiveness

4. Working through

5. Completion (Horowitz, 1976).

Crises not only follow relatively standard phases, they also have common characteristics. The most common characteristics of crises are the following:

1. Sudden onset

2. Unexpected

3. Quality of urgency or emergency

4. Potential to impact the entire community

5. Danger and opportunity coexist

Given the characteristics of crisis described in the preceding paragraphs, short-term, time limited interventions such as crisis intervention are the treatment of choice (Caplan, 1964; Aguilera, et al., 1974; Burgess and Baldwin, 1981). Since high stakes such as physical or emotional deterioration as a result of stress reactions to crisis events are present in crisis situations, the speed of intervention is important. (Slaikeu 1984) suggests that assistance be available immediately after crisis events occur. One crisis intervention expert discusses the importance of immediate intervention in the concept of "Hansel's Law" which states that the effectiveness of a crisis intervention service increases directly as a function of its proximity in both time and place to the crisis event (McGee, 1974).

Crisis intervention is the immediate and temporary, but active entry into another person or group's life situation during a period of acute stress and turmoil (Mitchell and Resnik, 1981). People do not have to be mentally disturbed to benefit from crisis intervention. In fact the majority of people who experience a crisis are not psychotic. Average healthy people experience crises routinely. Crisis intervention may be provided by professionals or by nonprofessionals in an effort to limit the impact of a disturbing event and to accelerate the normal recovery processes in normal people who are having normal reactions to abnormal events (Caplan, 1976; Rueveni, 1979; Slaikeu, 1984; Mitchell, 1981; Mitchell and Everly, 1993).

All crisis intervention, including CISM services and CISDs have four major goals:

1. Stabilize the situation

2. Mobilize individual or group resources

3. Normalize the reactions to the experience

4. Restore individuals and the group to routine functions (Mitchell, 1981; Slaikeu, 1984)

Conceptually, crisis intervention, which is also called psychological first aid, has five steps. The helper first makes *psychological contact*. In a debriefing this step is covered by the introduction phase. Second, the helper needs to *explore the dimensions of the problem*. The fact, thought, reaction and symptom phases cover the exploration of the dimensions. The third step of crisis intervention is to *examine possible solutions*. In the debriefing, this step is covered by the teaching and reentry phases. The fourth crisis intervention phase is to *assist in taking concrete action*. The teaching and reentry phases of the debriefing cover this step, but some of this work is done in the one-on-one sessions which occur immediately after the debriefing. The fifth crisis intervention step is to *follow up*. In debriefing work the follow up begins immediately after the debriefing is complete and continues over the next few weeks as team members assure that the group members are recovering properly (Slaikeu, 1984; Mitchell, 1983, 1988a, b; Mitchell and Bray, 1990; Mitchell and Everly, 1993). Chapter 6 described how these steps could be operationally translated in a one-on-one crisis intervention model, the SAFE-R model.

A crisis situation is considered resolved when emotional equilibrium has been restored and when individuals or groups have achieved cognitive

```
┌─────────────────────────────────────────────────────────────┐
│  OVERVIEW OF FIVE KEY ELEMENTS IN CRISIS INTERVENTION          │
│                                                               │
│    •  contact                                                 │
│                                                               │
│    •  explore dimensions                                      │
│                                                               │
│    •  discuss possible solutions                              │
│                                                               │
│    •  assist with concrete action                             │
│                                                               │
│    •  follow up                                               │
└─────────────────────────────────────────────────────────────┘
```

mastery of the experience and developed new coping skills including the use of appropriate resources (Viney, 1976). In other words, *reorganization and integration* of the experience into the fabric of one's life are essential for full recovery from the traumatic stress reactions produced by crisis events. Obviously these conditions are aims of the CISM services and of debriefings. CISM provides for *prevention* through its stress education programs, *intervention* through defusings, debriefings, demobilizations, one-on-one contacts and other services and aims continuously at *restoration* of people to the highest levels of functions in accordance with their capacities.

The overall emphasis in crisis intervention is on protecting vulnerable people, preventing harmful reactions and restoring individuals to maximal function in the fastest possible time frame. But individuals do not exist in the world in a vacuum cut off from others. Individuals are part of families and of organizations and communities. What negatively affects them, may also indirectly negatively affect those around them. Therefore, it is important that crisis intervention services be provided to the key elements of a person's environment including the families, service organizations and communities. There must be emphasis on the restoration of the groups as units to their fullest potential. This is one reason why group work, including education and debriefings have been key elements in CISM services from its inception.

Most people who specialize in crisis intervention agree that there are several important features of the process which appear to underlie its effectiveness. They are:

1. Active, directive and goal oriented helpers

2. Rapid mobilization of available resources

3. Flexibility

4. Those suffering through the crisis are encouraged to take responsibility for their own recovery

5. Helper empathy, genuineness and warmth

6. Helper knowledge of crisis intervention and skill in applying the principles of crisis intervention

7. Consistent, effective communication

8. Verbalization of the traumatic event

9. Education which teaches appropriate survival tactics

10. "Normalization" of the reactions to the experience (Lindemann, 1944; Berg, 1970; Fowler and McGee, 1973; Mc Gee, 1974; Aguilera et al., 1974; Viney, 1976; Hoff, 1978; Mitchell, 1981; Slaikeu, 1984; Meichenbaum, 1994)

The sections which follow will build upon the above paragraphs and describe how the applications of CISM procedures such as defusing and debriefings (CISD) utilize the basic principles of crisis intervention.

POSSIBLE MECHANISMS OF ACTION

Let us consider mechanisms which may underlie the effectiveness of defusings and debriefings. Consider the following aspects as they are represented within CISD and related processes:

1. EARLY INTERVENTION .... CISD is most typically utilized as an early intervention strategy, oft-times employed within hours of the actual traumatic stressor. Friedman, Framer and Shearer (1988) found that early detection of and early intervention with PTSD or post-traumatic stress syndromes led to lower costs and more favorable prognoses associated with victims of trauma. Two hundred clinical PTSD cases receiving treatment in the Los Angeles area were divided into two groups: 100 individuals who were diagnosed and treated within 6 months of the trauma were compared to 100 individuals who were diagnosed and treated from 6 to 36 months after the trauma. The average costs attributed to the "early" (within 6 months) cases were $8,300, while the costs attributable to the "late" cases were $46,000. The "early" cases averaged 12 weeks of recovery prior to return to work, the "late" cases required 46 weeks to recover. Finally, 13% of the "early" cases entered litigation while 94% of the "late" cases pursued legal action. Indeed, it is almost universally recognized that prevention and early intervention are preferable to having to pursue traditional treatment strategies (Yandrick, 1990; Duffy, 1979; Kentsmith, 1980; Butcher, 1980).

The concept of the "trauma membrane" may help explain why early intervention in the trauma process appears important. Lindy's notion of the "trauma membrane" (Lindy, Grace and Green, 1981) argues that after a traumatic event, victims begin to be insulated from individuals and processes external to the immediate trauma sequelae. This insulation process is thought to be analogous to the formation of a protective, insular membrane serving as a protective barrier. While this barrier attempts to protect from further intrusion, it may also inadvertently isolate victims from healing interventions as well. Thus, it becomes of paramount importance to intervene early while the trauma membrane is still permeable. Early intervention, then, allows for help prior to "concretization" of traumatic memories and perhaps prior to the formation of a potential host of maladaptive coping mechanisms (e.g., substance abuse, social alienation, acting out, etc.). Post (1992) argues that early intervention may prevent a neurologically based lowered threshold for excitation from developing within the central nervous system subsequent to intense stress. Thus, early intervention may prevent the development of a cellular "memory" of the trauma from forming in excitatory neural tissues.

2. OPPORTUNITY FOR CATHARSIS .... According to Heider (1974), there are few conditions that cannot benefit from catharsis. Catharsis refers to the ventilation of emotions. CISD provides a safe, supportive, structured environment wherein individuals can ventilate emotions. Kahn (1966) showed that expressing emotions lowers levels of arousal. In a review of studies specifically investigating the relationship between the disclosure of traumatic events and stress arousal, Pennebaker and Susman (1988) concluded that disclosure of traumatic events leads to reduced stress arousal and improved immune functioning. Most importantly, however, Roemer and Borkovec (1994) found that suppressing emotions was related to increased anxiety and depression over time, almost a sensitization effect, while expression of emotions was related to the habituation of anxiety over time. The importance of expressing one's emotions is not a very new concept. Shakespeare's MacBeth said, "Give sorrow words: the grief that does not speak whispers the o'er-fraught heart and bids it break." Getting emotions out in the open improves psychological and physical well being (Pennebaker, 1990). Emotional catharsis or ventilation is a critical feature of the healing process (Meichenbaum, 1994).

3. OPPORTUNITY TO VERBALIZE TRAUMA .... CISD not only gives individuals the opportunity to release emotions, but the opportunity to verbally reconstruct and express specific traumas, fears and regrets. van der Hart, Brown and van der Kolk (1989) recount the views of

master traumatologist Pierre Janet who noted at the turn of the Twentieth Century that the successful treatment of post-traumatic reactions was largely based upon the patient's ability to not just express feelings (catharsis) but was based upon the patients ability to reconstruct and integrate the trauma using the verbally expressive medium. The work of Pennebaker (Pennebaker, 1985; Pennebaker and Beall, 1986) appears to confirm the critical role that verbal reconstruction and expression of the traumatic event plays in the successful resolution of post-trauma syndromes for many individuals.

Bruno Bettleheim who studied holocaust survivors and other traumatized people stated, "What cannot be talked about can also not be put to rest; and if it is not, the wounds continue to fester from generation to generation." (Bettleheim, 1984, p.166). When people cannot put their traumatic experiences into words, they tend to dream about those experiences more often and they tend to obsessively think about those experiences for longer periods of time in an unresolved manner which creates more distress for them (Silver, et al., 1983; Harvey, et al., 1991). In a review of the literature on the benefits of verbalizing traumatic experiences Meichenbaum (1994) describes an unpublished work of Pennebaker and Francis in which they conclude that either verbally or in writing, the expression in language of one's traumatic experiences will:

1. Organize a person's thoughts and feelings about the event

2. Facilitate the labeling of feelings

3. Lower preoccupation with event related thoughts and feelings

4. Enhance insight and reframing and allow acceptance

5. Allow for an exploration of the meaning of the event

6. Encourage new perspectives and problem solving activities

The collective value of catharsis and the verbalizing of the trauma appear to reside in their ability to: 1) reduce stress, 2) reduce strain on the homeostatic mechanisms of the body, 3) reduce tendencies to ruminate / obsess and 4) increase the likelihood of "making sense" out of the trauma (reintegration of the individual's "Weltanshuuang" or "Worldview").

4. BEHAVIORAL STRUCTURE .... CISD provides a finite behavioral structure that is, a group debriefing represents a process with a finite beginning and a finite end, superimposed upon a traumatic event

representing chaos, suffering, and a myriad of unanswered questions. CISD is the antithesis of the traumatic milieu. Borkovec, and others, (1983) found that providing a structured environment within which to "worry" actually reduced the tendency for worry to contaminate or interfere with other activities on a daily basis.

5. PSYCHOLOGICAL STRUCTURE.... CISD and defusings follow a well-conceived structured psychological progression. The process is initiated engaging the cognitive domain (Introduction and Fact Phases in the CISD). This structure is ideal for those persons already engaged in that domain using cognitive analysis or even denial mechanisms. It aligns with their psychological posture rather than contradicting or opposing it thereby avoiding the risk of initiating group conflict. Consistent with a crisis intervention model, this structure is similarly useful for those engaged in the affective domain for it gently superimposes a cognitive structure so as to set some boundaries with the "promise" of the opportunity for further affective expression later in the process. It, thus, represents an exercise in self-control and self-efficacy as well. As the process moves through the Thought Phase, the cognitive domain is left and the affective domain may be entered. Affective ventilation may be achieved in the Reaction Phase. Being careful not to leave any "emotional loose ends," the process then passes

TABLE 11.1

CISD PHASES AND THE
COGNITIVE - AFFECTIVE PROGRESION

Phases	*Processes*
Introduction	Cognitive
Fact	Cognitive
Thought	Cognitive ⟶ Affective
Reaction	Affective
Symptom	Affective ⟶ Cognitive
Teaching	Cognitive
Re-Entry	Cognitive

through the Symptom Phase moving from the affective domain back to the cognitive. Lastly, the cognitive domain dominates the Teaching and Re-Entry Phases. This overall structure allows the affective domain to be experienced in the most useful manner possible given an acute, crisis intervention (not therapeutic) format. The cognitively based phases serve as entrance and exit portals to and from the affective domain, while also providing a useful cognitive structure and information in their own right. See Table 11.1 for a summary of this process.

6. GROUP SUPPORT .... CISD, in the classic application, employs a group model. The value of using a group format to address distressing issues is well-documented. Yalom (1970) notes that the group process provides numerous healing factors intrinsic to the group format itself. Among them are the exchange of useful constructive information, catharsis, the dissolution of the myth of a unique vulnerability or weakness among individuals, the modeling of constructive coping behavior, the opportunity to derive a sense of group caring and support, the opportunity to help oneself by helping others and perhaps most importantly with regard to trauma, the generation of feelings of hope. As Jones (1985) commented on the value of using group discussion formats following trauma, "There is real value, especially for young men, in understanding that others feel the same strong emotions under such circumstances, that each is not alone in the strength of his shock, grief, and anger" (Jones, 1985, p.307).

Numerous clinicians and researchers in the fields of crisis intervention, post-trauma treatment and group work suggest that the resolution of traumatic experiences is facilitated when people discuss those experiences in the presence of others who have lived through the same or similar situations (Yalom, 1970; Smith, 1985; Scurfield, 1985; Roth and Newman, 1993; Courchaine and Dowd, 1994). Some of the benefits of group process are:

- Exchange of useful constructive information
- Reduction of the sense of isolation
- Provision of mutual comfort and support
- Reduction of stigmatization
- Identification of common issue and goals
- Opening up of communication

- Safe exploration of hidden issues

- Encouragement and empowerment of participants

- Restoration of individual and unit pride

- Diminishing of guilt and shame

- Generation of feelings of hope

- Generation of optimism

- Enhancement of group cohesiveness

- Encouragement of mutual help

- Normalization of the experience

- Opening up paths of potential change (Meichenbaum, 1994)

7. PEER SUPPORT .... Although mental health professionals oversee the CISD process, it is a peer-driven process. Carkhuff and Truax (1965) long ago demonstrated the value of lay support models. Indeed peer support interventions offer unique advantages over traditional mental health services especially when the peer-group views itself as being highly unique, selective or otherwise "different" compared to the general population. Peers can most effectively eradicate the myth of unique vulnerability or weakness and can also most effectively offer advice on effective coping / stress management techniques. In the final analysis, peers have a unique credibility (the Aristotelian concept of "ethos") that no mental health professional could possess (unless he/ she is also a peer).

Peer counselors have been used in various settings including disaster situations (Orner, 1994). Peers who have been well-trained in the following peer counselor skills can be very effective in assisting people in their own professions through the turmoil produced in the aftermath of a traumatic event. The peer skills are:

- Attending

- Communicating

- Empathizing

- Summarizing

- Questioning

- Being genuine

- Being assertive

- Confrontation

- Problem solving (Tindall and Gray, 1985)

8. STRESS EDUCATION .... The stress education information provided in debriefings is not a lecture, but an interactive learning experience which helps people to leave the debriefing and cope better with more knowledge about the natural consequences of traumatic stress. Education in a debriefing is used to debunk myths; to provide information about possible stress triggers to be avoided and the symptoms which might arise and linger; to provide specific information on managing flashbacks, memory problems and relapse prevention. Stress education in debriefings instills hope, engenders meaning, and helps people to cognitively reframe their experiences (Meichenbaum, 1994). Often the education segment of a debriefing and many therapy programs is used to "normalize" an experience (Lipton, 1994). Providing an education segment in a debriefing provides people with a guide or a "road map" which helps them to recover from the traumatic experience (Ochberg, 1991; Herman, 1992).

9. ALLOWS FOR FOLLOW-UP .... The CISD process represents an entry portal where potential victims can engage in group discussion, information exchange and support. It also represents a mechanism wherein individuals who do indeed require formal psychological care can be identified and helped so as to maximize the likelihood of rapid and total recovery.

10. ACTION ORIENTED .... The CISD process follows a key principle of crisis intervention. It is a process of direct intervention during a period of extreme stress. The process does not allow people to remain in a state of confusion and disequilibrium. Instead the CISD team organizes the group, stabilizes the situation, mobilizes resources, actively normalizes the experience and encourages those affected by the trauma to take responsibility for their own recovery. When action is taking place, participants in a debriefing feel that their concerns are being taken seriously and that the leaders of the group are in control and knowledgeable about trauma support.

A RATIONALE TO CONSIDER

Having examined how CISD works, the question becomes, "Why establish such programs?"

According to the National Council on Compensation Insurance, excessive stress accounts for about 14% of all "occupational disease" workers' compensation claims (McCarthy, 1989). The Council notes that medical and other benefit payments average $15,000 for stress-related claims. This amount is twice the average amount paid per claim for workers with physical injuries.

Although even more difficult to document, the total financial costs of excessive stress to business and industry, beyond just workers' compensation claims, appear quite formidable. Estimates place the overall cost of stress on the economy as high as $150 billion per year (Miller, et al., 1988).

In an epidemiological investigation conducted by Helzer, and others, (1987), it was discovered that PTSD occurred in the general population of the United States at a prevalence of about 1%. This prevalence is comparable to that of schizophrenia. In a population of young urban adults the prevalence was found to be over 9%, lifetime (Breslau, et al., 1991). The statistical risk of PTSD can be very misleading, however.

For those in high risk professions, any single traumatic incident could engender symptoms of post-traumatic stress or fully developed PTSD. Consider, then, the following:

1. Work-related stress claims represent the fastest growing and most costly, per incident, type of workers' compensation claim affecting American commerce (McCarthy, 1988).

2. PTSD is a severe and incapacitating form of stress-related disorder, capable of ending its victim's functional life in a matter of moments while changing, forever, the life of the victim's family, (Everly and Lating, 1995).

3. The risk of becoming a victim of PTSD is mostly a function of being in a high-risk, potentially traumatizing situation / experience, thus individuals in "high-risk" occupations (such as emergency services professions) are at a higher than normal risk for PTSD.

4. The career prevalence of PTSD in a major urban fire department was estimated at over 16% (Corneil, 1992); and it may be that the risk of developing PTSD over the span of a career in any of the emergency service professions is in the 15% to 20% range.

In a study of the London Ambulance Service in the United Kingdom, 40 randomly selected ambulance personnel were tested to determine if they were stressed by the types of calls they handled. Sixty percent (60%) could be classified as having stress responses and 17% of the personnel were in the severe category of symptoms on the General Health Questionnaire and on the Impact of Events Scale (Thompson and Suzuki, 1991).

In another study of 1420 personnel of the London Ambulance Service, which happens to be the largest ambulance service in the world, it was found that 15% of front line staff crossed the threshold for the diagnosis of post-traumatic stress disorder and had as many as 16 symptoms of the disorder at significant levels. For example, in addition to the key PTSD symptoms of intrusion, avoidance and arousal, 46% of the group felt angry; 43% had.lost hope in the future; 25% felt "coldness" toward the patients; 33% were having sleep disturbance; 29% were restless and "jumpy" (Ravenscroft, 1994).

Similar results were found among ambulance personnel on another continent. The Victoria Ambulance service in Australia performed an extensive study of 1380 ambulance officers and 1223 of their significant others. Dr. Robyn Robinson (1994, p. 3) stated,

> "A disturbing finding is that sixty-five percent of Officers
> report that they currently experience trauma reactions as a
> result of prior ambulance jobs [calls]. Seventeen percent
> report pervasive, strong response. Though this study
> does not define staff with Post-Traumatic Stress Disorder,
> the findings suggest that a high incidence exists."

5. The suicide rates in some law enforcement agencies may be three times the national average and have been associated with the stress of being exposed to, and dealing with, other people's traumas (see for example, Newsweek, Sept. 26, 1994).

6. It is generally accepted that the psychological states of first responders greatly affect the overall outcome of any given emergency situation to which these personnel are asked to respond, including the health of the primary victims themselves.

7. These points and more argue compellingly for intervention efforts to be directed toward the prevention of post-traumatic stress syndromes (Duffy, 1979; Kentsmith, 1980; Butcher, 1980).

TABLE 11.2

COMPARISON OF SAN DIEGO AND CERRITOS AIR DISASTERS

	San Diego	_Cerritos_
Total killed	125	82
Plane survivors	0	0
Homes destroyed	16	16
Civilians killed on the ground	15	15
Emergency personnel engaged	300	300
Body parts recovered	>10,000	>10,000

(compiled by J. T. Mitchell, Ph.D. from NIMH, 1979; 1983; Duffy, 1979; Freeman, 1979; Honig, 1987)

TABLE 11.3

SAN DIEGO AND CERRITOS AIR DISASTERS' IMPACT ON EMERGENCY WORKERS WITH AND WITHOUT CISD INTERVENTION

	San Diego	Cerritos
Intervention	Sporadic 1 on 1 Crisis Intervention	12 CISD Demobilizations Hotline Follow-up
Loss of Ranking Police	5 in one year	Total of 1
Loss of Fire Personnel	7 in one year	in one year
Loss of Paramedics	17 in one year	
Increase in mental health utilization	31% in one year	1% in one year

(compiled by J. T. Mitchell, Ph.D. from NIMH, 1979; 1983; Duffy, 1979; Freeman, 1979; Honig, 1987)

8. CISD and traumatic stress defusings have over a 12 year history of application in high risk occupational venues across the globe making them the most widely used formalized intervention for the prevention of traumatic stress in the world.

While well-controlled, true experimental designs have not yet been used to assess the efficacy of CISD and defusing interventions, a 12 year history of thousands of applications has generated a compelling array of empirical evidence that attests to their value. Further, from a meta-analytic perspective, it might be argued that continued utilization across venues and across time tends to randomize error and therefore neutralize specific error terms. Nevertheless some systematically acquired data seem useful. For example, Table 11.2 and 11.3 compare the severity of two air disasters. Table 11.3 contrasts the effects of those disasters given very different post-disaster interventions. The Cerritos disaster was the beneficiary of CISD and related interventions. The results seem striking in this naturalistically derived empirical comparison.

While true experimental designs are difficult to achieve in field research, Rogers (1992) has conducted a quasi-experimental analysis of the effects of CISD on emergency personnel. Data suggest that there may be a powerful symptom mitigation effect achieved from the use of CISD. This effect may not be evident, however, until several weeks after the CISD. According to Rogers' data, the immediate 36 - hour post - CISD effect appears minimal. This study, obviously, needs to be replicated and expanded. The use of comparable control groups needs to be pursued as does the general quest for valid and reliable outcome data subsequent to defusings and CISD interventions.

Since the first edition of this book was published in 1993, new data on the effects of CISD have become available and other studies are currently underway. Each piece of this body of research is welcomed because it sheds further light on the evolving field of Critical Incident Stress Management and the use of debriefing services. Research will help to determine what is working and why, and it will help us to make plans, modifications, more effective protocols and procedures and set a direction for additional research in the future. The following paragraphs will shed some light on the latest research which has been accomplished to date.

Dr. Atle Dyregrov, a key European researcher in the field of traumatic stress, suggests that the early use of Critical Incident Stress Debriefing is helpful for disaster victims (Dyregrov, 1989). His suggestions for the use of group debriefings are supported by other researchers (Turner, Thompson and Rosser, 1993). The CISD process was utilized after a ferry bearing British school children sank in the Mediterranean Sea (Johnston, 1983). In the United States it has been suggested that debriefings would be useful in a variety of workplace traumas (Williams, 1993). Critical Incident Stress Debriefings are recommended for police officers (Blau, 1994) and for nurses (Burns and Harm, 1993). CISDs have been utilized extensively in the military (Miller, 1994). Numerous clinicians and researchers have utilized various forms of debriefings in their work with traumatized individuals and groups (Wilson and Raphael, 1993; Mitchell and Dyregrov, 1993; Meichenbaum, 1994).

In 1985, the Commonwealth Banking Corporation in Australia experienced 30 hold-ups affecting 107 employees. No debriefing or traumatic events response team was in existence in that year. The bank totalled 281 lost staff work days directly related to the hold-up and another 668 sick days within six months of the hold-ups. The average cost of compensation to employees was $18,488 (Aus.). A critical incident stress team called the "Post Hold-Up Support Program" was established in late 1986 and early 1987. In 1987-88, after the team had been established, there were a total of 36 hold-ups which also affected 107 staff members.

With trauma support by the Post Hold-Up Support Team there was a lowering of lost days and a lessening of workers compensation payments. Only 112 sick days directly related to the hold-ups were utilized by affected staff members. This was a 60 percent reduction over the 1985 statistics. Only 265 other sick days were used within six months of the hold-ups. This figure also represents a 60% reduction over the 1985 figures. Even more dramati-

TABLE 11.4

COMMONWEALTH BANK OF AUSTRALIA WORKERS COMPENSATION COMPARISONS			
	1985	*1987-88*	*Change*
hold-ups	30	36	+ 16%
staff affected	107	107	0%
support services	————	Support team	
sick days directly related to hold-up	281	112	- 60%
other sick days not directly related	668	265	-60%
compensation payments	$18,488	$6,326	- 68%
(Leeman-Conley, 1990).			

cally, the compensation payouts decreased substantially. The average after the support team was put in service was $6,326 (Aus.). This is a 68% decrease in workers compensation payouts. See the table 11.4 for a summary of these statistics (Leeman - Conley, 1990).

Other studies also suggest rather positive benefits from debriefings. Robyn Robinson's study of ambulance personnel indicates that 45% state that one or several major critical incidents were the cause of significant stress reactions for them. Of the 823 ambulance officers surveyed, 64% were aware of the debriefing services which were offered to them by the Victoria Ambulance Crisis Counselling Unit. Of these, 71% felt that debriefing services were very important, 26% felt that debriefing services were quite important and only 3% felt debriefings were not important (Robinson, 1994).

When the debriefings themselves were evaluated 37% of ambulance personnel in the study found them very helpful. Another 45% found the debriefings moderately helpful and 18 % found them not helpful.

Since the CISD process is believed to lower stress symptoms (Rogers, 1992), specific questions were asked about symptom reduction in Robinson's study. Twenty-one (21%) of the personnel who went through a debriefing said that they had considerable lowering of symptoms. Another 51% said their symptoms lowered a little, and 28% said the debriefing had no effect on their symptom levels.

When asked how long the benefits of CISD lasted, 48% believed the benefits of CISD were long lasting. Another 10% said the benefits of CISD lasted a few weeks; yet another 14% said the benefits lasted up to a few days and 28% said they did not perceive any benefits of the CISD (Robinson, 1994).

The effectiveness of CISDs was evaluated in a study of 288 emergency, welfare and hospital workers who were involved in 31 "Mitchell Model" debriefings held between 1987 and 1989 in Melbourne, Australia. The incidents which were debriefed included a line of duty death, five multi-casualty (with multiple fatalities) incidents, child fatalities, injury of a colleague, a patient suicide and other traumatic situations. All respondents in the study agreed that the critical incidents had moderate to considerable impact upon them.

Two weeks after each of the debriefings, questionnaires were distributed to all of the CISD participants. The two week time frame is important to note because a number of other studies have allowed much greater times to elapse and those delays may distort the results.

The majority of the participants in the Melbourne study indicated that the CISDs were considerably helpful to themselves and they perceived that the process was considerably helpful to others in the group. In fact, "96% of emergency service personnel and 77% of the welfare / hospital staff who experienced stress symptoms after the incident stated that they had experienced a reduction of stress symptoms which they attributed, at least in part, to the debriefing." (Robinson and Mitchell, 1993, p. 376).

The most prominent reasons presented by the participants for why the debriefings were helpful were:

- Talking with people involved in the event about the incident helped to deal with it better

- Talking about the incident (which they stated they would not have done without the debriefings)

- The debriefings helped personnel to gain better understanding of themselves

Although the questionnaire contained questions which invited criticisms of the CISD process, the only substantial criticisms offered by the participants revolved around procedural issues such as the lack of comfort of the chairs, the debriefing was held too long after the event and everyone involved in the event should have been present in the debriefing. Others cited the fact that the process was a new one and they did not know enough about it in advance. They suggested that if they had known more about CISD they might have gotten more out of the sessions. No one reported experiencing harm from the debriefings (Robinson and Mitchell, 1993).

Overall, CISDs were found to be generally positive for the participants in the Melbourne study. "The positive impact and the value of debriefing on personnel was marked. Most personnel who reported symptoms of stress following a critical incident also stated that these had been reduced as a consequence of attending the debriefing. Further, the greater the impact of an event on staff, the greater was the rated value of the debriefing." (Robinson and Mitchell, 1993, p. 380).

In another researcher's study similar reasons were given for the effectiveness of the debriefings. Of 219 nurses who received CISDs 193 reported the process was helpful to them. Twenty-six (26) reported that the process was not helpful. The nurses stated reasons why the debriefings were helpful or not helpful. (Brurns and Harm, 1993) See table 11.5 for these reasons.

It is important to pay attention to the reasons given for the ineffectiveness of debriefings. Not following the basic CISD principles outlined in this

TABLE 11.5

NURSING STUDY ON CISD

CISD Helpful	*% indicating*
1. Talking about the incident helped	86.6%
2. Realizing that I wasn't alone in my responses to the incident	85.1%
3. Hearing others talk about the incident	83.0%
4. Being part of a group that had also experienced the incident	73.2%
5. Hearing how others were handling the stress	58.2%
6. My stress responses decreased in intensity	46.9%
7. Learning about stress from the leaders	22.2%

CISD Not helpful	*% indicating*
1. The leaders had no relevant experience	26.9%
2. There were people present in the group with whom I was uncomfortable	23.1%
3. Too long after the event	19.2%
4. I was not comfortable discussing the event in a group	9.6%
5. I resented the time the debriefing took from my personal life	9.6%
6. Too soon after the event	3.8%

(Burns and Harm, 1993)

book and in numerous articles can set the stage for a "failed" debriefing or at least one that is uncomfortable for the debriefing team. Such a violation of core CISD principles is described in a paper on the Lockerbie air disaster. One "debriefer" wrote:

> "We also rapidly learned a cardinal rule in debriefing - that it is not advisable to begin with inquiring about the emotional reactions of 'exposure hardened' individuals. It was more effective (and easier) to collect together the overall experience of the group before exploring individual reactions. The correction of individual misinterpretations and misconceptions using this technique was very impressive." (Melchenbaum, 1994, p. 521).

Debriefing processes have been used on children with positive results. For example, one and one half years after the Armenian earthquake, children were given debriefing sessions and individual and group follow up sessions. The debriefing significantly reduced the severity of post-traumatic stress reactions in the children. Control groups did not fare as well (Pynoos, et al., 1994).

As can be seen by the numerous recent articles cited in the preceding paragraphs, CISD and its associated interventions have entered the realm of research and an expanded literature base. Shalev (1994, p. 209) notes that the works of Raphael and Mitchell are the "most widely cited" in the debriefing field. Meichenbaum (1994) echoes Shalev's comment and provides a description and critique of the "Mitchell Model" of CISD.

Today there is an even greater need than ever before for additional research and further development of the concepts of debriefing. For system managers to continue to support the services provided by CISM teams, they need additional evidence that debriefings and other support services are having a positive effect. Further efforts to detail and test the core concepts of CISD are enthusiastically encouraged. There are cautions, however, for both the practice and research of CISD. The next two segments of this chapter will highlight those cautions.

CISD CAUTIONS

No one psychological support process, no matter how well-designed and practiced, can be equally effective for all people under all circumstances. Where some gain maximal benefit others may feel little or no effect. The success or failure of the Critical Incident Stress Debriefing process depends on several interlocking factors which include, but are not limited to the following:

1. Using the CISD for the purposes for which it was intended (*mitigation* of the impact of a traumatic event, *prevention* of post-traumatic stress reactions and *acceleration* of recovery processes in non-psychiatric populations who have experienced significant psychological trauma). It should be noted that the CISD process was *not* developed as a treatment for Post-Traumatic Stress Disorder (PTSD) or any other mental disorder. Its main usefulness has been and continues to be as a tool which may prevent or mitigate various forms of traumatic stress including PTSD. One recent review of the broad utilization of CISDs in disaster work cautioned, "We recognize that CISD procedures may help some disaster victims. We are concerned, however, that an unreasonable expectation of CISD

usefulness may be developing among field practitioners." (Hiley-Young and Gerrity, 1994, p. 17).

2. Timing. Interventions which are too early or too late after a traumatic event may be ineffective (Burns and Harm, 1993).

3. Readiness of the group members for help. All the help in the world will be useless if those who need it are not ready to accept it (Mitchell, 1994).

4. Level of involvement in the traumatic incident. It appears that the more intimately involved in an incident a person is, the more likelihood there is that debriefings alone will not be sufficient to overcome the negative impact of the trauma. For instance, a fire fighter or police officer who helps others who are victims of a natural disaster may feel that the debriefings were especially helpful after the event if his home and family were not personally affected. If an emergency services person, on the other hand, not only had to help others after a natural disaster, but also suffered the loss of his or her home or injury or death to a family member, the debriefing is not likely to be very helpful by itself (Raphael and Wilson, 1993; Hiley-Young and Gerrity, 1994).

5. Level of concurrent psychological distress in a person at the time of the critical incident. Some people will need more assistance than just a debriefing because they had already been dealing with significant stressful situations before they encountered the current critical incident or because they have several current stressful circumstances which are occurring simultaneously (Raphael and Wilson, 1993).

6. Level of psychiatric disturbance which might exist before a traumatic event occurs. In some cases people may have a serious psychopathology. Then they encounter a significant stress. The end result is that they are unable to cope with the stress of a critical incident and decompensate further. Psychotherapy is clearly indicated in these circumstances and CISD is not likely to be effective by itself (Hiley-Young and Gerrity, 1994).

7. Applications of the CISD by properly trained mental health professionals and peers. Inadequately trained debriefers and those who apply the process inappropriately because of a lack of experience may cause the CISD process to fail (Mitchell and Everly, 1993).

8. Adherence to basic CISD policies and procedures. The CISD

process has been well-documented and significant variations from the commonly accepted procedures may cause harm to the recipients or may cause the process to fail (Mitchell and Everly, 1993).

9. Level of pre-incident education on traumatic stress and the CISD process. Pre-incident education may be helpful in mitigating the impact of a traumatic event and may also make the participants in a debriefing more ready to accept and utilize the process effectively (Mitchell, 1992).

10. Level of follow up services provided. It would be fool hardy for anyone to believe that support services of any kind can be provided without appropriate follow up services. It is very important to check repeatedly on the well-being of those who have been given support services. Some will not need further assistance. Others may need additional support or possibly a referral for professional counseling (Mitchell, 1992; Mitchell and Everly, 1993).

11. Intensity of the critical incident. Some events are so powerful that the CISD cannot eliminate all of the negative effects. Even months after a debriefing some symptoms of traumatic stress may linger and may need additional work to clear them up (Sloan, et al., 1994).

12. Level of exposure over time to critical incidents. Time may not heal as effectively as some might wish to believe. Recent studies of emergency personnel indicate that there may be a link between time in the service, the types and number of critical incidents which emergency personnel encounter and the persistent long range stress symptoms which can be found in emergency personnel (Moran and Britton, 1994).

13. Level of administrative support.

14. Level of family and social support.

15. The existence of a comprehensive critical incident stress management program which has many more components than just debriefing (Robinson and Mitchell, 1993).

The reader is referred to chapter 14 of this book for additional information on common problems in defusings and debriefings.

CAUTIONS IN CISD RESEARCH

If anyone plans to do research on CISD, or if they plan to read research projects developed by others, the following guidelines would be worthwhile considering. The end product of the research would then be more useful to CISD providers everywhere.

1. Obtain appropriate training in the specific model of debriefing which is to be researched. This will insure that the appropriate applications of the debriefing model are understood by those who will be researching it. Training in a specific process eliminates guess work and faulty assumptions. Reading about a model is insufficient since many gaps in learning may be caused by incomplete understanding of the process which comes from a review of only the writings in the field.

2. Define the model to be researched and describe it in detail. Many researchers today are claiming that they have studied debriefings, yet they cannot describe a specific debriefing process. They may refer to everything from a brief unstructured interview to a highly structured group process as a "debriefing." Their research would be more useful if they described what is meant by "debriefing." A lack of definition of the process causes significant confusion in those who study the research articles.

3. Clearly define the population to be researched. To state that one is studying "fire fighters" gives a very different impression to the reader than to state that one is studying average citizens whose homes were threatened by a fire storm and thus fought the fire to save themselves and their property. Clearly the groups are different in training, experience and in their reactions.

4. Do not mix groups within a population which is being studied. A police officer who provided perimeter control at a scene has a very different experience and a different viewpoint than a police officer who was on an assault team which was involved in a fire fight at the same incident. It is also not a good idea to lump average citizens or victims together with rescue personnel even though they experienced the same event. Their training, experience, personalities and reactions may be very different from each other.

5. Make sure that those who are providing the debriefings as part of the study are well-trained and experienced in the provision of the service. Also be aware that one person's style of providing a debriefing service

may vary substantially from the style of another debriefer. Likewise, one team's skills may vary considerably from that of another. As much consistency as possible needs to be built into the design of a study. **In the final analysis what we measure in any outcome research is *not* so much any given model or behavioral protocol, but rather *is* the clinicians' ability to implement or operationalize a given model or protocol.**

6. If a study is comparing a number of different events, they should be as similar as possible. For example, comparing the effectiveness of the CISD process when used on a multiple vehicle accident with multiple fatalities and another multiple vehicle incident with only minor injuries is not a fair evaluation since the stress effects of the two events are very dissimilar.

7. The best CISD study would compare people who received a debriefing to those who did not have a debriefing but who experienced roughly equal levels of exposure to the same event.

8. The researcher should not discuss items in the research paper which were not actually studied. In other words good researchers avoid writing in such a manner as to imply certain findings which were not actually included in the research project. It would be inaccurate to state that only voluntary debriefings have a positive effect if the only thing the project was designed to study is whether or not debriefings should occur within 24 hours of an incident.

9. Researchers need to avoid drawing conclusions which are well beyond the data. For example, if a study on the effectiveness of utilizing CISD for the treatment of schizophrenia were to conclude that the CISD process had no positive effect on the schizophrenia patients, it would be inappropriate to conclude that debriefings do not work on emergency personnel who are not schizophrenic.

10. Perform the research in close time proximity to the occurrence of the debriefings. Many researchers have waited several months to collect the data. Long time lapses from the time of the intervention subject the study to many variables which can cloud the overall picture and distort the results.

11. Never allow ongoing research projects to interfere with the provision of support services to groups who might benefit from the processes after a traumatic event.

12. Any research project should take into consideration the previously published works which address the same issues.

There is clearly a great need to have research in the CISM field. But research projects should be carefully designed and managed. The minimal guidelines above should be helpful to potential researchers and readers as well.

SUMMARY

In this chapter, we've tried to offer insight into the "whys" and "hows" undergirding the impetus to establish and maintain debriefing and defusing protocols.

As for mechanisms of action, the following concepts appear important:

1. Early intervention

2. Opportunity for catharsis

3. Opportunity to verbally reconstruct the trauma

4. Establishment of a behavioral structure within which to conduct the group process (a behavioral "road map" of sorts)

5. Establishment of a structured psychological progression (a psychological "road map" of sorts)

6. Group support

7. Peer support

8. Opportunity for follow up

In the final analysis, debriefings and defusings demonstrate that someone cares.

To paraphrase William James, the deepest craving of human nature is the desire to be appreciated! Upon such a foundation there may be no limit to what humanity can achieve for itself.

Chapter 12

MASS DISASTER CISD INTERVENTIONS AND COMMUNITY RESPONSE TEAMS

Within recent years there has been much discussion of the applicability of the CISD model, as originally developed and promulgated by Mitchell and others, to situations other than the acute critical incident variation of traumatization. Admittedly, the CISD as originally formulated was, indeed, designed to mitigate post-traumatic stress as caused by the acute critical incidents most commonly encountered by emergency service personnel. Herman (1992) and others have described a variation of PTSD referred to as "complex" PTSD. The "complex" variant PTSD is engendered by prolonged chronic traumatization and /or acutely chronic repeated traumatization. With "complex" PTSD in mind, a "mass disaster" CISD model (Everly and Mitchell, 1992) was derived from the original CISD model (Mitchell, 1983).

DEVELOPMENT

For years, experienced crisis interventionists have utilized the CISD model as originally formulated by Mitchell (1983) to successfully mitigate what has been referred to as "complex" PTSD. A few slight alterations were required to render the original protocol usable.

Recent experiences with Hurricane Iniki, Hurricane Andrew, the Yugoslavian conflict, the ongoing Middle East turmoil and finally the interventions in Somalia convinced the authors to formalize the alteration in the original CISD model so as to create a "mass disaster" CISD model designed to mitigate "complex" PTSD whether it be engendered by combat, prolonged civil unrest, mass disasters or prolonged community response operations. This model could prove useful in combatting "burnout" or cumulative stress as well.

COMPARING ACUTE CISD MODEL TO THE MASS DISASTER MODEL

Perhaps the easiest way to introduce the mass disaster CISD model is by way of comparison. Table 12.1 lists the stages of the original acute critical incident CISD model (Mitchell, 1983, 1988). Table 12.2 introduces the "mass disaster" CISD model (Everly and Mitchell, 1992).

Close scrutiny reveals that the mass disaster variation of the CISD places slightly more emphasis on direct ventilation of emotions (stage 4) and also places great emphasis on the importance of the constructive aspects of the experience (stage 5) with the goal being to aim toward rebuilding and "moving on" emotionally. In situations where there are no lessons to be learned (hard to believe!) or there is nothing constructive or positive, emphasis can be placed upon shear survival, or the like. Remember, survival itself is often an accomplishment. Obviously different situations will dictate different consideration.

TABLE 12.1

STAGES OF CISD

Stage 1	Introduction	To introduce intervention team members, explain process, set expectations
Stage 2	Fact	To describe traumatic event from each participant's perspective on a cognitive level
Stage 3	Thought	To allow participant's to describe cognitive reactions and to transition to emotional reactions
Stage 4	Reaction	To identify the most traumatic aspect of the event for the participants
Stage 5	Symptom	To identify personal symptoms of distress and transition back to cognitive level
Stage 6	Teaching	To educate as to normal reactions and adaptive coping mechanisms. (i.e., stress managment) Provide a cognitive anchor
Stage 7	Re-Entry	To clarify ambiguities and prepare for termination

TABLE 12.2

```
┌─────────────────────────────────────────────────────────────┐
│          THE MASS DISASTER / COMMUNITY RESPONSE               │
│                  VARIATION OF CISD                            │
```

Stage 1	Introduction	To introduce intervention team members, explain process, set expectations
Stage 2	Fact	To have each participant describe the nature of their participaion, from a cognitive perspective
Stage 3	Thought Reaction	To solicit cognitive response to: "What aspect held the most negative impact?" or "What aspect was the worst for you?" Then, transition from cognitive to emotional processing
Stage 4	Emotional Reaction	Given the response to stage 3, to solicit emotional reactions or consequences
Stage 5	Reframing	To transition from emotional domain back to cognitive. "What lessons could be learned from this experience?" and "What is something positive that you will take away from this experience?"
Stage 6	Teaching	To educate as to normal reactions and teach basic stress management if applicable
Stage 7	Re-Entry	To summarize experience with emphasis on positive or learning aspects

USES OF MASS DISASTER CISD MODEL

The mass disaster CISD model was designed to be utilized with disaster work crews who have been exposed to multiple traumatic incidents during a disaster. It has also been developed to assist in situations in which disaster workers have experienced work in numerous disasters over time or a single prolonged exposure to one disaster. First response emergency personnel and Red Cross disaster workers have effectively utilized the mass disaster model. The use of the mass disaster CISD model assumes that several important factors have been considered. They are:

- *Work crews have been released from their duties and have been returned to their home bases for rest.*

- *Personnel have been "processed out."* That is, they are not expected to return to that particular disaster for at least one week and preferably not for two to three weeks.

- *They have had time to reconnect with their families and friends.* If this has not occurred, workers will frequently resist any efforts to assist them by means of debriefings or other support services.

CONDUCTING A MASS DISASTER CISD

The Mass Disaster CISD is conducted in much the same manner as a debriefing for emergency personnel who have experienced a severe but much smaller incident in the course of their normal work. There are, however, some significant differences. The main differences show up in the third, fourth and fifth phases of the debriefing. In fact, the names of the phases have been changed to accommodate the differences in the technique (see Tables 12.1 and 12.2).

In phase number 3, for example, the name of the phase has been changed from the *"thought"* phase (as it is applied to emergency personnel such as paramedics, fire fighters and police officers) to the *"thought reaction"* phase. To assist the group in the transition from the cognitive aspects of an experience to the emotional aspects, the emphasis shifts from a nonspecific question such as "What was your first thought after you got off the auto pilot mode?" to a more direct question such as, "What aspect held the most negative impact for you?"

It is likely that the CISD team will hear more emotionally laden content in this type of debriefing than what would ordinarily come up in a debriefing of an emergency services unit. Sometimes the participants are so distraught that they describe their thoughts during the fact phase. If the participants join up the two phases, accept it and move on with the emotional re-action phase.

The fourth phase asks very direct questions about the emotional aspects of the situation. For example, it may be asked "What emotional reactions did you experience?" Unlike the debriefings held for police, fire and emergency medical persons in which the discussion of emotions is somewhat covert, disaster workers are asked direct questions about their feelings and reactions to facilitate catharsis.

The Reframing phase departs from the discussion of symptoms which is traditional in the police, fire and medical debriefings. Instead the participants in the group are asked about what they have learned from the experience. A common question in this phase is, "What lessons have you learned from this experience?" Another common question is, "What is something positive you will take away from this experience?" or "At what moment were you most proud of your involvement?"

The CISD team members play a very active role in attempting to get the participants to reframe their experience in a positive light. For example, if a person in the group was feeling guilty or cowardly because they ran from the danger while others were being killed or injured, the CISD team helps that person to see how wise it was to save oneself so as to be able to help those who were injured. The whole idea behind reframing is to find a positive in the midst of the chaos and negatives. Again the CISD team efforts are more overt in this form of debriefing than they are in the emergency services debriefing.

The other phases of the debriefing remain essentially the same.

COMMUNITY RESPONSE TEAMS

Many communities have utilized emergency based CISD teams to render assistance to community groups which have been seriously traumatized. Other communities are formulating independent teams which only respond to community situations involving citizens but not to emergency organizations.

The needs and responses of community groups will be considerably different than the needs and responses of emergency organizations so some adaptations have to be made to assist the community groups.

It is not always necessary to apply debriefing services to the community. Other interventions will work (perhaps even better than debriefings).

When there are many hundreds of people in a community who have been traumatized, providing full debriefing for all of them is not only a difficult task, it may be a totally unnecessary or counterproductive approach.

Instead of trying to organize time consuming and expensive debriefings for each group or subgroup in a community, it would be more efficient to bring large groups of people together in a meeting facility and present a brief class on traumatic stress and its effects in the community. Information could be given and questions answered. Informative handouts could be distributed. The usual time frame for such an approach is one to one and one half hours.

Those groups which still need special help could be given debriefings conducted by the Community Response Team (CRT). Individuals could also be discovered who would benefit from individual brief counseling and others would benefit from referrals for psychotherapy.

Community Response Teams need to assure that whatever services are provided are:

- Appropriate

- Adapted to the needs of the group

- Carefully coordinated with local resources

- Age appropriate

- Organized around a follow up or referral system

- Provided quickly

- Provided with planned follow up services

SUMMARY

Critical Incident Stress Debriefing (CISD) and its parallel intervention, post-traumatic stress defusing are interventions designed by one of the authors (Mitchell, 1983; 1988a; 1988b; 1991) specifically for the prevention of post-traumatic stress and PTSD among high risk occupational groups such as fire fighters, emergency medical personnel, law enforcement personnel, public safety, nurses, dispatch personnel and disaster and combat personnel. The recently modified CISD appears especially suited for mass disasters and community response applications. It is clear that as trauma preparedness training expands, the CISD model will find its way into ever new and exciting applications. Minor alterations in the CISD process may need to be made to maximize its effectiveness. Nevertheless, these modifications are best made, when necessary, by those highly trained in the fundamentals of CISD as originally designed and field tested for over a decade.

Chapter 13

ADVANCED CONCEPTS IN CISM

INTRODUCTION

As described in previous chapters of this book, Critical Incident Stress Management concepts, in general, have undergone a phenomenal development during the last two decades. Likewise, the Critical Incident Stress Debriefing (CISD) technique has developed substantially and has had to adapt to a variety of challenging situations. Although the core of the debriefing process has remained the same since 1984, applications of the process have been made, with relatively minor adjustments, to accommodate complex situations. Some applications of CISD to complex situations will be described in this chapter.

The advanced concepts of CISD which are described in this chapter are intended for use by experienced CISD teams which have had the advanced CISD course provided by the International Critical Incident Stress Foundation, Inc. The applications of CISD processes to complex situations should not be attempted by teams without specific training. Reading about special applications alone does not equate to specific training.

TIME LINE FOR CISM AND CISD

Some confusion exists as to when is the best time to provide certain CISM processes to distressed individuals and / or groups. The following chart and the paragraphs which follow should be helpful in determining an overall CISM strategy. One caveat to be kept in mind is that *people generally accept help when they are most ready for it.* No chart will be capable of providing all of the information necessary to make all of the decisions about the applications of specific interventions to all situations. Providers of services must think their way through situations. They should start by assessing the circumstances of the situation first and then determining the status of the people in need of support. Once they have that information, CISM team members can then decide which applications of CISM will be necessary to achieve the goals of the intervention.

CISM TIME LINE

Time	Circumstance	Intervention
Minus zero	Pre-incident status	• Plan • Educate • Prepare • Brief • Practice • Evaluate • Write protocols • Assess potentials • Choose staff • Train
Zero	Event	• Deploy assessment team • Assess • On-scene support services • Advise command • Brief individual support • Care for primary victims and family members and witnesses • Plan next steps
First 8 hours	Ongoing operations	• Continue on-scene support as necessary • Establish nearby demobilization center if warranted (First one or two shifts only) • Call in additional CISM support if necessary • Provide one-on-one services as required • Set up defusings
First 24 hours	Operations wrapping up or completed	• Continue one-on-one contacts • Continue on-scene if necessary • Arrange debriefing(s) • Plan other possible interventions

Time	Circumstance	Intervention
24 - 72 hours *(May be weeks longer if disaster work is prolonged)*	System returning to normal (ideal time for CISD(s))	• CISD(s) • One-on-ones follow up for all previous CISM interventions • Significant other support to start as necessary • Community outreach programs to start • Informal discussions encouraged • Follow up on all previous CISM interventions
72 hours to one month *(May be longer if disaster work is prolonged)*	System restored to normal	• Continue follow up or near normal conditions • Continue one-on-one contacts • Make referrals as necessary • Evaluate • Plan • Educate • Practice

Some may find the following diagram (Figure 13.1) useful. It describes the process of psychological traumatization with the types of CISM interventions and the most appropriate times of application superimposed.

CISD: A PROTECTIVE BARRIER

When CISD is applied properly and in a timely fashion, it can act as a protective barrier which may help to prevent the development of Post-Traumatic Stress Disorder (PTSD). The development of PTSD depends on several factors converging together. First, there must be a traumatic event which is beyond the usual experience of everyday life. Then there must be a reaction to the traumatic event. This reaction is usually made up of cognitive and affective evaluations of the traumatic event which produce a state of physical and emotional arousal. The cognitive and affective evaluations of the event lead to an overall interpretation of the trauma experience. If the interpretation is one that can produce a significantly changed view of the world, PTSD can result. The diagram (Figure 13.1) depicts this process.

If CISD is applied before the altered worldview which leads to PTSD can be established, it may, in many circumstances, help to prevent PTSD. CISD may have this positive effect by providing an enhanced knowledge base about the traumatic experience. With a broader knowledge base about the event, which has been contributed to by everyone in the group, individuals may be able to reprocess the experience and develop an interpretation which is less likely to lead them toward PTSD. For example, if a person goes through a traumatic event and then begins to cognitively and affectively evaluate the incident and concludes (even if it is a false conclusion) that he

FIGURE 13.1

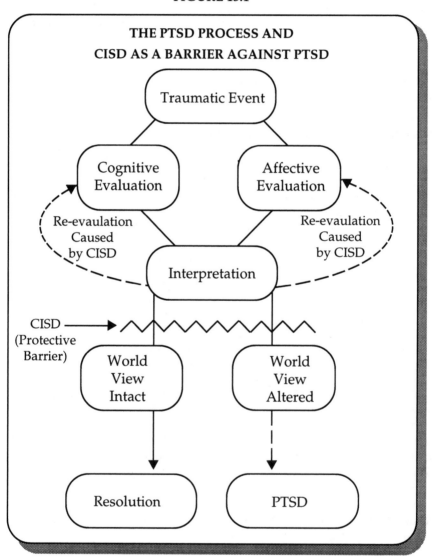

is at fault because he should have been able to prevent an injury to a colleague during the operations at the incident, he is more likely to develop PTSD.

If, on the other hand, that same person participates in a CISD and learns that the injury to his friend was produced by his colleague's own failure to follow proper procedures, it is far less likely that he will interpret the event in a manner which leads to PTSD. The diagram in Figure 13.1 demonstrates how a CISD may act as a protective barrier against PTSD by causing people to re-evaluate cognitive and affective factors. The broken line leading to PTSD indicates that some traumatic events are so severe that they may produce PTSD despite CISD services. In general however, the chances of developing PTSD are lessened when CISD services have been properly provided.

TOO MUCH TOO FAST

A string of disasters, which stretch back to the very beginnings of the Critical Incident Stress Management, movement have taught us many valuable lessons and CISM teams have generally been able to apply these lessons effectively to more recent disasters. Unfortunately, there are a few lessons which seem to be harder for some organizations, individuals and even for some CISM teams to learn and apply. In fact, it appears that certain organizations, individuals and teams practically ignore or refuse to accept some very important lessons from past disasters. Perhaps that occurs because they have some inexplicable need to be involved in the drama of the disaster or to be a part of history. Who really knows? Their motivations are unclear. For whatever reasons which may apply, serious mistakes are being made in the application of psychological support services in disasters.

The problem is not the presence and use of CISM services. The appropriate application of support services is welcomed and important for the overall management of the disaster. The painful facts are, however, that there is a history of serious overreactions to almost any disaster from the support services point of view. Overreacting to a disaster is a dangerous course of action which deserves some rethinking and considerable alteration.

Timing of appropriate psychological support services appears to be among the most critical problems in disaster management. Despite very clear patterns which have been repeated numerous times in various disasters over the past decade, some people still respond to an internal, almost irresistible urge to dash immediately into a disaster scene with potentially disruptive CISM and other psychological support services. Rushing in ignores an important concept of crisis intervention. People have to be *ready* for help before it becomes useful to them. Providing help too early usually sets the stage for the rejection of the help and failure of the effort.

When emergency services people are involved in the response, rescue, fire suppression, triage, treatment, transport, body recovery and wrap up phases of a disaster they are rarely ready for psychological help. They are caught up in the operations and they suppress their emotions and focus on the cognitive processes which help them to complete their jobs. This is so even if the disaster operations last from several days to a week or more. It is only when they have moved away from the situation sufficiently that they begin to move from the cognitive processes to the emotional processes which might generate their stress reactions. Figure 13.2 based on real disasters and the appearance of significant stress symptoms within the emergency services groups, may help to demonstrate the necessity of providing help when the personnel are most ready for it.

The chart is based upon the experiences of the senior author (J.T.M.) in a variety of major disasters after which he led debriefings. The Amtrak wreck in Baltimore required two days of operations. Although some individuals showed symptoms of stress earlier and needed assistance in the form of individual consultations, the majority of emergency personnel did not show stress symptoms significant enough to warrant a group debriefing until three to five days after the operation ended.

Seven days of on-scene services in El Salvador caused emergency workers to suppress their symptoms so much that they did not show up until seven to ten days after the end of the operation. Likewise, in Cerritos, California, after eight days of constant work at the plane crash site the symptoms remained relatively dormant until 10 to 14 days after the end of the incident. Figure 13.2 shows other examples from the author's experience.

Figure 13.2 should help CISM teams to understand that CISDs are usually not required right away. On-scene support services such as one-on-ones with obviously distressed *individuals*, advice giving to command staff, and direct assistance to distressed victims and bystanders at the scene are required. Disaster demobilizations or defusings (see chapters 8 and 9) may be required as units are being released from service. But hold off on the formal debriefings (CISD) until things settle down a little (usually a week to ten days). There may be exceptions to this general rule under some extraordinary circumstances, but exceptions should be well thought out.

Another related problem is asking people how they feel during the operations at the disaster site. Emergency personnel are in a highly defended cognitive state during operations and they resent anyone making efforts to make them concentrate on their emotions. In fact, taking them out of their cognitive defenses and opening up their emotions could literally jeopardize their safety and / or their lives.

In a recent plane crash disaster, some obviously poorly trained mental health professionals who were completely unfamiliar with basic CISM principles, were following emergency workers around with a survey attached to a clipboard on which they were checking off the appropriateness of emergency workers behaviors and whether or not they were showing emotions. They also tried repeatedly, and annoyingly to get emergency personnel to open up and discuss their emotions related to the event while they were still involved in the most sensitive aspects of the disaster operation. This technique is totally inappropriate. It screams out a complete ignorance of basic crisis intervention principles and demonstrates an incredible insensitivity on the part of those who participated in this absurd procedure. It certainly points to a severe lack of understanding of both the jobs and personalities of emergency workers.

The actual victims of the disaster may respond earlier to their emotional reactions, so various types of help are usually accepted by them much earlier than by the emergency workers. Victims do not have to worry about "image armor" or the need to keep up a good front as the emergency services personnel do. They let go of their cognitive defenses earlier and are therefore ready for help much faster.

FIGURE 13.2

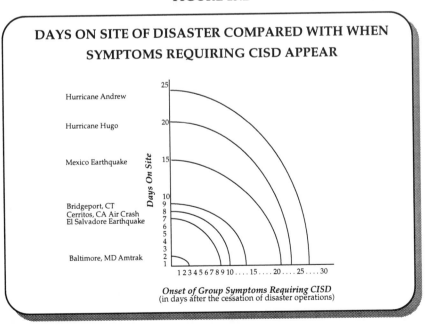

Disasters are different than ordinary CISM services. They are a terrible learning experiences for inexperienced or inadequately trained CISM team members or representatives of disaster relief agencies because they are so different from the usual CISM and psychological services. Disasters demand the most highly skilled CISM helpers, not the least experienced. Less than that standard opens up an enormous potential to create a situation which does far more harm than good. So, let us all be careful in the management of a disaster support service. Assess first, provide one-on-one help as might be necessary at the scene, and defusings or demobilizations in a secure zone after personnel are released from the scene. Then carefully design CISD groups to follow up in a week to ten days after the conclusion of the incident. Some prolonged disasters may necessitate holding off CISD services for several weeks after the event concludes.

With a cautious, well-designed approach, we can assure that the right type and the right amount of help is given at the right time when people are most ready to receive it.

LESSONS LEARNED

The last twelve years of CISD work has taught us many lessons. Mistakes have been made and corrections have occurred. The lessons of the past are important for us now and for the future of CISM services in general and CISD in particular. Some of the lessons learned about CISD have been written in other portions of this book. At the risk of a little repetition, but with the understanding that there is learning in repetition, some of the key lessons learned from the past will be presented here.

1. *CISD is not psychotherapy.* It was never developed to be a therapy nor a substitute for psychotherapy. It was designed to be a team facilitated, organized and structured group discussion of a traumatic event with two main goals: 1) mitigation of the impact of a traumatic event and 2) acceleration of normal recovery processes in non-pathological populations who are having generally normal reactions to abnormal events. The very general descriptions in the Table 13.1 indicate the main differences between psychotherapy and CISD.

2. *CISD is a team approach.* The most effective approach to the facilitated group process of CISD is a team approach. In the emergency services, corrections facilities, air line industries, hospitals, military organizations and other front line operations or in companies with large stable work forces, teams made up of mental health professionals *and* peer support personnel drawn from those populations are always utilized.

TABLE 13.1

CONTRAST OF PSYCHOTHERAPY AND CISD

Psychotherapy	*CISD*
Therapeutic model: intervention for an established problem to change defense mechanisms and initiate life style changes or relationship changes	Crisis Intervention model: stabilization, mobilization of resources, normalization, restoration of function
Generally long term (12 or more sessions)	Very short term (3-8 total contacts, one of which is a CISD)
Emphasis on individual needs	Group emphasis
Treatment	Prevention
May require change in defenses	Reinforces effective defenses
Must deal with transference issues	Transference minimal due to brevity of contacts
Treatment continues until problems resolve and symptoms recede or disappear	Referral is made if symptoms persist or worsen
An extensive amount of therapy may be required in cases of significant psychopathology	No attempt is made to treat those with significant psychopathology, instead referrals are made to mental health professionals
Therapist driven	Peer driven, mental health guidance
Skilled therapist(s)	Peer / mental health team

In small companies and community groups which are not associated with emergency operations, a team of two or three mental health professionals are more likely to be the intervention team.

It has been found that peers drawn from the same professions are best. That is, police serve police best and nurses serve nurses best. Likewise, every emergency profession gains the best benefits from the CISD when they are served by peers from their own profession.

3. *CISD is more helpful when applied within a brief time after the traumatic event.* In most cases, the debriefing is *ideal* when it is offered within 24-72 hours of the incident. In the majority of situations, a debriefing will lose its effectiveness after four to eight weeks depending on the intensity of the event. It may, however, be provided later and will still be beneficial even several weeks after an event. The more powerful the situation, the more likelihood there is that a CISD will have a positive effect.

    There is a caution, however, and that is, if the CISD is offered a very long time after the event, such as more than two months later, it may actually be counterproductive. It could open up the psychological wounds and rip down defensive barriers which the people need to maintain themselves in their work environment.

    In some very rare cases it has been necessary to provide debriefings several years after a traumatic incident. This has been done, with considerable success, in circumstances in which no help had been provided to the group at the time of or since the incident. The events stand out as highly traumatizing to the group members and are not easily forgotten. Such events tower over all of the events in the history of the organization. In these situations, CISD alone is typically not effective. One-on-ones, neuro-cognitive or other forms of therapy such as Eye Movement Desensitization and Reprocessing, education programs, significant other support and administrative education and support programs are necessary.

4. *CISDs should be short in length.* The CISD process has been designed to be completed in approximately 2 to 3 hours. It may be done more rapidly when the group is small. It may take a little longer when the group number is higher or when an incident is particularly distressing. It is extremely rare, however, for a CISD to last longer than three hours. Avoid having debriefings which last four or more hours. Marathon CISD sessions indicate one or more of the following problems:

- The incident is extremely powerful.

- The team is allowing too much to be said in the fact and thought phases.

- The team is very inexperienced.

- The team leadership is poor.

- The team is unfamiliar with the CISD process.

5. *Probing is out of place in CISD.* Debriefing teams have to be satisfied with the information they are given by the participants in a debriefing. Every person in the debriefing has a right to refuse to participate actively in the process if they so choose. It is especially important that a CISD team never probe to gain personal information about a person in the debriefing.

6. *Never embarrass a participant in a CISD.* Drawing attention to an individual participant in a debriefing is inappropriate. Avoid mentioning the fact that they are weeping, wringing their hands or showing emotions in any way. Do not pass boxes of tissues around to the distressed participants. Also avoid touching distressed people during the debriefing. Remember emergency personnel have a high need for control and anything which embarrasses them will threaten that control and cause them to react negatively.

7. *Maintain the confidentiality of CISDs.* Any violation or a perceived violation of the confidentiality of a debriefing threatens the integrity of the CISM team and may cause great harm to the debriefing process itself.

8. *Avoid giving too much advice in CISDs.* The debriefing has been designed to provide the opportunity for ventilation. It is not an opportunity for team members to wax eloquent about their favorite advice. The team obviously needs to give some helpful advice about stress management, but they should not overdo this advice giving.

9. *Never tell personal "war stories."* Team members who tell their own stories in the CISD harm the process by detracting from the incident which is being discussed by the group. "War stories" take the focus off the incident to be discussed and places it instead on the CISD team members.

10. *The CISD team should quiet down in the reaction phase and let the participants talk more.* The CISD team is most active in the introduction, teaching and reentry phases. The participants, on the other hand, are usually very active in the fact, thought, reaction and symptoms phases. Allow silences to work for very brief periods of time (ten seconds in most cases). If the silence goes on too long, it may be necessary for one of the team members to ask the question again or to encourage someone to speak if that person wants to or looks like they do.

11. *An education session is NEVER a substitute for a debriefing.* Although stress education is very important, it can never be used as a substitute for a debriefing. To do so would deprive the participants of the opportunity to vent their emotions and find out from one another the details of the incident which might help them to resolve the pain they may be experiencing.

12. *There is always a need for follow up after a CISD.* Sometimes a brief follow up meeting (**not** another debriefing) is held about a week after the debriefing. People may be asked how it has been since the debriefing has taken place and if they are still having any left over reactions which need to be discussed. Whatever the group members need to discuss is worked through and information which might help them is presented.

Most of the follow up work is provided in one-on-one sessions. It is important that peer support personnel obtain peer counselor training so that they may be more effective in their individual follow up sessions.

DIFFICULT DEBRIEFINGS

When one considers the amount of information in this text, no one should have the idea that debriefings are easy processes which anyone can provide even when they have no training. Nothing could be further from the truth. Debriefings, in the best of circumstances, can be a challenge which demands well trained and experienced team members whether they be peers, clergy or mental health professionals.

Adequate training in the advanced CISD course is essential if a CISD team is going to be involved in any of the following debriefings. These types of debriefings are very complex and things can go wrong quickly. CISD teams managing the following types of events must be resourceful and capable of altering their approach rapidly while maintaining the core elements of the debriefing process.

MULTIPLE INCIDENT DEBRIEFING

The multiple incident debriefing or multiple events debriefing is used when the same personnel in an organization experience several horrible events in a brief period of time. A maximum of four events can be debriefed simultaneously. More would overburden the CISD team and they would likely fail in their attempts to help the group. If there are more than four events the CISD team should choose the four worst ones.

A line of duty death is never part of a multiple incident debriefing. It is so powerful that it would overshadow any other event. Line of duty deaths should be handled completely separately.

The events may be very similar to one another or they may be quite different but may have just occurred in a brief time frame. The usual time frame is between one shift and no longer than fourteen days.

The CISD team assesses the situation and makes a conscious decision to utilize the multiple incident debriefing format. CISD teams should never be surprised and have a multiple incident debriefing spontaneously begin within a regular debriefing. In other words, a multiple incident debriefing is a planned process not a haphazard one.

To assess the potential for a multiple incident debriefing, a CISD team should ask the following question in their initial assessment of a request for debriefing:

- Besides this incident for which you are requesting a debriefing, are there any other significant events which have occurred within the last fourteen days? If the answer is "no" make preparations for a standard single incident debriefing. If the answer is "yes," then ask for the following information:

  * How many events have there been?

  * What types of events have occurred?

  * Are any of the events very similar?

  * What is the exact time frame for the events?

  * Were the crews the same for each event or were some of them only on one or two of the events but not all of them?

  * Is each of the events serious enough to be debriefed by itself even without having had the others?

* Is there one event which people seem to be focusing most upon?

* How are the crews from these events right now?

* Are there any unusual reactions or symptoms noticeable among crew members?

* Any other pertinent information?

Once an assessment is made and the CISD team decides to provide a multiple incident debriefing, it should begin to organize the members of the team who will actually do the debriefing. It will be necessary to have at least one extra team member for the team. If it would only take two CISD team members to do a standard single incident debriefing then three are chosen for the multiple incident debriefing. If it would take three to do a standard debriefing, then four are chosen for the multiple incident debriefing, and so on. More time must also be planned. Most multiple incident debriefings require one half hour to one hour extra to complete.

The CISD team must know about each of the events as if each one of them was the only event to be debriefed. This means that the team has to do some "homework" before they go to the multiple incident debriefing.

A team member should be assigned a "specialist" role. Each team member is instructed to pay close attention whenever the incident to which he or she has been assigned is mentioned in the debriefing. During the teaching phase the team member who is assigned to a specific event teaches on that event. Any team member can teach on any of the incidents, but the "specialist" has to teach on the incident to which he or she has been assigned. This spreads the team work load out so that one team member does not have to do all of the work.

It is okay to mix in people who only worked on one of the incidents with others who have worked more of them. More than likely they have already heard of the event through the organization in which they work. There is little chance it will negatively affect emergency personnel because they are usually unaffected by events in which they did not participate.

The events are debriefed simultaneously. The various events are blended into the discussion randomly and no attempt is made to organize the discussion into blocks. The sorting out of the various events is accomplished in the teaching phase of the debriefing. This is a real challenge for a CISD team. The team members try to follow each situation as it is expressed and intermixed. It is essential that each event be discussed in the teaching phase. If not, the participants will get the impression that one of the events is considered unimportant by the CISD team. That could cause a person to be distressed if they just happened to be upset by the one event which was not discussed in the teaching.

To begin the multiple incident debriefing, the CISD team asks, "Tell us who you are, your regular job, the incidents you were involved with and the one which was the worst for you. A very brief description of what happened in each event will be helpful. You do not have to discuss them in any particular order."

In the thought phase the question is asked, "What thoughts came to mind on each of the events? Are there any thoughts which stand out overall as you look back on these events?"

Likewise, in the reaction phase the question is modified from the standard debriefing in the following way, "What is the worst thing about any of these events for you personally? You may wish to state something about each of the events or just pick the overall worst thing about any one of them."

In the symptoms phase the participants are asked if any signals of distress showed up in them in any of the events.

The teaching phase of the multiple incident debriefing process is just like the teaching which goes on in any debriefing. The difference is that each event must be discussed in the teaching phase. Another difference is that the team makes considerable effort to link the events together and point out any themes which seem to exist.

SYMBOLIC DEBRIEFING

On occasion, a debriefing for a single incident will trigger many old memories of past traumatic events. The discussion in the debriefing makes an unexpected shift into a broad range of old events. The CISD team members are usually surprised by the shift from the current event to the old events. It occurs naturally.

The shift from the present event to the older ones is produced because there is something which triggers the old memories. Sometimes the events are very similar, or similar feelings exist in the new event as were present in the old ones. Occasionally the five senses play a role in stimulating the old memories. The current event represents or "symbolizes" the older ones.

To manage a "Symbolic Debriefing" the CISM team must first recognize the possibility of such an occurrence. The possibility is always present. The team needs to listen carefully as the old events start showing up in the debriefing. They need to see how the old and new events are linked. The CISD team, once it becomes aware of the shift, makes one or two gentle attempts to reintroduce the current event. An example of an attempt to reintroduce the current issue would be, "We can see how this situation reminds you of many past events and we appreciate you bringing that out. The connections you make with the past are important, but we would like to ask another question about this current situation." Then a question pertinent to the current event is brought out. If the discussion drifts off to old events again it may be a signal that the old painful experiences have never been worked out and need to be discussed. Efforts to recover the current event are stopped and the team pays close attention to whatever the group discusses.

If the old events have no significant emotional power and the group just seems to be avoiding the current, more painful incident, the drift into old topics is resisted and the group is kept on track in the current event. Under those circumstances, the drift away may be a smoke screen to avoid the pain of the current event.

If the symbolic debriefing is progressing and many old events are being brought in, the CISD team must listen carefully and attempt to find any common themes. These themes will be taught in the teaching phase as the team attempts to tie all the loose ends up and make sense out of the various events which have been discussed. The CISD team has to be flexible in the number and types of questions it asks. The scatter in the events requires such flexibility. A wide range of questions also assures that the old and new events will be properly connected so that at the end of the symbolic debriefing the issues are more resolved for the participants.

LINE OF DUTY DEATH

Line of duty death is, without doubt, one of the most difficult of all debriefings to manage. The death produces intense levels of shock, denial, anxiety and grief for the participants in the debriefing. Great tact and sensitivity must be displayed to the individuals in the group. There is a considerable need for individuals to receive one-on-one services before and after the CISD. A CISD team managing a line of duty death will have a formidable amount of work to accomplish from the time the death is announced until several weeks after the funeral. The early stages of grief are difficult times for an organization and for the individuals in that organization. Emotions will remain high although they will be changing as the group and the individuals pass through the grief stages.

These feelings are frequently transmitted to the CISD team members. The team members may endure vicarious traumatization from the experience of the debriefing. They need detailed briefings before they provide the CISD. The team members will also need a more intense post-debriefing meeting at the conclusion of each CISD and the other CISM services.

Line of duty death requires a broad range of CISM services. Once the team is notified of the death, it goes into action. The team may assist the organization in developing a quick plan for death notifications to family members. Many CISM teams have actively participated in providing death notifications to the deceased's family according to contingency plans. When this occurs, a team approach is recommended. Usually a department chaplain, a high ranking officer of the department, a mental health professional from the CISM team and a peer support person are brought together to make the death announcement. If it is not possible to bring such a joint team together quickly, then a high ranking official of the organization should make the announcement. In any case, the announcement to family members is always the worst experience. No amount or type of training can adequately prepare anyone to present such bad news to the loved ones of a deceased member of the group.

Once the death announcement has been made, the team turns its attention to the organization of the first group contact with the members of the group. On the day of the death the first debriefing is held. It should be noted, however, that this debriefing does not follow the same format as the seven phase debriefing which is used after the funeral. It is also much shorter in length than a seven phase debriefing. In fact, the first debriefing is more like a defusing than it is like a debriefing. The two major goals of this first debriefing are:

1. To establish a baseline of facts about the situation

2. To assist the group members in preparing for the funeral

In the first debriefing the CISD team asks the group if they could briefly explain what happened so everyone will have the same information. The comments usually come slowly and with great pain. People are very shocked and have trouble sorting out some of the details. The thought phase is skipped since no one has had adequate time to sort out their thoughts. When the reaction phase is brought out, the CISD team has to emphasize specifically that it wants to know if people can identify the aspect of the situation which is giving them the most pain at the time of the debriefing. Do not expect that they will be able to give much coherent information during the debriefing. Only a few people usually speak at this time. The symptoms phase is usually skipped since they have had little time to experience any symptoms except shock and denial. The teaching phase gives a very brief overview of the early stages of grief and some time is spent preparing the personnel to cope with the intensity of the next few days and especially the funeral.

CISM team members provide one-on-one services on request and whenever necessary during the next few days as funeral preparations are made. A small delegation representing the CISM team may attend the funeral out of respect to the organization and its membership. No specific CISM functions are outlined for this delegation. There is usually no need for specific services. The funeral tends to preoccupy everyone's thoughts and few seek direct assistance at this time. Immediately after the funeral, some individuals do seek out team members for an opportunity to ventilate. Team members may assist as requested but they should not "push" themselves on anyone. *Grief is a natural process and too much help can actually interfere with natural coping and recovery processes.* So CISM team members generally take on a watch and see approach to this stage in the grief and mourning process. Help when requested to do so, but do not overdo efforts to help. The funeral delegation from the CISM team should not be expected to conduct the debriefings after the funeral. It will be too hard for them to do both the funeral and the debriefings.

The second debriefing occurs usually three to seven days after the funeral. This debriefing is designed to round out the details of the loss and to set the path forward through the long range grief process. The standard seven stages are followed unlike the debriefing done on the day of death which was previously described. Issues which may trigger painful reactions at this point are associated with events which occurred during the funeral, or the fact that the organization is making efforts to return to normal. For example, the administration may have arranged to have the person's locker emptied and that triggered anger in other personnel. The team needs to process all of the various issues which are brought out in the debriefing. Toward the end of the CISD, the team asks the participants how they would most like to remember the deceased. Then they must discuss in detail the grief process and present realistic estimates about how long it will take for the group to work through grief. Often the team provides advice on how to keep the memory of the deceased alive within the organization by plaques, live tree plantings, scholarship funds and other activities.

Follow up over the next few weeks are important. Some individuals will need to talk to CISM team members. There may be a need for a brief group meeting to find out how they are doing since the funeral and the last CISD. Administrators and supervisors may seek advice on how to handle one or another aspect of the recovery process. The family of the deceased may need additional support or recommendations on finding grief counselors to help them if they are getting stuck in the grief process. The CISM team usually provides debriefings and other services as required to the department's spouses and significant others. They are usually terrified by the loss and need help in re-balancing their lives after a death which could have just as easily been their own loved one. Sometimes debriefing support may need to be provided to the children of operations personnel.

One month, three months, six months and one year anniversaries are rough times which tend to trigger additional reactions. CISM teams should be aware of these time frames and be prepared to provide individual services if they should be requested.

MULTIPLE LINE OF DUTY DEATHS

If the effects of one line of duty death are devastating to the organization then the word to describe the impact of a multiple line of duty death on an organization is "catastrophic." Recovery from multiple line of duty deaths is a grueling task. CISM teams will certainly work very hard if they are brought in to assist after a multiple line of duty death. The experience is very emotionally draining on the team members and replacements may be required to prevent the team members from "burning out" as they render assistance.

The paragraphs above on the issue of line of duty death certainly apply here. There are, however, some specific items which should be mentioned here since multiple line of duty deaths are so out of the ordinary.

First, it is important to treat each of the affected families in an individual manner. Never group all of the bereaved families together. Each family has different needs. They generally pull together and depend on family members, not outsiders, to assist them with their immediate needs. Putting all of the bereaved families together may stir unusually intense grief feelings which can get out of control. Also, if one family perceives (even if it is completely false) that the deceased person in another family caused the death of their loved one, there will be an explosive situation established if the families are put together. They may choose to get together on their own, but the department does not attempt to put the families together before, during or immediately after the funeral. Months later the families may choose to get together or they may be brought together for some special ceremony. By that time the facts of the loss of their loved ones will have been established and the individuals will have had time to deal with the early stages of grief. Each family should initially be given crisis intervention support. Later they may benefit from grief counseling when they are ready for it.

Significant other support services including debriefings and one-on-one support are essential for all of the families associated with the organization. Many times children's groups and teen groups have to be established to calm the fears generated in the children by the dramatic loss of personnel. This is a CISM team function since these services are not provided by any other program in the organization or the community.

The CISM team may have to assist the organization in buffering the media. Making statements approved by the organization can alleviate some of the distress caused by intense public interest.

The CISM team must remember the people who work in support functions for the organization. Such groups might include those who are clerks, secretaries, computer operators, supply personnel and many others. These people will feel the loss even if they were not regularly working around those who were killed.

Many who survived experience "survivor guilt" and may need brief counseling or even therapy to overcome the impact of the losses. Others may be angry that one person was killed and not another. This is called "survivor resentment" and is a natural, although uncomfortable, reaction to loss. If it becomes severe, those who suffer from it may also need support.

DISASTER SERVICES

The material in this section has special applicability for both emergency services and disaster workers on Community Response Teams (CRT).

Disasters, in one sense, are great learning opportunities. This is especially so if one hopes to learn how to manage the operations of the disaster. Being present at a disaster can teach a person a great deal about what to expect about those large scale incidents. In another sense, disasters are horrible learning environments. This is so if a person is trying to learn how to provide crisis intervention services and Critical Incident Stress Management. Sending inexperienced people to a disaster to learn the skills of crisis intervention can be a dangerous process which can cause harm to the people to be served and which often teaches all the wrong things. Disasters are so unusual and so overwhelming that unprepared people are shocked by the situation and have a hard time learning anything more than personal survival skills to help them to get through the experience.

Crisis intervention skills and CISM should be learned gradually in smaller events and then the experienced person is exposed to the disaster where he or she can apply their well developed skills. What is learned in a disaster is so different than what is experienced in day to day life that it is hard to apply the lessons from the disaster to what a person does every day in CISM.

The best way to approach disaster support services is to train, practice and pre-plan. Small events and drills gradually expose a person to the crisis concepts which can be employed in providing support at a disaster. The people in need of help are given the very best services by trained and experienced personnel and not mediocre services by personnel who are struggling to orient themselves to a highly unusual circumstance.

Here are some general CISM rules which can be useful in a disaster situation.

1. Avoid the urge to bring too many CISM personnel to the scene. Too many people might be exposed to the gore of the scene and may not be able to help others when they have been traumatized. Also, timing is a very important consideration. See the section of this chapter entitled "Too much too fast" for additional information.

2. Never interfere with people who are performing their jobs adequately. The display of emotions is less important as an indicator of how well a person is doing than the ability to continue to function.

3. Expect emotional suppression on the part of emergency operations personnel at the scene. It may take days before operations personnel have any reactions to the situation. The victims and the survivors will be more likely to have immediate reactions.

4. Never provide group service in the midst of the disaster. Group services of any kind are not utilized until the personnel have completed their work at the disaster and are being released from the scene.

5. Demobilizations are used after a disaster. These are then followed in a week to ten days with a full CISD.

6. Any decisions made by CISM teams which affect staffing or operations must be approved by operations field supervisors.

7. Those who provide disaster support services should always follow the same rules for good health that they are promoting for the personnel at the disaster. That includes proper food, rest and time away from the scene.

8. Support personnel should not be physically involved with the operations. To do so risks injuries, and distress so that they might not be able to support the operations personnel well enough.

9. CISM personnel work within the rules established by the operations authorities in the field.

10. Call for additional CISM teams as required.

Debriefings held after disasters may be a little unusual because the events were so intense that people develop many reactions to the experience. They may have ten or more "worst things" to share in the reaction phase. Often people remain silent in the debriefing until the very end and they bring up some item that has not been stated earlier by anyone. When they bring up the item they wish to discuss, the entire group may slip out of the teaching or re-entry phase and go back to the reaction phase. This can be worked through if the CISD team is tactful and confident. When the discussion dies down, a little more teaching from the team will help to bring the group back up to a positive ending of the debriefing.

SUMMARY

This chapter presented an overview of some of the core advanced concepts and issues in the CISM / CISD field. A time line for CISM interventions was presented along with information on the lessons learned from past CISDs. Considerable space was allocated to a discussion of complex situations and debriefings. Included in this discussion was information on disaster work, multiple line of duty deaths, symbolic debriefings and multiple incident debriefings.

It was emphasized that no individuals or team members should attempt to employ these advanced techniques without proper training in Advanced CISD concepts. Newly organized teams in particular are cautioned not to attempt to manage situations which are well beyond their knowledge and experience because it is possible that they might do some harm to the people they are trying to help.

Chapter 14

TROUBLE SHOOTING THE CISD PROCESS: COMMON PROBLEMS IN DEFUSINGS AND DEBRIEFINGS

With over a decade of experience and literally over twenty thousand actual debriefings, a formidable body of "lessons learned" has accrued. In this chapter, we shall highlight the most common problems encountered in leading a successful defusing or debriefing.

The most common problems arise, interestingly enough, from the failure of the individuals leading the defusing or debriefing to fully understand the dynamic processes inherent in these interventions and the consequential failure to adapt effectively to these challenges. While there are certainly numerous problems that can arise during a debriefing the vast majority will fall into one of five categories. These are listed in Table 14.1.

Let us now take a brief look at each of these categories.

OVERLY RIGID APPLICATION

This volume is intended to be an operations manual; a "how to" for CISD, defusings, demobilizations and related interventions. The guidelines contained herein are designed to be general prescriptions and reflections on strategies and tactics that have proven useful in the past. New traumas present new challenges, and often there is a need to adopt a dynamic flexibility in the face of crisis or chaos. The guidelines offered in the text are thought to be valuable in the vast majority of cases but one needs to understand that, upon occasion, unique situations will arise that dictate adaptation.

Common variables that may dictate adaptation would include challenging or unique geographical settings; cultural, ethnic or racial diversities; unique intensity or unusual chronicity of the traumatic event; and often, the sheer magnitude of the traumatic event. When in doubt as to how to adjust to a new and challenging debriefing simply remember to practice some common sense tactics: 1) listen effectively, 2) employ crisis intervention

TABLE 14.1

COMMON PROBLEMS IN CISD

1. Overly rigid adherence to general CISD guideline with no sensitivity for unique situational, personal, cultural or social circumstances.

2. Overzealous application of interventions without appropriate assessment of the state of psychological functions and receptivity of the individuals to be briefed.

3. Failure to conduct the defusing or debriefing in a discrete psychological structure that progresses from the cognitive domain, to the affective domain and back to the cognitive domain for termination.

4. The team members' dysfunctional counter transference, that is, over identification with the trauma experience and / or failure to maintain an objective perspective on the debriefing process as it progresses.

5. Failure to comply with basic defusing and debriefing principles and techniques which have been developed and practiced by CISD teams throughout the world and are now commonly accepted as the standard for applying CISD techniques to emergency personnel and disaster workers.

concepts, 3) do not open any emotional issues that you cannot bring to a closure and 4) depend on peer support personnel who can often obtain a much clearer understanding of the needs of the group.

The advent of defusings, debriefings, demobilizations and disaster mental health services has the potential to do a great service to society, but we must use care in our application of these powerful interventions. Overzealous or excessive application of crisis intervention or therapeutic strategies can be as harmful as under utilization of the same services.

Any psychological intervention is going to produce its greatest benefit if the person receiving the intervention is psychologically receptive to the process itself. For example, earlier in the text we offered general guidelines in terms of the timing of when interventions should be applied. That which ultimately dictates appropriateness is not how many hours / days have passed since the trauma, but rather is how psychologically receptive the victim is to the help being offered.

Every reader can probably recall a difficult time in their lives when he / she just wanted to be left alone. Similarly, one can just as easily recall a difficult time when companionship was considered healing. What makes the difference? Answer: the state of psychological receptivity, that is, that one is ready and willing to accept the form of help or assistance. Forced companionship is as potentially traumatizing as the original trauma to some victims who need isolation and solitude at that particular point in time.

In concert with this discussion of psychological receptivity is the issue of psychological defenses. Perhaps the most commonly used initial defense mechanism in trauma and disaster is *DENIAL*, that is, insistence that everything is okay or that its really not that bad despite objective evidence to the contrary. Some refer to this as a "shock" phase.

A common mistake made by trauma intervention personnel is to overzealously challenge or confront defense mechanisms. If one recalls the goal of crisis intervention as being re-establishing psychological homeostasis, or baseline functioning, we see that defense mechanisms can play a useful role in coping with an otherwise overwhelming psychological challenge. Remember, don't attempt to remove a defense mechanism unless you can replace it with something else that the victim can rely upon for emotional protection until the crisis passes or resolves.

A good example of overzealous intervention can usually be found immediately after large scale disasters. Helpers flock to the scene in record numbers. Many are not sure what they will do when they arrive at the disaster site, but they are irresistibly drawn to the tragedy. Without an organized approach to disaster relief, they may only add to the chaos.

Some CISM teams and CISM trained individuals have unfortunately contributed to the chaos in disaster by arriving at the scene even though they have not been called. They usually have not developed a plan of action in coordination with the local CISM resources. Some have attempted to provide debriefing services when the rescuers and disaster workers were still involved in search and rescue operations or when they were in a state of shock and denial.

CISM teams should slow their overzealous response to disasters. Outside of some brief on-scene support services or some one-on-one contacts with individuals needing assistance (which is provided by locally based CISM teams), debriefing work in disasters does not begin until three to six weeks after the event. The best response of a CISM team to another community is to coordinate those efforts with that community and with the efforts of the International Critical Incident Stress Foundation, Inc. An unrequested presence at a disaster is an overzealous and inappropriate response which may produce harm for CISM teams everywhere as well as for the people who need their help.

FAILURE TO UTILIZE THE NECESSARY PSYCHOLOGICAL STRUCTURE

The CISD process was carefully designed to follow the natural psychological structure of cognitively (intellectual) processing information first and then formulating an affective (emotional) evaluation of their experience. To jump immediately to a discussion of the affective factors and skip the normal cognitive factors is disruptive to psychological processes. In emergency personnel, such a movement will cause anger and rejection. Some emergency workers could actually be harmed psychologically by such a dramatic violation of their normal psychological process for handling traumatic experiences.

Table 14.2 outlines the debriefing process and the psychological structure which should be followed during each phase.

Note that the thought phase and the symptom phase are transitional phases which allow for a smooth as possible movement from one psychological process to another. Too rapid a transition produces discomfort in people who are dealing with traumatic material

Failure to follow this structure during a debriefing will generally lead to a series of problems including but not limited to: 1) participants feeling

TABLE 14.2

CISD Phases	*Psychological Process*	
Introduction	Cognitive	
Fact	Cognitive	
Thought	Cognitive ⟶ Affective	
Reaction	Affective	
Symptom	Affective ⟶ Cognitive	
Teaching	Cognitive	
Re-Entry	Cognitive	

pressure to discuss affective factors before adequate trust of the team and the process has been established, 2) participants feeling cut off once they begin their affective discussions and 3) participants feeling that the CISD team is incompetent and out of control.

LEADER COUNTER TRANSFERENCE

Counter transference develops when the CISD team begins to over identify, on a personal or professional basis, with the personnel being debriefed. CISD personnel must be careful to walk a difficult course of showing sufficient caring, understanding and empathy without becoming immersed or overwhelmed with the intensity or familiarity of any given critical incident. It is not an easy task, but debriefing teams need to keep an objective view of the critical incident and the people they are helping.

One of the best ways to assure an objective CISD is for the team members to keep the experience a cognitive one. For example, instead of looking for similarities between the current event which is being debriefed and one's own past painful experiences, debriefing team members should focus on the current debriefing. They may ask themselves for instance, "What questions do I need to ask, what steps do I need to perform, what do I need to teach to bring these people the maximum benefit from this debriefing?"

FAILURE TO COMPLY WITH BASIC CISD PRINCIPLES

The vast majority of CISM teams have provided high quality debriefing services and have helped many thousands of emergency personnel. Their work has been consistently positive during the last decade. Those dedicated people deserve a great deal of respect and admiration for their work.

A small number of teams, however, have made serious mistakes during defusings or debriefings. And virtually every team has made some minor mistakes as they provided services. The paragraphs to follow should not be perceived as finger pointing accusations. Rather, they should be seen as opportunities to learn from others and remind ourselves of the limitations of CISM services and the pitfalls to be avoided while providing those services.

One of the most serious problems encountered in the debriefing work is the attempt to turn a debriefing into psychotherapy. A CISD is not psychotherapy nor is it a substitute for psychotherapy. A CISD is a stress prevention oriented group discussion of a traumatic event. Psychotherapy, on the other hand, has been developed to "cure" or "fix" an already existing problem or disorder. CISD work should avoid taking on traditional psychotherapeutic roles and stick to its primary goals of: 1) reducing the impact of a traumatic event and 2) accelerating the normal recovery process for normal people who are experiencing normal reactions to totally abnormal events.

The second most serious problem faced by CISD teams is associated with and often the root cause of the first. It is the fact that some teams falsely believe that some of their members can serve without appropriate CISM training. As it has been pointed out elsewhere in this book, the lack of training for professional and peer support personnel is a formula for potential disaster.

Another serious mistake made by CISD teams is the false belief that every person in a debriefing must speak during the debriefing or they will not receive any benefit from the session. The very few CISD teams which believe this myth have, on occasion, come close to violating the absolute right each person has to maintain one's privacy.

CISM teams which believe that all the supportive work of the team must be accomplished during the actual debriefing are also making a serious mistake. The CISD is more of a screening tool than a recovery tool. After the debriefing much work remains. The team members need to follow up by means of phone calls, station visits and other methods. The belief that a single two or three hour contact is going to complete all of the work necessary for resolving the thoughts and feelings associated with the traumatic experience is indicitive of a team that misunderstands the limitations of the debriefing process.

Yet another serious problem is the misapplication of the debriefing to events outside the power of the process. To attempt, for example, to resolve long standing social problems by applying CISD is a prescription for failure.

Debriefings fail for many other reasons. Here is a brief list of some of the more common pitfalls to be avoided:

1. Insufficient use of peers in CISD.

2. Teams which provide too much advice.

3. Writing of anything during a debriefing.

4. Inadequate knowledge of the incident before starting a CISD.

5. Providing CISD services to close relatives or friends or to people who team members supervise or work with very closely.

6. Choosing debriefers who were directly involved in the incident to be debriefed.

7. Interrupting a person who is expressing their emotions during a debriefing.

8. Inadequate introductory remarks.

9. Inadequate teaching and summary remarks.

10. Public discussions of the debriefing by CISD team members once it is concluded.

SUMMARY

This chapter explored the five main problems which can jeopardize the effectiveness of CISD teams. Readers were cautioned about too rigid an application of CISD guidelines as well as overzealous use of the CISD process. One of the most significant problems is the failure to utilize the proper psychological structure for the debriefing. The issue of losing one's objectivity was also presented as was the failure to comply with a standard set of operating procedures in debriefings.

The chapter concluded with a list of pitfalls to avoid to insure the most effective and efficient performance of CISD teams.

Appendix A

COMPONENTS OF AN EMERGENCY SERVICES CRITICAL INCIDENT STRESS MANAGEMENT TEAM

INTRODUCTION

In this appendix, we will discuss the specific components of a CISM team developed for use specifically with emergency service workers and public safety personnel. In reading this appendix it is important to keep in mind that the comments are made in the context of an emergency services CISM team. Some of this material is redundant to that presented earlier, but the decision was made to utilize this format, nevertheless, so as to provide a complete, discrete compendium within this appendix.

Crisis Response Teams (CRT) which serve industrial and commercial settings as well as community groups may need to be structured differently than CISM teams that serve predominantly emergency personnel. CRTs may or may not use "Peer Support" personnel. The use of peers may depend on the existence of a large and stable work force from which to choose peers. CRTs may rely more on mental health professionals and medical staffs than the use of peers. They may also serve only small designated populations such as companies, schools and communities but not the emergency services organizations. The interventions of such a team usually follow the same models described here for use with emergency personnel. Under certain circumstances, however, some modifications to the intervention strategies may be necessary to suit the needs of particular industrial, commercial or community groups.

OVERVIEW

In most cases, a CISM team is a voluntary (unpaid) partnership between various individuals and groups who work together to achieve common goals — lessening the impact of traumatic stress on emergency personnel, accelerating the recovery from stressful events and the enhancement of the psychological health of the emergency worker. The motivation for their service is a sense of dedication and commitment to people in the helping professions who give so much of themselves to their communities.

Most teams are multi-agency and multi-jurisdictional. They provide services to any emergency personnel who need them. Teams may also serve community groups under certain circumstances and on a case by case basis.

A CISM team is made up of two distinct, but interrelated, groups of members who rely upon one another's expertise to prevent critical incident stress, to reduce it when it is not preventable and to hasten the recovery from it when it occurs. The two groups of members are:

- Professional support personnel

- Peer support personnel

Professional support staff include mental health professionals and clergy personnel. Mental health professionals and clergy have somewhat different roles which will be described later in this appendix. Peer support personnel are police officers, fire fighters, nurses, paramedics, emergency medical technicians, dispatchers, physicians and other primary operations personnel. (see Table A.1)

CISM teams are peer oriented crisis intervention programs that depend on guidance and assistance from mental health professionals. Their main function is to attempt to stabilize chaotic and highly stressful situations before those events can cause damaging stress reactions in emergency personnel. Prevention is far more heavily emphasized than treatment.

There have been attempts to establish critical incident support services for emergency service workers without incorporating all of the essential elements of a Critical Incident Stress Management team. For example, some have tried to establish a stress team without appropriate mental health personnel. Others have tried to develop a team without peers. We believe both alternatives are misdirected. If mental health consultation and guidance are absent, peer support personnel could easily miss significant psychological problems. If peers are not included on the team the emergency workers involved in an incident may suffer long delays in obtaining support services from mental health personnel. In effect, peers may serve a valuable role in the early recognition of unusual or dysfunctional behavior in other peers in the emergency organization. In addition, mental health professionals are frequently resisted by emergency personnel and they may often have difficulties in entering into effective helping relationships with the emergency personnel whose jobs may be "foreign" to them. Peer team members may form a psychological bridge from the emergency service worker to the mental health professional.

Interventions from CISM teams are short term. Teams refer to mental health professionals anyone who does not show signs of improvement within three to five contacts. The primary functions of a CISM team do not include long term counseling or psychotherapy. Interventions may have therapeutic elements but they do not substitute for psychotherapy.

TABLE A.1

MEMBERS OF AN EMERGENCY SERVICES CISD TEAM

Professional Support Personnel

1. Mental Health professionals

2. Clergy

Peer Support Personnel

1. Fire Fighters

2. Police Officers

3. Paramedics

4. Emergency Medical Technicians

5. Nurses, especially critical care and emergency

6. Dispatch personnel

7. Search and Rescue personnel

8. Park Service Rangers

9. Corrections Officers

10. Ski Patrol

11. Search Dog Team Members

12. Wild Land Fire Fighters

13. Disaster Workers

14. Professional Life Guard Services

15. Physicians

16. Other first response personnel

TYPICAL TEAM STRUCTURE

LEAD AGENCY

CISM teams have a lead agency (police, fire, EMS, hospital, etc.) which serves as an umbrella organization under which the CISM team organizes itself and, at least in its early stages, functions. The lead agency establishes the environment in which the CISM team can be developed and supported. The services of the lead agency may vary somewhat from jurisdiction to jurisdiction, and, they may change as the team evolves. In some cases, the lead agency dissolves its role as the team develops and the steering committee takes over the management of the team. This is especially so when a community decides to have a "combined emergency services steering committee or board of directors" that takes on the general management of the team. In other words, instead of a single lead agency, all of the participating agencies share in the responsibility of team management. There are, however some basic functions of a lead agency regardless of how it is structured. They are:

- Provision of funding or arrangements for the funding of initial team development

- Development of a steering committee or board of directors for the CISM team

- Staffing for meetings during the developmental stages

- Establishment of a team membership committee

- Coordination of initial (basic) team training

- Assistance in recruiting team membership

- Assistance in locating appropriate team leadership

- Provision of general support for the activities of the CISM team

- Assistance in developing research and evaluation methods as well as quality assurance

- Collection of data for statistical reports and research

- Provision of office space when necessary

- Provision of necessary equipment and supplies (phone, communications, stationery, etc.) to adequately manage the team

- Provision of release time for staff members to manage the team

- Arrangement of continuing education for team members

- Adoption and promulgation of rules and policies and procedures for team operation

- Maintenance of an up to date call out list of all team members and a background file on each team member

TEAM COORDINATOR

Each team needs at least one coordinator who is in charge of the day to day operations of the team. The best people to utilize in the coordinator positions are members of one or more of the emergency organizations. Mental health professionals and chaplains are usually less knowledgeable of the inner workings of the first response organizations. They are also not present in the stations, squad rooms, break rooms and other common gathering places for emergency personnel. They, therefore, seldom hear about the tough incidents early enough to maximize intervention effectiveness.

Teams should build in redundancy. That is, they should have back ups for coordinators. One coordinator, no matter how efficient, can be overwhelmed from time to time and will not work as effectively. Besides, people need to be able to carry out life's other responsibilities. When there is a family gathering or a vacation, or even illness, someone must carry on the coordination functions for the team. Missed calls or delays in responding to the needs of distressed emergency personnel deteriorates trust and incapacitates a CISM team.

Some CISM teams have different coordinators for each of the organizations served by the team. For example, there may be two coordinators for police, two for fire, two for emergency medical services and two for nursing. Almost any combination of coordinators or almost any number of them is fine as long as the tasks of team coordination are properly managed. The tasks to be handled by coordinators are:

- General management of the CISM team

- Evaluating the need to dispatch a team or to provide any other services once a call has been received

- Receiving the call from the dispatcher and then calling the necessary team members to respond to the situation

- Assisting in developing team membership

- Representing the team at emergency and community meetings

- Assistance in the selection of appropriate members for the team

- Providing for opportunities for continuing education of the team

- Coordination with the clinical director to assure appropriate support services

- Developing positive relationships with agency administrations, Red Cross and other community groups

- Handling requests from community groups for assistance and dispatching team members if those requests are appropriate for team intervention

- Soliciting support from the emergency services organizations

- Assisting in the writing of the team policies and procedures

- Co-leading team meetings with the clinical director

- Assuring that distressed debriefers are given appropriate help

- Establishing a peer review board to correct problems on the team

- Sponsoring periodic team meetings

- Developing a program of quality assurance for the team

- Maintaining any records of team activities

- Maintaining a referral list

- Arranging for workshops, seminars and for lectures to enhance team education

- Teaching some of the stress management programs to emergency personnel

- Keeping up to date on the most current research, findings and theories of emergency services stress, occupational stress, critical incident stress, Post-Traumatic Stress Disorder and related topics

- Maintaining association with national and international organizations which foster critical incident stress work

- Maintaining up to date call out list of all team members

CLINICAL DIRECTOR

Teams, as previously mentioned, must have mental health professionals who serve them. Mental health professionals include psychologists, social workers, psychiatrists, psychiatric nurses and certified mental health counselors. Although it is not necessary to have different types of mental health professionals on a team, it is usually necessary to have more than one mental health professional on a team in order to avoid overworking the one professional. One of those mental health professionals is chosen as the clinical director. The clinical director provides oversight to the intervention activities of the team and assures that the right kind of service is provided and that all team members work within the limits of their training and experience. The clinical director performs the following tasks:

- Works closely with the team coordinator to assure proper team performance and quality assurance

- Represents the CISM team before the public and before the organizations the team serves

- Monitors the debriefings provided and offers suggestions for future debriefings and suggestions regarding follow up services

- Assists the coordinator in developing appropriate CISM team continuing education

- Provides some of the continuing education training for the team

- Assists the coordinator and team committees in developing written policies and procedures for the team

- Assists the team in developing a cross familiarization program for mental health professionals so that they might observe emergency personnel in action

- Assists in the selection of team members

- Participates in the peer review board to correct team problems

- Conducts periodic reviews of team records and services

- Assists the coordinator in maintaining a comprehensive list of referral sources

- Assures that follow up services are provided to those in need

- Offers clinical guidance to coordinator and team members

Note: The issue of insurance is one that is less than clear at this point in time. Nevertheless, it is highly recommended that all mental health members of the CISD team carry malpractice insurance.

TEAM LIAISON

Every team has some business, correspondence and other administrative responsibilities. Every team has to negotiate for some necessities such as phone service, a checking account, a desk for its work, meeting space, etc. The team liaison manages all of the team's business while coordinating his or her efforts with the team coordinator and the clinical director. The team liaison serves as the book keeper, secretary, treasurer and logistics coordinator for the team. The person who holds this position should have sufficient rank within an emergency services organization to assure that the team's needs are managed in a timely and efficient manner. It is also important that the person in the liaison position be a firm believer in the team effort and willing to work for the benefit of the team.

MENTAL HEALTH TEAM MEMBERS

Mental health professionals are people who hold advanced degrees (master's or doctoral) in a mental health field and work as a mental health services provider in one or more professional settings such as hospitals, crisis centers, community mental health centers or in private practice.

Mental health professionals are obviously vital for the team's functions. They are frequently given the name "professional support personnel." They provide several important services for the team. They are the mental health professionals who work with a Critical Incident Stress Debriefing (CISD) team when a debriefing is being provided. They provide consultation and clinical guidance to the peer support personnel on the team. They may also assist in the education of the team members. They may provide a few counseling sessions when individuals have been overwhelmed by the stressful event and it becomes evident that the debriefing alone will be insufficient to resolve the problem. Mental health professionals frequently serve as referral resources when long term counseling is required. It should be noted, however, that if a referral for long term counseling is made, the usual fees and requirements of regular counseling sessions will then apply. It would be unreasonable to expect that a mental health professional would provide free services beyond the very few contacts which fall under the CISM banner. When possible, mental health providers who are members of CISD or CRT teams should refrain from referring victims of trauma and disaster to their own private practices. Mental health professionals perform CISM services under the guidance of the clinical director and those services include:

- Assistance with the education of the team

- Psychological leadership during the debriefing

- Assistance in the development of referral services

- Assisting the coordinator in determining the appropriateness of a debriefing request

- Assistance with follow up services after the debriefing

- Service, when necessary, on the peer review board

- Accept long term therapy referrals when appropriate (see above)

- Participate actively in cross familiarization training

- Attend periodic team meetings

- Representing the CISM team before emergency organizations and the public

- Providing clinical guidance to peers who have intervened in traumatic events

- Assistance with the interpretation of data collected by the team

- Assistance in the selection of team members

CLERGY

Most of the CISM teams in the United States have clergy personnel who serve as part of the professional support staff. If they have appropriate degrees in the mental health field (see section on mental health team members above), they may take on mental health roles on the team. If, on the other hand, they serve their communities as active emergency personnel, they may take on peer support roles. In rare instances, clergy are both active emergency personnel and certified mental health professionals. Because it is confusing to those they serve to constantly be switching from one role to another, they would be best to serve their teams as mental health professionals if they hold mental health degrees.

Usually they provide their ministry on a CISM team by a concerned presence in which they function as active listeners to the pain of emergency personnel. Clergy may provide spiritual support when it is clear that the emergency worker is seeking such support. Clergy must be careful, however, not to impose a given religious perspective on emergency personnel who may not be ready to hear such a message. This is true for one-on-one interventions as well as in groups. Religion and philosophy are deeply personal issues. Many people like to keep those issues to themselves. The best discussions of these topics will take place when people are voluntarily

TABLE A.2

MENTAL HEALTH PROFESSIONALS

The minimum criteria for choosing mental health professionals are:
- At least a Master's degree in one of the following areas:
    - A. Psychology
    - B. Social Work
    - C. Psychiatric Nursing
    - D. Pastoral Counseling
    - E. Mental Health Counseling
    - F. Training and Certification as a Physican Who Specializes in Psychiatry
- Regular employment or services in one of the following areas:
    - A. Social Services
    - B. Psychological or Psychiatric Services
    - C. Crisis Intervention Services
    - D. Pastoral Ccounseling
    - E. Psychiatric Nursing
    - F. Other Counseling Services
- Professional training in the following areas is essential:
    - A. Critical Incident Stress Debrieifing (CISD)
        1. Basic CISD Training is Required
        2. Advanced CISD Training is Required
        3. Post-Traumatic Stress Disorder Training is Required
    - B. Crisis Intervention
    - C. General Stress
    - D. Group Processes
    - E. Human Communication Skills
    - F. Directive Intervention Strategies
    - G. Familiarization Through "Ride Alongs" with Emergency Personnel in Their Environments
- Professional training in the following areas is beneficial:
    - A. Substance Abuse
    - B. Alcoholism
    - C. Family therapy
    - D. Neuropsychology
    - E. Physiological Basis of Behavior
- Professional support personnel should have their own professional pursuits insurance.
- Unless some specialized local arrangements are made, professional support staff should be willing to donate their time to the emergency services for CISM activities.

involved and when they feel ready for those discussions. The clergy can, in the final analysis, reassure those who have encountered a faith crisis as a result of their work in a traumatic event. In that sense, clergy play a uniquely powerful role in CISM.

Upon occasion, the clergy may be asked to lead a group prayer in an especially distressing situation or community wide event. It is obviously a good practice to comply with the requests of the traumatized group.

CISM trained clergy will be far more prepared for their role on a CISM team if they go through the familiarization program with emergency workers. They need to know as much as possible about the job and personalities of the operations people they hope to serve. Obviously, the same guideline can be equally applied to the mental health professionals who serve on a team.

PEER SUPPORT PERSONNEL

In situations involving commercial establishments, industries and educational programs, it is not necessary to utilize "peer support personnel." However, in the emergency services, the use of peers is absolutely essential. Nurses understand nurses and, in most cases, are more easily accepted as support personnel than mental health professionals or clergy. Likewise, fire fighters prefer to receive help from one of their own and police officers report that they can receive unique insight from other police officers. The list can go on by category of emergency workers, but the reader has the basic idea by now. The use of peers from one's own professional group cannot be overemphasized for emergency personnel. This is especially so in the period shortly after the traumatic event. If the situation is not resolved by the crisis intervention efforts of peers, then referrals to mental health professional and clergy personnel will be necessary. It is important to keep in mind that many Critical Incident Stress Management services are peer oriented and peer driven, but clinically guided by mental health professionals.

Peer support personnel on a team are drawn from all of the organizations which could use the team. Any emergency or specialty service organization can contribute membership to a team. Specialty service groups include ski patrol, corrections, life guard services, dive teams, national park service personnel, mountain rescue groups, search dog teams and any groups which are likely to regularly function in a first response mode.

Peer support personnel are chosen because of their maturity (not age), and ability to work with people. They have an understanding of the harmful effects of stress and have a desire to lessen stress in their fellow workers. They are dedicated and caring people who are willing to give of their time and their talents to assist distressed fellow workers. Peers are usually the prime movers on a CISM team. During the last decade their role on CISM teams has been dramatically expanded. They have received more training and now have a wealth of experience. They have proven themselves to be extremely competent in rendering assistance to their fellow workers. They:

- Often initiate the first contacts with those who are showing signs of distress after exposure to a critical incident.

- Assist in assessing the need for defusings, debriefings, individual contacts, family support services, referrals and others.

- Contact the team coordinator to begin the set up process for the services of the CISM team.

- Serve as the eyes and ears of the CISM team and are alert to the signs and symptoms of developing stress problems.

- Perform services such as defusings, under the guidance of mental health professionals on the team.

- Take on a very active role in the debriefings.

- Provide basic on-scene support services to individuals who are showing signs of distress during the incident.

- Call for mental health assistance when their training and resources are exceeded.

- Assist the CISM team in educational programs for their fellow emergency personnel.

- Provide peer counseling if they have been properly trained.

- Serve on the peer review committee when necessary.

- Assist in providing follow up after defusings, debriefings and other interventions.

- Assist the team coordinator and mental health professionals as required.

- Provide individual consultations as required.

- Report their interventions to the mental health professionals on the CISM team who guide them in their work.

- Assist the team in CISM related projects.

- Function only within the limits of their training.

Table A.3 describes minimum criteria for peer personnel.

TABLE A.3

PEER SUPPORT PERSONNEL

The minimum criteria for choosing peer support personnel are:
- Emergency service experience
- Emotional maturity
- Respect of one's peers
- Ability to keep information confidential
- Sensitive to the needs of other people
- Willingness to work as a team member
- Willingness to learn psychosocial behavior
- Agreement to work within one's limits
- Agreement to follow the established criteria
- Training in Basic CISD required
- Training in Advanced CISD required
- Training in psychology and /or social work preferred
- Training in human communication preferred
- Training in traumatic stress and Post-Traumatic Stress Disorder preferred
- Training in Crisis Intervention preferred
- Training in Peer Counseling preferred
- Training in Advanced Peer Counseling is preferred

Figure A.1 illustrates the typical relationships between the main components of a CISM team. The entire team is able to communicate directly and indirectly with any one of its members or the steering committee. It is extremely important that the clinical director and team coordinator work closely together with the support of the steering committee or board of directors and also the team liaison.

TEAM MEMBER SELECTION

It is crucial for a team's survival and efficient function that the very best people be chosen to serve on the CISM team. "Political" appointments to the team are not only inappropriate, they can be dysfunctional. The wrong kind of help may be more destructive than no help at all. The task of finding and recruiting the best individuals can present some significant challenges to the steering committee or the membership committee.

The first task is to choose a membership committee and then determine the best methods to find and recruit the team's membership. The membership committee must be trained themselves in the CISM and CISD processes or they will be unable to choose the right people to perform the task of helping others. At times, the right talent for the team is readily available and willing to participate. At other times, active recruitment efforts will be necessary to contact the right team members. One way to actively recruit team members is to provide stress education programs and invite a broad range of participants. Frequently, people attending educational stress programs develop sincere interest in the team and wish to join it. Occasionally potential team members must be approached and asked if they would be willing to assist on the team.

FIGURE A.1

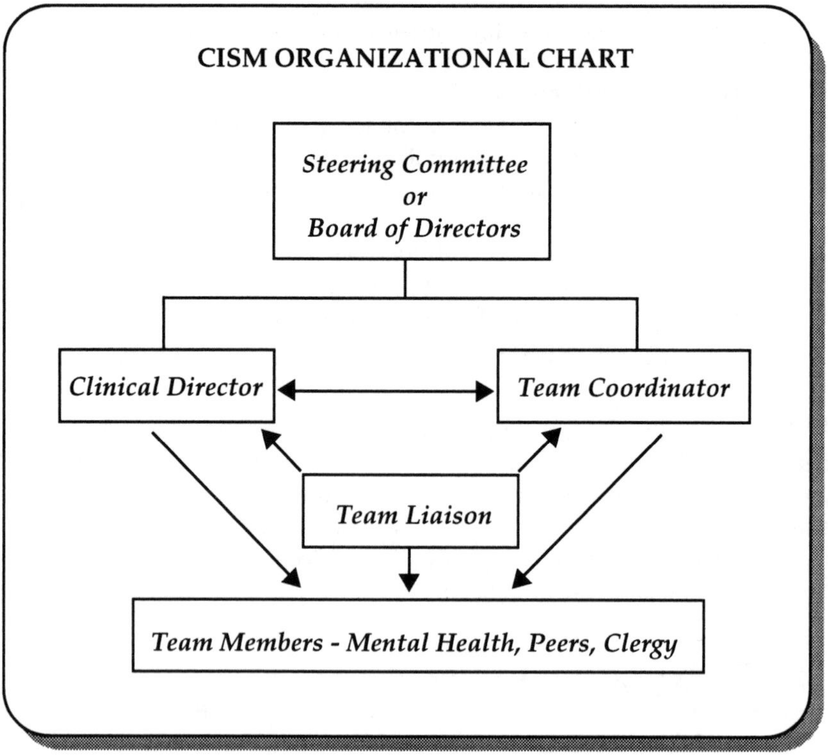

CISM ORGANIZATIONAL CHART

Steering Committee or Board of Directors

Clinical Director ↔ *Team Coordinator*

Team Liaison

Team Members - Mental Health, Peers, Clergy

COMPREHENSIVE APPROACH TO CISM

A team which believes it only has to do debriefings to manage stress in the emergency services is only functioning at less than a fraction of its capacity. It takes much more than debriefings to change a CISD team into a CISM team. The following programs are vital for a comprehensive approach to CISM:

- Extensive basic stress and continuing education program(s)

- A CISD team in place and ready when needed

- "Significant other" support programs

- Family support and family life programs

- Administrator / supervisor education and support programs

- Peer support (counseling) strategies

- Mutual aid and community outreach programs

- A wide range of flexible intervention techniques such as:

    A. Mid-action support (on-scene)

    B. Individual consults for peers

    C. Defusings

    D. Demobilizations (disaster only)

    E. Debriefings

    F. Follow up services

    G. Informal discussions

    H. Chaplain services

    I. Professional counseling services

    J. Mutual aid programs with other organizations

    K. Community education programs

    L. Other services as required

SUMMARY

This appendix has described the structure and components of the emergency services CISM team. An overview of the components of a critical incident stress team was presented. Considerable emphasis was given to the criteria for team membership. Also emphasized were the roles and responsibilities of the leadership and general membership positions on the team. The appendix closed with a description of the general functions of a CISM team.

NOTE: Lynn Kennedy-Ewing of Delaware County, Pennsylvania CISM Team deserves special thanks for her contributions to this appendix. The written guidelines which she has developed for CISM team operations and policies has served as a model for this appendix as well as for the policies and procedures of almost every CISM team in North America, Europe and the South Pacific.

Appendix B

ESTABLISHING AND MAINTAINING A CRITICAL INCIDENT STRESS MANAGEMENT TEAM IN THE EMERGENCY SERVICES

INTRODUCTION

Some readers of this book will be struggling to establish a brand new CISM team. Others will be trying to recondition a much older team which has lost a considerable amount of its membership. This Appendix (B) has been written to assist those who face the problems of team organization or reorganization. It is designed to serve as a set of guidelines which can help the team organizer reach the goals of team development in the shortest possible time. It has been based on the experiences of many who have struggled through CISM team development during the last decade.

Assistance in developing a CISM team may be obtained by contacting the International Critical Incident Stress Foundation, Inc. (a non-profit organization) at (410) 730-4311, or by contacting established CISM teams.

FIRST STEPS

CISM teams do not appear overnight. They are always the end result of careful study, planning and a great deal of hard work on the part of many dedicated people. Team development requires effective leadership, a dedicated development committee, clearly stated goals and objectives and a drive for excellence in service to one's fellow workers. Several groups have failed in their efforts to establish a CISM program in their locality because they lacked the essential elements for team development described in the sentences above.

Experience with CISM team development suggests that one of the most essential elements is a person in the emergency services who is a strong believer in the CISM program and who has an energetic personality. Such a person usually becomes the leader in developing a CISM team. The development of a team can be enhanced and facilitated if the developer has the following characteristics:

- Knowledge of CISM
- A drive to establish a CISM Team
- A dynamic personality
- Persistence
- Positive outlook
- A sense of humor
- Positive interpersonal style
- Incessant care for others
- Some dedicated supporters
- A plan of action
- A guidance support
- Administrative support

DETERMINING THE NEED FOR CISM AND CONVINCING ADMINISTRATION

Determining the actual need for a CISM team is important because it makes a person credible when he or she approaches the administration to obtain permission to move ahead with CISM plans. Determining that a need exists usually goes hand in hand with a presentation of the need to the administration. There are several approaches which can be followed. The least desirable is guess work. Rarely does guess work carry any weight with doubting administrators. Other, more beneficial approaches include, but are not limited to the following:

- Bring in experts to address the administration.
- Have experts present at large conferences and thus begin a "grass roots" approach.

- Collect personal accounts of individuals within the jurisdiction and present these to the administration.

- Be careful of confidentiality. Do not name people or use too familiar events without permission of the person(s) involved.

- Develop an informal data collection process and find out how many and what types of events have occurred in a three, five or ten year (retroactive) period of time.

- Develop a formal data collection and or research project to look at the experiences of the past three, five or ten year periods. Find out what events have happened, what were the stress reactions, how long did the symptoms last, what effects did the critical incident(s) have on one's family members, what changes took place in the emergency workers' lives as a result of the incident and so on. Present the data to the administration.

- Bring in senior officers or supervisors from organizations which have used the services of a CISM team.

- Present reading materials to the administrators.

- Develop a cost /benefit analysis for the administration, if possible.

- Collect the accounts of other organizations which have teams and present that information to the administration.

- Utilize the assistance of the International Critical Incident Stress Foundation, Inc. and other teams to guide new or restructured team development.

- Utilize any combination of the above techniques.

IMPORTANT ISSUES IN TEAM DEVELOPMENT

The set of questions which follows has been developed to serve as a guide to the organizers of a CISM team. It is suggested that the questions be reformulated into subdivisions on a check list or survey. Team organizers can use the check lists and survey to assure that they achieve the development of the very best team possible. Local problems and issues may influence the development of a team and those special circumstances can be included in subdivisions of the questions in the list below.

- Does the data collected indicate a need for a CISM in the area?

- Is there already a nearby team in operation?

- Are arrangements made to bring in an existing team when necessary?

- Can existing resources suffice or is it necessary to have a new team?

- How often would a new team be used in an average year?

- Is there a realistic start up date for the team?

- What are the objectives of the team?

- Have membership criteria been established?

- What is the team member application process?

- Who will choose the team members?

- Will the team incorporate itself?

- Are the mental health professionals self insured?

- Would it be better to develop a new team or join an existing one?

- How large will the area served be?

- Is there an appropriate lead agency?

- Do the emergency personnel want the team?

- Are there sufficient knowledgeable mental health professionals willing to serve on a team?

- Does a good referral system of mental health professionals exist?

- Is one of the mental health professionals willing to serve as the clinical director of the team?

- Are the available mental health professionals willing to train with the peer support personnel to serve on the team?

- Will all of the agencies cooperate in running the team?

- Is there a pool of peer support personnel willing to be trained and to serve on the team?

- Is there an available leader for the team development?

- Is a steering committee or organizing committee being formed?

- Is there a team membership committee and a membership application?

- Is nearby basic CISD training available or are arrangements being made to bring in a training consultant or training team?

- Have any attempts been made to educate the potential users of a team about its services?

- What plans exist for familiarization programs for the emergency personnel in the area to be served?

- Is the organizing committee prepared to write a set of team operating protocols based on the basic CISM concepts described within this book and utilized by other well organized teams?

- Are team members willing to meet regularly to assure the best possible development of the team?

- Is there sufficient financial support available to establish a CISM team? (Experience indicates that it costs about $6,000 to $10,000 to train a team to the basic level of CISM).

- Is there a 24 hour communications system willing to handle the incoming calls for a debriefing team or other CISM service?

- Are sufficient team coordinators prepared to screen incoming calls on a twenty four hour basis and assign priorities to CISM services, alert team members and deploy teams as required?

- Are team members willing to obtain regular continuing education in at least the following areas:

  Crisis intervention

  Human communication skills

  General stress

  Physiological response to stress

  Post-Traumatic Stress Disorder

  Conflict resolution techniques

  Peer support techniques

  Directive intervention skills

  Incident command

  Disaster services

  Line of duty death

Significant other support

Group dynamics

Knowledge of emergency services

Advanced CISD training

Suicide recognition / intervention

Making referrals

Grief and mourning

Understanding children in stress

Cumulative stress

CISM team protocols

Ethics and confidentiality

Multi-agency support services

Updates on CISD

Updates on defusings, one-on-one and so on

MIDDLE AND FINAL STEPS IN TEAM DEVELOPMENT

Rather than repeat most of the issues presented in the previous section as steps to developing a team only a brief summary will be presented here.

The **FIRST STEPS** are concluded once:

- The need has been determined.

- The program has been approved by the administration.

- Peer and mental health support of the program has been reasonably assured.

- Existing CISM programs have been reviewed.

MIDDLE STEPS

- Establish an organization committee.

- Decide on a lead agency.

- Develop team structure.

- Solicit applications from potential team members.

- Schedule training.

FINAL STEPS

- Train.

- Select team members.

- Establish effective leadership.

- Establish written protocols.

- Maintain team operations.

- Evaluate team performance.

TEAM TRAINING

There are many issues which a CISM team must face as it develops and maintains its operations. Training stands out as the most important of all. Without training, the team cannot perform its mission and the chance of causing damage to another person increases sharply. Even the most knowledgeable mental health professionals need to have the CISD training to assure that they are familiar with the terminology utilized in the field. They also need to interact with emergency personnel and gain an understanding of their personalities and their jobs. The training program provides an opportunity to begin the necessary interactions with emergency personnel.

Unfortunately, in the great majority of cases, mental health professionals do not receive training in stress, job related stress, critical incident stress and related crisis topics when they are in graduate school. Most pick up that type of information when they are in the work environment. Typical mental health professionals come to the CISM team with a vast array of backgrounds. The CISD training serves to bring everyone to the same level. It confirms the fundamentals of what is known to be successful in working with emergency personnel and with the community at large.

Critical Incident Stress and the intervention programs which have been developed to reduce it and to accelerate a person's recovery is a specialty field. It requires people with specialized training. Mental health professionals, clergy personnel and peers must be well versed in the special problems and interventions which are involved in working with traumatic stress (Critical Incident Stress). They will be providing preventative support services, not psychotherapy. It is also important that they understand that the intervention techniques which have been designed for use with emergency personnel may be used, with only minor adjustments, in the general community as well as in industrial, educational and commercial settings. But the techniques which were developed for use specifically with the general population cannot be used with the emergency personnel.

Prior to service in any CISM or CISD activity:

- All team members must complete a minimum 16 hours of Basic CISM Training and Instruction.

Detailed descriptions of the information to be provided during the training program appear in the *Human Elements Training* text (Mitchell and Everly, 1994). A brief overview of the training program is provided here for the convenience of the reader.

1. Overview of stress, its causes, sources, effects and management

2. Emergency services stress (work related): intrinsic, environment, critical incidents, and cumulative stressors.

3. Types of critical incidents.

4. Personality profile of emergency services personnel.

5. Rudiments of team development: steering committee, team structure, team leadership, member selection, team maintenance, quality assurance, record keeping, legal issues, team limitations, insurance, continuing education.

6. Training in the specific methods and protocols for the interventions used in CISM including:

   a. Pre-incident education

   b. On-scene support services

   c. Demobilization

   d. Defusing

   e. Debriefing

   f. Individual consultations

   g. Follow up services

   h. Significant other support services

i.   specialty debriefings

j.   informal discussions

7. Resource recognition and making referrals.

8. Family stressors associated with the emergency services.

9. Demonstration debriefing.

10. Communications and crisis intervention skills.

Each team member should attend at least one continuing education session per year. This requirement for a CISM team member may be achieved by attending a Peer Support Training; an Advanced CISD training or a team, state or regional CISM training activity.

ORGANIZATIONAL STRUCTURE OF A CISM TEAM

Detailed information on the structure and components of a CISM team is contained in Appendix A of this book. The following is an overview of the minimal organizational structure of a CISM team.

Each team shall have the following components:

- Steering committee or a board of directors

- A clinical director

- A senior team coordinator

- As many team coordinators as needed to assure 24 hour coverage

- A sufficient number of mental health professionals to fulfill team requirements

- Numerous peer support personnel from the various agencies. Peers may be currently active or former members of emergency service organizations. Every agency served by the team shall have representation on the team when possible. Generally there should be two thirds or more peer support personnel and one third or less mental health and clergy personnel

TEAM MEMBER SELECTION

The criteria for selecting team members is described in detail in Appendix A. This segment merely describes the process by which members are chosen for the team. The reader is urged to review the team member selection criteria which is presented in Appendix A.

The first step in choosing members is to establish an application for team membership. The applications are collected and then reviewed by the selection committee which is usually made up of two or three mental health professionals or clergy personnel and five or six peer support personnel. The selection committee then makes reference contacts, arranges for interviews when more information is necessary and finally selects the candidates who seem to be most suitable for service on the team.

In cases in which the team does not know the candidate or when there is a need for more information or when there are doubts about the suitability of a candidate, the membership committee may hold an interview to help resolve the doubts or find the information which may be missing. Typically four or five committee members meet with the candidate, ask questions and try to determine if their doubts are groundless or warranted. An example of when an interview is necessary is when a team candidate has recently experienced a highly traumatic incident and there is some question as to the readiness of the candidate to handle other people's pain when he or she is still struggling with his / her own.

Once the interview is complete the interviewers make recommendations to the remainder of the membership committee. The committee then completes the selection process and writes to inform the candidates of the results of the membership selection process.

COMPREHENSIVE APPROACH TO CISM

In Appendix A it was suggested that a comprehensive CISM program was extremely important. Organizations which attempt to deal with traumatic stress by utilizing a single focused strategy, such as the development of only an educational program or only the provision of debriefing services are doomed to failure. A more sensible approach to traumatic stress management is a multifocal or comprehensive approach which includes a strategic plan for a wide spectrum of stress control programs.

Building a comprehensive Critical Incident Stress Management program seems like an overwhelming and extremely expensive task. It is not if it is done properly by combining resources with other agencies, services and organizations within the community. It is not necessary for each organization to create its own comprehensive program to manage traumatic stress. A much more efficient and effective approach to managing traumatic stress is to become a part of an extensive system of Critical Incident Stress Management services provided jointly by a number of organizations within a community or shared between several jurisdictions.

At present, in the United States, there are over 300 Critical Incident Stress Management teams spread out throughout the country. In Australia, there are seven to nine teams, at least one for each of their states. Canada currently has about 25 teams and more are being developed to cover every province. Norway has two teams, Germany has two and Sweden has two. Practically every CISM team is a "combined emergency services" team which serves hospitals, fire services, law enforcement agencies, paramedic and emergency medical technician programs, communications personnel, corrections officers, search and rescue groups, ski patrols, disaster workers, military services and other primary response organizations.

If the CISM team is properly organized and if sufficient mental health professionals are available to serve on the team, a Community Response Team (CRT) can be developed as a subcategory of the CISM team. The Community Response Team takes on the responsibility of managing support services after crisis events within the community which are affecting the citizens. The victims of traumatic incidents need rapid intervention from mental health professionals who are trained in managing traumatic stress. Emergency personnel have very different needs and responses to traumatic events. In addition, their personalities are very different from the personalities of average non-emergency people. It is usually best to have the CISM component of the team deal with the emergency personnel and the CRT component of the team deal with the victims who are traumatized.

In some areas of the country, the American Red Cross disaster mental health network is joining its resources with the CISM team to develop the Community Response Team. This cooperative arrangement is encouraged. The interventions with emergency personnel should be provided by the peers and professional support staff of the CISM team. The interventions for the community are managed by the CRT with less emphasis on the use of peers.

The combined emergency services teams described in the paragraphs above can work quite well. All of the organizations feed members onto the CISM team. They all benefit from each other's experiences. They share in training of the team; they utilize the same mental health professionals and can rely on each other in a disaster. Other benefits of working together are that the various groups develop respect and understanding for the other emergency professions, and they learn that there are many similarities among the various emergency service professions. Most importantly, combined CISM teams have a major advantage of being able to emotionally support one another in the difficult work of traumatic stress management.

This approach can easily be used by any emergency organization. There is no need to duplicate services. Combining one organization's resources with another's in a consortium of support saves money, effectively utilizes resources, improves the breath and depth of the experience and enhances the training efforts. One organization may contribute a clergy person to the team. Another may have a mental health professional who would like to serve. Yet another has a physician who joins the CISM team. Nurses, fire service personnel, law enforcement officers and other emergency personnel are usually drawn from the organizations in the area.

AVOIDING A MAJOR PITFALL

One of the key guidelines for success on a CISM team is never to provide services on a formal debriefing team to people with whom you are very close friends. It is alright to help a friend by means of a one-on-one consultation or an on-scene support service. Those interventions by CISM team members are generally very brief contacts which hold little danger of getting involved too deeply. When no other trained CISM personnel are available in a timely fashion, a peer support person may provide a defusing to his or her fellow workers if he or she was not involved in the incident. Caution is advised in these circumstances, however, because the CISM person is operating in a gray area which could produce some problems. The formal debriefing service is a point of potential problems. When a debriefing is necessary, it is not advisable for the peer to provide support services to his close friends. Debriefings are more complex and emotionally involved and they also allow for more in-depth discussion of traumatic events which can cause an atmosphere of confusion for the peer who is too close to the personnel or to the situation.

There are reasons why a broad spectrum team is more efficient and effective than a CISM team which is developed to serve only one organization. It is generally unsound for the providers of Critical Incident Stress services and for the recipients of those services to know one another too well. Every medically trained person recognizes the inherent psychological dangers of providing medical treatments to seriously ill people who happen to be one's relatives or close friends. Similar dangers exist for those who serve on CISM teams. The same problems arise when supervisors try to provide support services to their subordinates. Too close an association between those who give the help and those who receive it can cause emotional turmoil related to role and boundary distinctions.

It is strongly recommended that a person on a CISM not provide debriefing services if any of the following conditions exist. Instead, some other peer support personnel should be chosen to work at the debriefing

Do not serve as a member of the team chosen to do a debriefing if:

1. You have played a significant role in the actual event.

2. You have direct command or supervisory responsibility for the personnel involved in the incident even if you were not there.

3. You are very close friends with the members of the group involved in the debriefable event.

4. You are working with the group involved in the incident on a regular basis, (as part of a unit or station) even if you were not with them during the incident

5. You are part of the internal affairs or operations investigation unit and have responsibility or the potential responsibility for investigating the event.

6. You are a close relative of one of the affected people.

A combined emergency services CISM team is one situation where competition between organizations is decreased and an atmosphere of mutual cooperation and support is enhanced. It is clearly a recommended course of action.

GUIDELINES FOR EFFECTIVE CISM

Emergency organizations, if they are going to provide the services which will preserve their personnel in their careers, must first make a proactive commitment to the appropriate development of a Critical Incident Stress Management program.

The first commitment is to find an appropriate emergency person to chair the development committee. A major mistake emergency organizations and hospitals may make is to assume that critical incident stress management is solely a mental health professional's task. No one will deny that mental health professionals play a highly significant role in a comprehensive CISM program. They are vital to the program's success. They often do not have the time to develop, coordinate and administer a CISM program. They also suffer another handicap. They are seldom providers in the emergency operations environment and, therefore, lack an understanding of how to work with the emergency services.

The development committee should coordinate its efforts with CISM teams which may already exist in the area. The fact that there are over 300 teams in the United States makes it likely that an active CISM team may be already working in the region. Every effort should be made to join their resources rather than to set up a competitive team which serves only one organization. The best interests of a team and the community are usually served when there is a multi-agency and multi-jurisdictional team structure.

The tasks assigned to the steering committee include selection of professional and peer support staff to serve on the team, as well as the establishment of a policy and procedures committee to develop appropriate written operating procedures. Most steering committees have a subgroup which assures close coordination with the CISD team(s) in the local community and region and with the International Critical Incident Stress Foundation, which serves as an international coordinating, standard setting and education body for CISM teams. Steering committees also must provide appropriate training and education opportunities for the CISM team members.

The CISM team needs to be a peer focused support service which utilizes mental health professionals and chaplains as consultants. When effectively led and given the freedom to do its work, a CISM team can be a powerful force in maintaining personnel. So, the next commitment the administrator of the emergency organizations have to make is the commitment to trust the members of the CISM team to carry out their mission without threatening the operation of those organizations.

CISM teams can only function if they have an open network of communications. There must exist an effective means for emergency personnel to call for CISM team assistance. In addition, to be consistent, frequent communication with the local, regional and national CISM networks for information exchange and mutual aid is a must.

PROTECTING THE TEAM FROM LEGAL ACTION

Up to the time of printing of this book no known law suits have occurred which involve CISM teams and none are known to be in preparation for litigation. The record so far, especially in light of the fact that over 20,000 debriefings have been provided since 1983, is a good one. We believe that the newness of the field and the fact that teams have been following the guidelines are the main reasons why law suits have not occurred involving CISM teams.

No one wants a law suit and no one expects one when providing support services to emergency personnel. Not wanting or expecting a lawsuit is no protection from encountering one. There are some steps, however, which can be taken which can offer a team a great deal of protection against legal complications. This section will detail some of those protective steps. If there is a need for specific legal advice, that should be sought through attorneys familiar with emergency services operations, disaster relief work and possibly CISM.

- The very best protection against legal action is excellence in the practice of CISM services.

- The next protection is to carefully follow the written policies, protocols and guidelines of local and international organizations associated with CISM. In some jurisdictions such guidelines may become "standards of care."

- CISM teams would be wise to incorporate.

- Any time a person in a debriefing demonstrates a clear and imminent danger to themselves (suicidal threat) or others (homicidal threat or actual or threatened other serious crimes), the team is required to act in the best interests of the individual and / or the person(s) who may be in danger. This might require disclosure of certain pieces of information to the person's family or to the person's supervisor. It might also entail involuntary hospitalization or other actions deemed necessary to save a life. Saving a life has a higher priority than stringent adherence to absolute confidentiality. Team members should follow the guidance of their clinical director or the mental health professional involved in the debriefing. It should be pointed out now that the examples given here are merely theoretical. There is no known case of an emergency worker who disclosed such information in the midst of a debriefing. It is more likely that a civilian (one not involved in the emergency services) would bring such information up in a debriefing. Teams which serve non-emergency populations need to be alert to the fact that they may see this particular situation arise more than teams which serve emergency personnel.

- Laws vary from jurisdiction to jurisdiction. Team members should be familiar with the laws which apply in their own jurisdiction.

- Respect the right of refusal. In some cases personnel are ordered into a debriefing for the good of the individuals and the organization. Since part of the debriefing is an educational session, the mandating of the debriefing can be appropriate. No one can be ordered to talk in a debriefing if they choose not to. If a person's objection to attending the debriefing is extreme, it might be best for the CISD team to allow that person to exclude themselves from the process. The person should be advised that his or her choice for exclusion may not be in his or her own best interests. The individual should be advised that various types of help are available if he or she should decide it is needed at some other time. The names of team members and their telephone numbers and the types of services which could be provided should be given to the person who chooses to exclude oneself from the debriefing.

- Informed consent is necessary. The process followed in a debriefing should be no surprise to people. They should be told about debriefings in pre-incident stress education programs and as part of the introductory remarks made by the CISD team.

- Advice which is given in a debriefing should be limited to those things which are considered reasonable and prudent and would be the kind of advice given by anyone to people who are coping with stress. The advice given should be backed up by literature in the field of stress mitigation.

- The advice provided in a debriefing should be limited only to the current situation.

- Participants should be advised not to discuss anything which could jeopardize an investigation, cause them to be disciplined or which would cause them to admit deliberate violations of the policies or procedures of their organization.

- Do not turn a debriefing into psychotherapy. It is not psychotherapy, nor is it a substitute for psychotherapy.

- Do not take notes, make recordings or allow cameras at a debriefing.

- When you tell people you will keep the contents of the debriefing confidential, keep it confidential.

- Licensed professionals must always follow the dictates of their professional code of ethics and the law as it may be applicable to their functions within the context of CISM services.

MAINTAINING A CISM TEAM

There are three primary techniques and several secondary considerations which will keep a CISM team healthy and functioning once it has been established. Ignoring these guidelines for team health, especially the primary techniques, sets the stage for the eventual failure of a team.

PRIMARY GUIDELINES FOR TEAM HEALTH:

1. Education

2. Cross familiarization

3. Regular team meetings

EDUCATION

Stress education is one of the primary elements of CISM team health. It is divided into two main areas: 1) education of the personnel in the organizations who will be using the team's services and 2) education of the team itself.

No one will think of calling the CISM team during or after a crisis event if the team is not known. One of the first steps to be taken by a new team is to present an educational program to each emergency services organization. The education programs (typically 2 - 3 hours in length) usually cover the following topics:

- Nature of stress

- Emergency services stress

- Causes of critical incident stress

- Signs and symptoms of distress

- Survival strategies for stress

- The CISM team

- Accessing the team

It may be necessary to modify the education program into twenty minute or half hour modular presentations to accommodate groups which are on shifts and unable to get together for more than brief periods of time. It is inconvenient to teach the stress material in small segments, but it is effective if organized and coordinated properly.

It is also very important for the team that the leaders of the various organizations are given information on the functions of the team and the reasons for calling upon the team. When supervisory staff understand the functions of the team and how to call upon the team they are more likely to use the team to assist their personnel.

For more information on education in Critical Incident Stress Management see Mitchell, J. T. and Everly, G. S. (1994) *Human Elements Training,* Ellicott City, M.D., Chevron Publishing Corporation.

CROSS FAMILIARIZATION

Cross familiarization or cross training of CISM team members is essential for team survival and appropriate team function. Cross training means that peer support personnel are trained in issues which are usually the domain of the mental health professionals. For example, peers are trained in crisis intervention, human communications, stress management, Post-Traumatic Stress Disorder, grief and critical incident stress.

Cross familiarization also means that mental health professionals and clergy personnel are familiarized with the equipment, personalities, organization and the strategies and tactics of operations personnel. The professional support staff cannot learn this information in a classroom. They must spend several hours in an emergency department of a hospital, ride along with fire fighters on the engine, ride with the police on patrol, make runs with the emergency medical crews and visit the communications center. Cross familiarization takes place over a long period of time. No one can gain all of that exposure in one night. A few hours in one organization and then a few in another will help. Over time the experiences mount up and the professional support staff become more well versed in dealing with emergency personnel.

We believe it is not possible to be truly effective with emergency personnel without this cross familiarization process. Emergency personnel will tend to have difficulty trusting anyone who does not have a substantial awareness of their jobs and their personalities.

REGULAR TEAM MEETINGS

Teams which do not meet regularly are likely to develop problems. Lack of contact with the team members isolates the leaders and fragments the team. Teams without meetings lose a sense of direction and purpose. The lack of contact encourages team members to go off in their own directions. The end result is often team disintegration. To survive, a CISM team should meet every four to six weeks. Every eight weeks is probably a little too long of a time frame but it is better than not at all.

There are usually three segments to a CISM team meeting. They are:

- Intervention Review

- Team Business

- Education

The intervention review segment is open only to team members since the information discussed relates to the critical incidents managed by the team members during the last four to six weeks if possible. In the intervention review segment each situation managed by the team is briefly presented and the team response is discussed and analyzed. Advice may be offered by the team members to assure that the follow up is provided as necessary. Any points to be learned for the benefit of the team members are discussed as necessary. Team members are reminded that the information discussed in the intervention review segment is confidential.

The second segment of the team meeting is team business. Any correspondence to the team is discussed and decisions are made to respond in one manner or another. Issues related to membership, training, funding, future plans and other elements of team business are openly discussed. All team members should be encouraged to participate in the discussions.

The emphasis in a CISM team meeting should be on a casual, democratic meeting in which everyone feels that they are equal. When a team gets stuck on minute issues of parliamentary procedure, they have lost sight of what they are all about. There are certainly more important issues to be faced by a team than who is to speak and in what order. Keeping the meeting light and functional is the objective. The lighter style will keep people interested in coming to meetings in the future. *Remember, one of the functions of CISM team meetings is team building and development of cohesion.*

The third segment of the team meeting is the educational segment. Continuing education is the objective for this segment. A team that does not continuously upgrade itself will stagnate. A suggested list of continuing education topics was presented in the section of this chapter above entitled "Important Issues in Team Development." Those topics and a number of others are important for the team education program. The usual education segment of a team meeting is 30 to 45 minutes.

SECONDARY GUIDELINES FOR TEAM HEALTH: IN-SERVICE EDUCATION FOR TEAM MEMBERS

In addition to the regular educational sessions which take place during team meetings, team members should have at least eight hours of continuing education per year at regional, national or international conferences on stress, crisis intervention or other related topics. Staying within the team's own jurisdiction for additional training does not afford team members the opportunity to network with other stress management teams from other areas of the country or the world. People who do not interact with other CISM organizations tend to lack depth and become fixed within a limited number of intervention strategies. As a result they become less effective in rendering assistance to their fellow workers.

A MECHANISM FOR TEAM RECORD KEEPING

Team members like to be credited with the work they have performed. Some records should be kept for statistical purposes and to determine which team members have the most experience and which have the least. Check-off sheets which show the number of times a person has performed defusings, debriefings or other interventions can help to determine which strategies need to be reviewed at team meetings.

WRITTEN PROTOCOLS AND PROCEDURES

Few things can be as frustrating for a team as not having written guidelines by which they function. The lack of written guidelines also causes disruption between the CISM team and the operations units during the incidents. Written guidelines, protocols and procedures help to insure that all team members are functioning according to acceptable standards. It is possible that written protocols and procedures may afford some degree of protection to the team in the unlikely event of a legal contact or a disciplinary action against a team member who has violated the procedures.

NEW MEMBER RECRUITMENT

There is some attrition on every team. People in the professional support staff and the peers from the various organizations are busy. They may have family responsibilities as well as professional responsibilities. Since most are not paid to participate on CISM teams, they do not always have the luxury of putting CISM activities at the top of their priority list. Some aspects of team member lives are constantly changing. When those circumstances change, team members may take a temporary or permanent leave from the team.

It is necessary to keep the team membership up to near maximal levels to assure effective response to crisis events and the best use of the team membership. Both peer and professional staff should be interested in adding team members to replace those who have left the team. Sometimes just a suggestion to a friend that they might be very helpful on a team is a sufficient enticement for a potential new team member to join. At times it takes announcements and a more active recruitment program to find the right candidates for the team.

Once a new team member decides to join the team, full CISD training should take place as soon as possible. No one should provide CISM services without the proper training. In addition, new team members should be placed on a trainee status until they have had sufficient experiences on the team to allow them to move into a full member position.

IN SERVICE EDUCATION OF EMERGENCY SERVICES

It is not enough to present a broad educational program one time and expect that it will be sufficient to keep emergency personnel knowledgeable about the team's existence and functions. Most CISM teams have found it necessary to go back into the fire and police stations and to the communications centers and into the hospitals to provide periodic updates about the team. One of the main functions of the team is to mitigate stress reactions. Continuing education programs which provide additional insight into stress management for the staffs of the various organizations can do much to help prevent or mitigate stress. Those programs will also keep the team before the groups which could best benefit from it. (See Mitchell, J. T. and Everly, G. S. (1994) *Human Elements Training*, Ellicott City, M.D., Chevron Publishing).

COMMUNITY EDUCATION PROGRAMS

In many areas of the country, particularly in areas in which Community Response Teams (CRT) have been established, significant efforts are underway to alert the community to the threat of traumatic stress. Where the CRT program has been attached to the Critical Incident Stress Management team there tends to be greater involvement from the general membership of the CISM team with the community. The prevention of stress through education is a key element of the CRT team. And when a major incident occurs in an area, the provision of crisis education programs and debriefing services may be necessary.

Although CISM teams have been developed to assist emergency organizations and personnel, they have a strong record of responding to the community during times of disaster and have proven their benefit on numerous occasions. They should take a leadership role in preparing mental health professionals to assist stricken communities after a crisis event. They should also stand ready to render humanitarian aid to the community when their services are required. A close coordination and cooperation between the CISM team, the Red Cross, the Community Response Team and the local mental health services is necessary if adequate stress reduction services are to be provided to the citizens.

If the Red Cross and the local mental health services have not yet organized a Community Response Team, and if the CISM team is asked to provide services to groups other than emergency personnel, several considerations should be made before committing the CISM team to support services for the community. Those considerations can best be made in the form of the following questions:

1. Are there organizations or agencies which should be managing the psychological needs of the community during the crisis?

2. Are the members of local mental health services adequately trained to manage the psychological trauma produced by this crisis situation?

3. Can the organization respond in a timely fashion to assist the community? The response to a major community disaster must be within hours, NOT days.

4. Do the organizations which have training and responsibility to respond to the psychological needs of the community have sufficient personnel to manage the situation?

5. Are the trained organizations requesting assistance or is the call originating from sources outside of those organizations?

6. If the request for assistance is coming from the organizations which are trained to handle the crisis response, what exactly do they need from the crisis team?

7. Are there adequate lines of communication between the CISM team and the CRT program or the other relief groups?

8. How quickly can the CISM team draw upon its resources to respond to the situation? Where do the team members report and who is in charge of the situation and the psychological response teams?

9. Is the intervention being provided for humanitarian reasons only? (Accepting fees for services may be unwise for a CISM team developed for the emergency services.)

10. If the CISM team is deployed to assist community groups, will they be unable to achieve their primary mission of providing support services to emergency personnel or are there sufficient team members to cover both the community and the emergency personnel?

Whenever a CISM team is requested to assist a CRT or provide direct services to the public, the team's clinical director should be notified of the request. Usually there is no negative reaction to the request for help, but on occasion, there are some jurisdictional issues which may need to be addressed before the help can be provided. The decision to render assistance is usually reached within minutes.

See the index of this book for the location of additional information on Community Response Teams.

SIGNIFICANT OTHER EDUCATION / SUPPORT SERVICES

At this point in this chapter, it should be obvious that a CISM team has many more tasks than that of just providing debriefings. The CISM team employs a holistic approach. That is, it is concerned with many aspect of the emergency worker's life. CISM teams take a proactive stance not just a reactive position. Providing debriefings after the incident is considered reactive. Providing preventative stress education programs and significant other and family life programs is proactive.

It is not sufficient to support only the person in uniform. Instead, it is necessary to support the entire environment in which the uniformed person operates. That includes the person's family. Also, sufficient evidence already exists which indicates that the families of emergency personnel have frequently been ignored after critical incidents in the past.

To rectify that unfortunate situation, CISM teams have developed support programs which reach out to significant others of the emergency personnel. Support programs include stress prevention education programs and debriefings and follow up services for significant others after particularly distressing situations have affected their loved ones in the emergency services. Significant others are given information on a number of topics designed to lower their anxiety and prevent the harmful effects of stress. The following is a list of the typical programs presented to significant others by the CISM team. In some cases the emergency personnel are asked to be present during the education programs.

- The personality of the emergency worker
- Communications for couples
- Fair fighting
- Decision making in families
- Financial planning and budgeting for families
- Familiarization with emergency equipment
- Tours of the work place
- Ride along programs
- Spouse support programs
- Meet your loved one's commanders / supervisors
- Understanding grief
- Coping with anxiety
- Child rearing in the emergency services family
- Critical incident stress
- Getting help
- Supporting the distressed loved one
- Children in crisis
- Caring enough to confront
- Ongoing spouse education support groups

After tragic events, which seriously affect not only the emergency workers, but their families as well, several services may need to be provided to help the significant others recover from the stress they experienced because their loved ones encountered critical incident stress. Examples of direct services to significant others include:

- Debriefings to spouses of surviving personnel after a line of duty death in an organization

- Bereavement - crisis oriented counseling to the wife, children and parents of the deceased emergency worker

- Grief seminars for the families of deceased emergency personnel approximately six months to a year after the death

- Follow up contacts with the bereaved family members for several weeks after the death

- Teen groups for children of surviving emergency personnel after a line of duty death in an organization

- Young children's groups for children six to twelve years old after a highly distressing incident which may have affected their parents

- Debriefings for significant others after a particularly distressing incident in a community

- Advice to the significant others about child care during times of distress in the family which is directly associated with the work of the emergency services person

- Follow up services to significant others of emergency service personnel as the needs may require

MECHANISMS TO DEBRIEF THE DEBRIEFERS

The old adage, "a little knowledge can be a dangerous thing," may have some applicability for people trained to provide services to others through the CISM team. They seem to develop an idea that they are totally invulnerable to stress reactions themselves since they have some stress knowledge and some stress experience. Obviously that false belief can be the foundation for some serious problems. Debriefing teams are on the cutting edge of services to people with raw human emotions. They can get hurt. They need to take many of the same precautions to protect themselves from being too stressed as the people they serve.

Team members stay healthy and functional on a team when they follow the same guidelines for breaks, food, rest and the amount of time on-scene that they teach to others. It is not only a good practice from their own health perspective, it is the very best example they could give to others. As individuals, CISM team members need to ask for relief when they are getting overwhelmed. If there are family problems which they are working on in their own homes, they might need a break from debriefings for awhile. The same might be true if they have done too many debriefings in a short period of time. Team members should always have a right to go on a temporary leave of absence from the team when their personal health or home life needs more attention.

One extremely important mechanism to preserve the CISM team members is to require that the actual team members who ran a debriefing meet immediately after the debriefing. This meeting is an opportunity to "debrief the debriefers." At the meeting the team should accomplish the following:

- Quick review of the debriefing / understand what just happened and why it happened.

- Assign tasks for follow up services to specific team members.

- Allow sufficient time for the debriefers to ventilate their own reactions to the debriefing.

- Make sure everyone is okay before releasing the team.

Some incidents are so powerful and the CISD team spends so much time and energy working on the debriefings and the follow up services that the CISD team members may need another team to debrief them. The events in which this is likely are line of duty deaths and disaster. A neighboring team or a specialty team from another state may be brought in to provide this type of debriefing. At the very least, team members who were not involved in the debriefing are called upon to debrief the debriefers.

The team which is debriefing the debriefers must realize that the debriefing team already knows many of the basic techniques of debriefing and may resist a debriefing which is too close to the exact seven phase model which they would use to provide a debriefing to any other group. The team which is debriefing the debriefers must be flexible and allow a broad range of questions to be inserted into the debriefing of the debriefers. The whole style of this type of debriefing is more relaxed and conversational. It often helps to allow team members to retell the entire story in a chronological order so that everyone can discuss when they got involved and to what extent they got involved in the debriefing. Somewhere in the discussion they need to discuss the point at which they felt the most emotions for the participants in the debriefing. The debriefing for the debriefers, unlike the formal debriefing with its seven phases, allows a bit more direct questioning of the CISD team. The debriefers of debriefers are more concerned to make sure no important issues are left untouched. They are, however, aware that they are working with their colleagues. Sometimes, the debriefers will insert clarifying statements or educational information for the benefit of all. The debriefing of the debriefers ends when everyone feels that the incident and the teams response has been sufficiently "worked over."

TIME OUT FOR OVER EXTENDED TEAM MEMBERS

It was mentioned in the section above that some team members might recognize their own needs to take a break from the CISM team and to stop doing debriefings for a period of time. Other team members will not be aware that they have become overextended. They often tend to forget their own pain. They begin to take on more and more CISM responsibility. Little by little, lifting someone else's pain drains their own resources. It happens subtly, almost imperceptibly. Everyone around them gets the idea that they are getting in too deep. They are becoming overextended. The only person who doesn't recognize the problem is the one who is in it.

Here are some warning signs of an overextended CISM team member:

- Excessive worry about the people one has debriefed. This worry goes far beyond what is necessary to achieve adequate follow up.

- Intense irritability when a fellow CISM team member attempts to advise a debriefer about something they believe they already know.

- Obsessive thinking about the debriefing experience.

- Constant replays of the incident described in the debriefing even though the debriefed was not present at the actual incident.

- Unfounded anger at one's fellow workers or one's loved ones after doing a debriefing.

- Loss of interest in one's own work after debriefings.

- Chronic feelings of fatigue for long periods after debriefings.

- Doing far more for individuals from a particular debriefing than one would do for any other person under similar circumstances.

- Maintaining a high degree of follow up contacts when they are not necessary.

- Attempts to work independently of the team without appropriate supervision from team professional support staff.

- Frequent, unexplained loss of emotional control after debriefings.

- Sleeplessness after debriefings.

- Agitation, restlessness after debriefings.

- Excessive withdrawal from contact with others after going through a debriefing.

- Excessive volunteering to take on more and more debriefings.

- Feeling upset and jealous whenever others are doing debriefings in which the overextended person is not involved.

- Excessive belief that no one else could provide the "proper" debriefing within the area served by the team.

Peers on a team are the more likely candidates for over extension. This is so because of their more frequent contact with distressed fellow workers. But mental health professionals and clergy personnel may also be subject to the distressing condition. Overextended CISM team members jeopardize their own health and the smooth operation of a CISM team. They need to be helped to regain control of themselves before they begin do harm. Their fellow team members may be able to point out the problem they are in, or the team coordinator could address it with them. If necessary the team's clinical director might need to be brought into the situation. Every effort needs to be made to help the person come to their own conclusions that they are getting out of control in the debriefing environment. They will generally be far more cooperative if they can see the problem themselves. The issue should be addressed in a direct and up front manner which leaves no room for doubt about the dangers of the situation. The person should be given whatever help and guidance which may be necessary and some reasonable monitored time frame in which to correct the problem. If no improvement is demonstrated in a reasonable time, the person will eventually need to be removed from the team. Although this is a difficult action to take when the team has such a "dedicated" worker, it is the only choice available for the protection of the individual and the team.

FOLLOW UP SERVICES

No community or organization should begin to develop a CISM team without recognizing the fact that follow up services are an integral part of the CISM services. This should be known from the beginning and not appear as a surprise once the team has been developed.

Follow up services help to keep team members interested in their work. They feel that they have a genuine purpose in between debriefings. They often get the greatest satisfaction from the feedback they receive after providing follow up services.

Good follow up services must be planned into the development of the team. They should be an integral part of the team's operating policies and procedures.

FUND RAISING

Since the majority of teams operate without paying their team members, the overall operating expenses of the team is generally quite low. There are some direct and hidden costs to operating a CISM team and team organizers must keep that point in mind. The direct costs of team development and operation are usually associated with the initial set up of the team. In most cases the costs are about $6,000 to $10,000. This includes the cost of bringing in a trainer, his or her fees, the costs of air fare or travel to the training site, lodging for the presenter, food and miscellaneous expenses. Other direct costs may be the telephone services, postage, travel to provide team services, office supplies and other items of that nature.

Indirect costs include such things as releasing individuals from their normal duties and replacing them with substitutes during a debriefing. Overtime for fill-in personnel is frequently the biggest hidden cost of operating a team. Other hidden costs include the emergency phone service which is managed by the communications center and billed to the team, the time the coordinators spend deploying teams and keeping team activities going, and the time spent in continuing education for the CISM programs.

Although the costs, outside of the direct developmental costs associated with establishing the team, are not always clear, the team's benefits may far outweigh the direct and indirect costs. Teams are designed to keep good people on their jobs. The costs of replacing those people is far higher than that of maintaining good people who are well trained and experienced.

If identifying the costs of operating a team is difficult, the funding sources to support team operating is even more nebulous. It ranges from the most efficient and effective source of funds -- a line item on the budget of the emergency services, to the interesting -- bake sales and raffles. Some sell T-shirts, caps and pins. Most teams try to gain some support from community business. Many have the benefit of presenting educational services for which they charge fees. Some have received limited grants from the International Critical Incident Stress Foundation, Inc. to help get their team up and running.

Whatever method of funding is chosen to support a team, involving the team members in the process is important to maintaining active membership. People who have a hand in creating or maintaining an organization stay its most loyal supporters. They feel that they have a real role to play in maintaining the health of the organization.

RAISING SUPPORT FROM EMERGENCY PERSONNEL

There are two main ways the emergency services personnel come to believe in the value of the CISM team. The first method of gaining support is for the CISM team members to teach stress related information frequently to all of the emergency service providers. The simple fact that there is frequent contact from peers who have become knowledgeable about stress and its effects and that these peers are willing to teach others some of what they have learned is a tremendous boost to the credibility of the team.

The second method for the team to gain support is to do an excellent job in debriefings and other direct support functions. When team members respond quickly to requests for help and when they provide efficient and effective services to those who need their help, the team's reputation quickly builds a positive foundation. Team members must also maintain a low profile and not lead people to believe that they are forcing their services upon any one. It is also necessary that a team quickly correct any mistakes which might occur. Ignoring mistakes is a disruptive way to manage the team affairs and may turn out to be an error which can, under certain circumstances, turn out to be fatal for the team.

GAINING FURTHER SUPPORT FROM SUPERVISORS AND ADMINISTRATORS

Supervisors and the organization's administrators deserve to know what the team is all about. There is no need for them to know the details of information and reactions discussed during the debriefings or other interventions made by the CISM team members on behalf of distressed emergency personnel. But they must have knowledge about the team, its functions the types of events it responds to and the manner in which it is called. They cannot use the team properly nor can they support it if they know nothing about it.

Team members would be wise to bring the leaders of the various organizations together in the early stages of the team's development and periodically once it has been established. Information about the team's functions and limitations is essential for the administration and supervisors. Sometimes it is helpful after the general familiarization sessions to arrange meetings between key team personnel and the administrators and highest ranking supervisors in each organization. The individual attention paid to the key people in the various organizations assure use and support of the team. Since teams may be a very new addition in some areas, the leadership of the organizations may have many concerns and questions. Administrators and supervisory personnel must be reassured of the following items:

- The CISM team is run by operations personnel who depend on mental health professionals and clergy personnel for guidance and professional consultations.

- The CISM team encourages recovery from stress, not disability claims, workers compensation and litigation against the organization and its leadership.

- The CISM is a prevention program far more than it is a treatment program.

- The cost of team operation are minimal, but the benefits are maximal (difficult to quantify, however). Although some research is currently underway and some studies have already been published with very positive results, CISM is a new field which is only a little over a decade old. It would be unwise to discount the thousands of anecdotal records which have been collected over the decade. A little more than a dozen years of experience in which almost 400 teams have been established and over twenty thousand debriefings have been provided to emergency personnel cannot be simply ignored. This is especially so when the overwhelming majority of the reports of debriefing services are extremely positive.

- The CISM team cannot overrule a commanding officer, especially when the team is working at the scene of an incident. Any decision which affects the staffing of the operation or the operational procedures must be cleared in advance by the team members. If the decision interferes with the operation, the CISM team member may express his or her concerns but the ultimate decision making in emergency services falls to the supervisor or administrator.

- The CISM team will assist the supervisors and administrators directly whenever necessary and will make whatever efforts are necessary to advise the command level personnel of situations which may need supervisor direction and leadership.

- The CISM team will keep the administration and leaders of an organization informed of the general nature of the teams activities.

- The CISM team will actively participate in educational programs for the organizations involved in utilizing the teams services.

- The CISM team will actively participate in disaster drills and other activities which will enhance their performance with each other.

- The CISM team will keep the administration informed of developments in the CISM field, particularly completed research projects which affect the services provided or drive further development of the team.

DISASTER DRILLS

Another way for the team to enhance the active involvement of team members in CISM functions is to participate actively in disaster drills. It is most important for the team to go through the call out procedures, go to the scene and check in with the command post. Team members should set up their operations under the safety officer at the scene. In the incident command system, the safety officer is in charge of all health and safety issues at the scene. Therefore, the CISM team should report to the safety officer who can bring special considerations to the incident commander.

It is not advisable for the CISM team to have "mock" distressed victims. It is too difficult to fake emotions. The personnel do not like this type of role playing and the team is often perceived as ludicrous when it attempts such artificial "crisis interventions." The best use of the team in a drill situation is to have them go through the steps of being called out, responding to the scene and setting up with the safety officer. The team members should learn about perimeter control points, command post operations, sectors, rehabilitation of personnel, the morgue set up, the media section and numerous other aspects of a disaster situation. Team members could hand out an informational brochure on the functions of a CISM team at the end of the drill. The handout should contain the names of team contacts and the phone numbers to use for emergency call out of the team.

TEAM EVALUATION

Evaluating team performance is one of the most difficult aspects of maintaining a CISM team. This is so for many reasons. Emergency personnel resist efforts to look too deeply into their organizations and their own personal inner thoughts and emotions. The emergency services are organizations which are long on tradition and short on introspection. They feel that outsiders looking into their organizations and not fully understanding their jobs, may issue a set of recommendations or mandates which could interfere with their ability to perform their jobs. From the individual perspective, emergency people do not like efforts to make them come into contact with their emotions because too close a realization of how much emotions are a part of their lives may jeopardize their abilities to work effectively under field conditions. Emergency personnel work very hard to suppress their emotions and any study which forces them to bring those emotions to the surface for examination will meet with significant resistance. They believe that they need to suppress their emotions to insure that they will be able to work through a crisis when they are needed. Emergency workers believe firmly that emotions are only distractions from their peak efficiency in handling a traumatic situation.

Another reason evaluation is difficult is that emergency personnel are constantly on the move. They are most reliable when it comes to the performance of their duties but they do not make good subjects for study because they cannot be held in one place long enough to be studied.

Any study of the effects of debriefing on emergency personnel will have to take into consideration the fact that traumatic events continue to occur after the debriefing. Those new events may keep symptoms of stress higher than if the person was able to rest for a week or two after a traumatic event. Studies which evaluate team performance must always be designed with the idea that the researcher is going to observe real world people in real world situations. No carefully designed laboratory exists in which emergency personnel can be examined under tightly controlled conditions.

Even a combination of all of the above reasons why studying the team performance is difficult does not excuse a team from its responsibility of attempting to determine if its interventions are effective and if its performance is efficient. Teams must search out new methods to examine their work. The task is important because without appropriate evaluation, changes may not be made in the interventions teams make, or changes will be made when none are necessary simply because some one suggests a new idea. In some circumstances, changes may be made which could be harmful. Without evaluation, those changes might do harm before the error is discovered.

Formal studies of the effectiveness and efficiency of the team are necessary, but some basic guidelines need to be adhered to. They are:

- Research and team evaluation must always be secondary to the provision of services such as debriefings, defusings and other processes.

- Individual confidentiality must always be observed.

- Participants should be involved in the study on a voluntary basis.

- People in a study should have appropriate information on which their decision to participate is based.

- The study should be designed around the real world nature of the personnel involved and their jobs.

- The objectives of the study should be clearly stated.

- The limitations of the study should be clearly stated.

- Feedback should always be given to the participants and their organizations at the completion of the study.

- Conclusions should never be drawn from data known to be faulty or from data which are incomplete or from too small a sample.

- The researcher has an obligation not only to present the data to the participants but, more importantly to help the participants to properly interpret the data.

Formal research projects are only one of the mechanism to evaluate team performance. There are several other important methods. Feedback from participants in the debriefings should be encouraged and, when it comes, it should be listened to very carefully. The participants in a debriefing are often the best sources of information regarding team performance. They can give good hints about the communications used by team members, the clarity of the teaching segments, the perceived genuineness of the team members and things which the team might have missed during the debriefing.

The team should review its cases at its regular meetings as described in the section on "regular team meetings" above. The case reviews give the team a significant opportunity to analyze a case and gather every one's opinion about how it was handled. Changes in one's personal style or minor changes in the team performance can be targeted during such discussions.

Another aspect of team performance evaluation can be managed by a Peer Review Board to review complaints (internal or external) about errors or deliberate disregard for commonly accepted CISM or CISD practices. The Peer Review Board is made up of between three and five members (both professional and peer support personnel) of the CISM team who are in good standing. They are designated by the clinical director and the coordinator. At least two should have served on the previous Peer Review Board. The other members may be assigned as necessary to review the complaint.

The Peer Review Board should gather the facts related to the incident as soon as within three days of the complaint or report of inappropriate activity. The board then meets with the member in question within three days of the complaint. The board will then evaluate the information gathered and issue a written report with recommendations to the clinical director and the senior coordinator for the team within two days of the meeting with the team member.

The clinical director and the team coordinator will either act upon the recommendations of the board or resubmit the report for further review.

REVOCATION / SUSPENSION OF MEMBERSHIP

Any organization which develops a mechanism for bringing in new members must also develop a mechanism for removing any of its members from service if their performance is below minimal standards. This is especially important in a situation in which a poor performance can lead to harm to a person or a group struggling through the stresses associated with a critical incident. Team membership can be revoked by the clinical director, the team coordinator or the Peer Review Board. Usually the decision is made when the team leadership has conferred together and has reviewed the facts of the situation which has caused them to consider the revocation of team membership of one of their team members. Any of the following could be grounds for dismissal from a CISM team.

- Any breech of confidentiality.

- Failure to follow local policies and procedures.

- Organizing or providing a debriefing without notifying the team coordinator.

- Organizing or providing a defusing without notifying the team coordinator.

- Not informing the team coordinator of an on-scene support service, a significant other support program, specialty debriefing, individual consults or any other CISM team activity, intervention strategy or educational endeavor.

- Using one's membership on the team to enhance one's private business concerns.

- Using one's membership on the team to enhance one's personal social life. This would be the case if a team member used team membership to gain access to another person for the purposes of a date.

- Going to a scene or location of a critical incident to function on behalf of the CISM team without the prior knowledge or consent of the team coordinator or a designee.

- Failure to be present at an assigned debriefing when the member has made a commitment to do so.

- Consistent failure to attend team meetings and team education programs.

- Acting against the expressed direction of the clinical director or the team coordinator.

- Misrepresenting oneself concerning the affairs or operations of the CISM program.

- Failure to complete the required team paperwork.

Appendix C

SUGGESTED VOLUNTARY TRAINING STANDARDS FOR PERFORMING CRITICAL INCIDENT STRESS MANAGEMENT WITH EMERGENCY SERVICES, DISASTER RESPONSE AND HUMANITARIAN AID PERSONNEL

SUGGESTED TRAINING STANDARDS FOR PEER SUPPORT PERSONNEL

A "peer" is defined as a volunteer or paid member of one of the generally recognized emergency service professions, disaster response professions or humanitarian aid professions. These include, but are not limited to, law enforcement, fire suppression, nursing, emergency medicine, emergency dispatch, chaplaincy, humanitarian aid services, disaster management, search and rescue personnel, ski patrol, life guards and other personnel.

Recommended Critical Incident Stress Management Training:

1. An entry-level Basic CISD course (2 days minimum)

2. An Advanced CISD course (2 days)

3. A Peer Counseling course (2 days)

4. A Family Support Services course (2 days)

SUGGESTED TRAINING STANDARDS FOR MENTAL HEALTH PROFESSIONALS:

A "mental health professional" is defined as an individual possessing a graduate or professional degree in one of the generally recognized mental health professions, that is, psychology, counseling, psychiatric nursing, psychiatry, social work and mental health counselors.

Recommended Critical Incident Stress Management Training:

1. An entry-level Basic CISD course (2 days minimum)

2. An Advanced CISD course (2 days)

3. A course on Psychotraumatology and/or the Assessment and Treatment of Post-Traumatic Stress Disorder (1 day minimum)

It is clearly acknowledged that these training standards are the "ideal" and should be viewed as voluntary guidelines. Given the infancy of the field of critical incident stress management for emergency response personnel, we recognize that it may be literally years before these standards can be met. Nevertheless, most would agree that emergency response professionals face unique challenges during the pursuit of their career. Those who are dedicated to supporting those professionals must be uniquely trained with the goal of excellence always in mind. By touching the lives of these professionals, one touches not only these professionals themselves and their families, but one has the ability to touch the lives of all who are served by the collective professions we call emergency services, disaster response and humanitarian aid.

Appendix D

SERIOUS ERRORS IN CISD

If a debriefing is going to fail, it is likely to fail on one of the following items. Some of these mistakes may cause harm to the participants in a debriefing. All of these mistakes should be carefully avoided.

- Using untrained CISD team members.

- Not using mental health professionals in a debriefing.

- Misunderstanding the CISD process which progresses from strongly cognitive, (**Introduction** and **Fact** phases) to a transition phase from cognition to affect (**Thought** phase) to a strongly affective phase (**Reaction**) and finally back through a transition phase (**Symptoms**) to cognition phases again (**Teaching** and **Re-entry**). See the table below:

Introduction ———————	Cognitive
Fact ———————	Cognitive
Thought ———————	Cognitive → Affective
Reaction ———————	Affective
Symptoms ———————	Affective → Cognitive
Teaching ———————	Cognitive
Re-Entry ———————	Cognitive

- Attempting to turn CISD into psychotherapy.

- Attempting to substitute CISD for psychotherapy.

- Not utilizing CISD trained peers for emergency, hospital, military or other operational groups.

- Not preparing adequately for debriefing.

- Not arriving early enough to circulate around and meet the participants.

- Not doing an adequate case review.

- Not having a CISD team strategy meeting before the debriefing.

- Picking a team full of inexperienced debriefers.

- Picking a team member with significant current personal problems.

- Not providing appropriate follow up services for CISD.

- Not meeting after a debriefing to make sure the CISD team is okay.

- Not assessing the need for appropriate CISD (under use of the process).

- Over using CISD by utilizing the process on minor events.

- Not following the CISD model.

- Altering the CISD model.

- Telling "war stories" during a debriefing.

- Team members not periodically looking at each other during a debriefing in order to communicate with their eyes.

- Writing notes during a debriefing.

- Arguing with the participants.

- Acting or speaking in a manner which indicates insensitivity to the participants.

- Bringing up information from other debriefings.

- Breaking confidentiality.

Appendix E

FOR ADDITIONAL INFORMATION ON:

A. CISM Team Registry

B. CISM Training

C. CISM Support Services

D. Other CISM Issues

Contact:

International Critical Incident Stress Foundation, Inc.

4785 Dorsey Hall Drive
Suite 102
Ellicott City, Maryland
21042

Phone: (410) 730-4311
Fax: (410) 730-4313

Emergency: (410) 313-2473

REFERENCES

Adams, J. D. (Ed.). (1980). *Understanding and managing stress*. San Diego, CA: University Associates.

Aguilera, D.C., Messick, J.M., and Farrell, M.S. (1974). *Crisis intervention: Theory and methodology*. St. Louis, MO: C.V. Mosby.

American College of Sports Medicine. (1980). *Guidelines for graded exercise testing and exercise prescription*. Philadelphia: Lea & Febiger.

American Psychiatric Association. (1964). *First aid for psychological reactions in disasters*. Washington, DC: American Psychiatric Association.

American Psychiatric Association. (1968). *Diagnostic and statistical manual of mental disorders*, Second Edition. Washington DC: Author.

American Psychiatric Association (1980). *Diagnostic and statistical manual of mental disorders*, Third Edition, Washington DC: Author.

American Psychiatric Association (1987). *Diagnostic and statistical manual of mental disorders*, Third Edition, Revised. Washington D C: Author.

American Psychiatric Association (1994). *Diagnostic and statistical manual of mental disorders*, Fourth Edition. Washington DC: Author.

Appel, J.W., Beebe, G.W. and Hilger, D.W. (1946). Comparative incidence of neuropsychiatric casualties in World War I and World War II. *American Journal of Psychiatry*, 102, 196-199.

Appel, J.W. (1966). Preventive psychiatry. In A. J. Glass and R. J. Bernucci (Eds.). *Neuropsychiatry in World War II* (pp. 373 - 415). Washington, DC: US Government Printing Office.

Appelbaum, S. H. (1981). *Stress management for health care professionals*. Rockville, MD: Aspen Systems Corp.

Arnold, M. (1970). *Feelings and emotions*. New York: Academic.

Arnold, M. (1984). *Memory and the brain*. Hillsdale, NJ: Erlbaum.

Back, K. J. (1991). Critical incident stress management for care providers in the pediatric emergency department. *Critical Care Nurse*, 12(1), 78-83.

Bailey, P. (1918). War neuroses, shell shock, and nervousness in soldiers. *Journal of the American Medical Association*, 71, 2148-2153.

Beck, A. (1979). *Cognitive Therapy of Depression*. New York: Basic.

Beck, A. and Emery, G. (1985). *Anxiety disorders and phobias*. New York: Basic Books.

Benson, H. (1975). *The relaxation response*. New York: Morrow.

Benson, H. (1983). The relaxation response. *Trends in Neuroscience*, 6, 281-284.

Benson, H., Alexander, S., and Feldman, C. (1975). Decreased premature ventricular contractions through the use of the relaxation response. *Lancet*, 2, 380-382.

Berg, D. (1970). Crisis intervention concepts for emergency telephone services. *Crisis Intervention*, 4, 11-19.

Bettleheim, B. (1984). Afterword. In C. Vegh, *I didn't say good-bye*. New York: E.P. Dutton.

Blau, T.H. (1994). *Psychological services for law enforcement*. New York: John Wiley & Sons, Inc.

Borkovec, T.D., Wilkenson, L., Folensbee, R., and Lerman, C. (1983). Stimulus control applications to the treatment of worry. *Behavioral Research and Therapy*, 21, 247-251.

Breslau, I.N., Davis, G.C., Andreski, P. and Peterson, E. (1991). Traumatic events and post-traumatic stress disorders in an urban population of young adults. *Archives of General Psychiatry*, 48, 216 - 222.

Brett, E.A. and Ostroff, R. (1985). Imagery and post-traumatic stress disorder. *American Journal of Psychiatry*, 142, 417-424.

Breznitz, S. (1980). Stress in Israel. In Selye, H. (Ed.) *Selye's guide to stress research*. New York: Van Nostrand Reinhold Co.

Brown, M.W. and Williams. (1918). *Neuropsychiatry and the war: A bibliography with abstracts*. New York: National Committee for Mental Hygiene.

Burgess, A. W. and Balwin, B.A. (1981). *Crisis intervention theory and practice, a clinical handbook*. Englewood Cliffs, NJ: Prentice Hall, Inc.

Burns, C. and Harm, I. (1993). Emergency nurses' perceptions of critical incidents and stress debriefing. *Journal of Emergency Nursing, 19* (5), 431-436.

Butcher, J. (1980). The role of crisis intervention in an airport disaster plan. *Aviation, Space and Environmental Medicine*, 51, 1260-1262.

Caplan, G. (1961). *An approach to community mental health*. New York: Grine and Stratton.

Caplan, G. (1964). *Principles of preventive psychiatry*. New York: Basic Books.

Caplan, G. (1976). *Support systems and community mental health*. New York: Behavioral Publications, Inc.

Carkhuff, R. and Truax, C. (1965). Lay mental health counseling. *Journal of Consulting Psychology*, 29, 426-431.

Cherniss, C. (1980). *Staff burnout in human service organizations*. New York: Praeger Publishers.

Cohen, R. E. and Ahearn, F. L. (1980). *Handbook for mental health care of disaster victims*. Baltimore, MD: Johns Hopkins University Press.

Corneil, D. W. (1993). Prevalence of post-traumatic stress disorders in a metropolitan fire department. Unpublished Doctoral Dissertation. The Johns Hopkins University, Baltimore.

Couchaine, K.E. and Dowd, E.T. (1994). Group Approaches. In F. Dattilo and A. Freeman (Eds.). *Cognitive-behavioral strategies in crisis intervention*. New York: Guilford.

Craren, E. J. (Ed.) (1992). *Nebraska statewide CISD program, rules and regulations* (vol. 1) and *Operational policies and procedures* (vol.2). Lincoln, NE: Nebraska Interagency CISD Council.

Davidson, L. and Baum, A. (1986). Chronic stress and post-traumatic stress disorders. *Journal of Consulting and Clinical Psychology*, 54, 303-308.

de Vries, H. (1981). Tranquilizer effect of exercise. *America's Journal of Physical Medicine*, 60, 57-66.

de Vries, H., and Adams, G. (1972). Electromyagraphic comparison of single dose of exercise and meprobamate as to effects of muscular relaxation. *American Journal of Physical Medicine*, 52, 130-141.

Donnovan, D. (1991). Traumatology: A field whose time has come. *Journal of Traumatic Stress*, 4, 433-436.

Duffy, J. (1978). Emergency mental health services during and after a major aircraft accident. *Aviation, Space and Environmental Medicine*, 49, 1004-1008.

Duffy, J. (1979). The role of CMHCs in airport disasters. *Technical Assistance Center Report*, 2(1), 7-9.

Dyregrov, A.. and Reidar T. (1988). Rescue workers emotional reactions following a disaster. *Scandinavian Journal of Psychology*.

Dyregrov, A. (1989). Caring for helpers in Disaster situations: Psychological debriefing. *Disaster Management*, 2, 25-30.

Ellis, A. (1973). *Humanistic psychology: The rational-emotive approach*. New York: Julian.

Epperson, M. M.(1977). Families in sudden crisis. *Social Work Health Care*, 2, 3.

Epperson-Sebour, M. M. (1985). Response. In Green (Ed.) *Role stressors and supports for emergency workers*. Washington, DC: Center For Mental Health Studies of Emergencies., U.S. Department of Health and Human Services.

Everly, G. S. (1979). A technique for the immediate reduction of psycho-physiologic stress reactivity. *Health Education*, 10, 44.

Everly, G. S. (1989). *A clinical guide to the treatment of the human stress response*. New York: Plenum.

Everly, G. S. (1990). Post-traumatic stress disorder as a "disorder of arousal." *Psychology and Health: An International Journal*, 4, 135 - 145.

Everly, G. S. (1992) "Psychotraumatology: A two-factor theory." Paper presented at the Fourth Montreux Congress on Stress, Montreux, Switzerland.

Everly, G.S. (1993a). Psychotraumatology: A two-factor formulation of post-traumatic stress. *Intergrative Physiological and Behavioral Science.*, 28, 270 - 278.

Everly, G.S. (1993b). Neurophysiological considerations in the treatment of post-traumatic stress disorder. In J. Wilson and B. Raphael (Eds). *Handbook of traumatic stress syndromes* (pp. 795 - 801). NY: Plenum.

Everly, G.S. (1994). Short-term psychotherapy of acute adult onset post-traumatic stress: The role of Weltanschauung. *Stress Medicine*, 10, 191 - 196.

Everly, G. S., and Benson, H. (1989). Disorders of arousal and the relaxation response. *International Journal of Psychosomatics*, 36, 15 - 22.

Everly, G. S. and Horton, A.M. (1989). Neuropsychology of PTSD, *Perceptual and Motor Skills*, 68, 807-810.

Everly, G.S. and Lating, J. (Ed.)(1995). *Psychotraumatology: Key papers and core concepts in post-traumatic stress.* NY: Plenum.

Everly, G. S. and Mitchell, J. T. (1992, Dec.). "CISD and the prevention of work-related PTSD." Paper presented to the Second NIOSH/APA Conference on Work-related Stress, Washington D.C.

Everly, G. S. and Rosenfeld, R. (1981). *The nature and treatment of the stress response.* New York: Plenum Press.

Figley, C. R. (Ed.). (1985). *Trauma and its wake,* (Vol. 1). New York: Brunner / Mazel.

Fowler, D.E. and McGee, R.K. (1973). Assessing the performance of telephone crisis workers: The development of a technical effectiveness scale. In D. Lester and G.W. Brockoop (Eds.), *Crisis intervention and counseling by telephone.* Springfield, IL: Charles C. Thomas.

Freeman, K. (1979). CMHC responses to the Chicago and San Diego airplane disasters. *Technical Assistance Center Report* 2(1), 10-12.

Friedman, R., Framer, M., and Shearer, D. (1988). Early response to post-traumatic stress. *EAP Digest,* September - October. pp. 45-49.

Freud, S. (1913). Further recommendations on the technique of psycho-analysis. In J. Strachey, translator, *The complete psychological works, vol. 12,* NY: Norton.

Girdano, D., Everly, G., and Dusek, D. (1993). *Controlling stress and tension, (4th ed.).* Englewood Cliffs, NJ: Prentice-Hall.

Gist, R. and Lubin, B. (Eds.) (1989). *Psychosocial aspects of disaster.* New York: John Wiley & Sons.

Graham, N. K. (1981). Done in, fed up, burned out: Too much attrition in EMS. *Journal of Emergency Medical Services*, 6(1), 24-29.

Graham, N. K. (1981). Part 2: How to avoid a short career. *Journal of Emergency Medical Services*, 6 (2), 25-31.

Greden, J.F. (1974). Anxiety or caffeinism: A diagnostic dilemma. *American Journal of Psychiatry*, 131, 1089 - 1092.

Greenstone, J.C. (1993). *Critical Incident Stress Debriefing and Crisis Management.* Austin, Texas: Texas Department of Health.

Harvey, J.H., Orbuch, T. L., Chwlisz, K.D., and Garwood, G. (1991). Coping with sexual assault: The role of account making and confiding. *Journal of Traumatic Stress*, 4, 515-532.

Heider, J. (1974). Catharsis in human potential encounter. *Journal of Humanistic Psychology*, 14, 27 - 47.

Heinman, M. F. (1975). The police suicide. *Journal of Police Science and Administration*, 3(3), 267-273.

Helzer, J., Robins, L. and McEvoy, L. (1987). Post-traumatic stress disorder in the general population. *New England Journal of Medicine, 317*, 1630-1634.

Herman, J. L. (1992). Complex PTSD. *Journal of Traumatic Stress, 5*, 377-392.

Herman, J. and van der Kolk, B. (1987). Traumatic antecedents of borderline personality disorder. In B. van der Kolk (Ed.), *Psychological trauma* (pp. 111-126). Washington, DC: American Psychiatric Press.

Herman, J.L. (1992). *Trauma and Recovery*. New York: Basic Books.

Hiley-Young, B. and Gerrity, E.T. Critical incident stress debriefing (CISD): Value and limitations in disaster response. *NCP Clinical Quarterly, 4*, 17-19.

Hoff, L.A. (1978). *People in Crisis: Understanding and Helping*. Menlow Park, CA: Addison-Wesley Publishing Co.

Holmes, R. (1985) *Acts of War: The behavior of men in battle*. New York: Free Press.

Holmes, T.H., and Rahe, R. (1967). The social readjustment rating scale. *Journal of Psychosomatic Research, 11*, 213-218.

Honig.A. (1991). *Cerritos air disaster: Psychological effects*. Paper presented at the First World Congress on Stress, Trauma, and Coping, Baltimore, MD, May 1991.

Horowitz, M.J. (1976). Diagnosis and treatment of stress response syndromes: General principles. In H.J. Parad, H.L.P. Resnik and L.G. Parad (Eds.). *Emergency and disaster management: A mental health source book*. Bowie, MD: The Charles Press Publishers.

Horowitz, M. (1976). *Stress response syndromes*. NY: Jason Aronsom.

Jasnoski, M., Holmes, D., Solomon, S., and Agular, C. (1981). Exercise changes in aerobic capacity and changes in self-perceptions. *Journal of Research in Personality, 15*, 460-466.

Johnston, S.J. (1993). Traumatic stress reactions in the crew of the Herald of Free Enterprise. In J.P.Wilson and B. Raphael (Eds.), *International handbook of traumatic stress syndromes*. New York: Plenum Press.

Jones, D. R. (1985). Secondary disaster victims. *American Journal of Psychiatry, 142*, 303-307.

Kahn, M. (1966). The physiology of catharsis. *Journal of Personality and Social Psychology, 3*, 278 - 286.

Keller, K. L. (1991). Stress management for emergency department personnel. *Topics in Emergency Medicine*, September, 70-76.

Kennedy-Ewing, L. (1988). *Operational and training guide for the Critical incident stress management program of Delaware County, Pennsylvania*. Media, PA: Department of Human Resources.

Kentsmith, D. (1980). Minimizing the psychological effects of a wartime disaster on an individual. *Aviation, Space, and Environmental Medicine, 51, 409 - 413.*

Kilpatrick, D.G., Saunders, B., Amick-McMullan, A., Best, C., Veronen, L., and Renick, H. (1989). Victim and crime factors associated with the development of crime-related post-traumatic stress disorder. *Behavior Therapy*, 20, 199 - 214.

Kliman, A.S. (1975). The Corning flood project: Psychological first-aid following a natural disaster. In H. J. Parad, H.L.P. Resnik and L.G. Parad (Eds.), *Emergency and disaster management: A mental health sourcebook*. Bowie, MD: Charles Press Publishers.

Kraus, H., and Raab, W. (1961). *Hypokinetic disease*. Springfield, IL: Charles C. Thomas.

Kroes, W. H. and Hurrell, J. J., Jr. (Eds) (1976) *Job stress and the police officer: Identifying stress reduction techniques*. Washington, DC: U.S Department of Health, Education, and Welfare (Pub. No. NIOSH 76-187).

Lang, P. (1971). The application of psychophysiological methods to the study of psychotherapy and behavior modification. In A. Bergin and S. Garfield (Eds.), *Handbook of psychotherapy and behavior change*. New York: Wiley.

Lazarus, R. and Folkman, S. (1984). *Stress Appraisal and Coping*. New York: Springer.

Leeman-Conley, M. (1990). After a violent robbery. *Criminology Australia*, April / May, 4-6.

Lindemann, E. (1944). Symptomatology and management of acute grief. *American Journal of Psychiatry*, 101,141-148.

Lindy, J.D., Grace, M., and Green, B. (1981). Survivors: Outreach to a reluctant population. *American Journal of Orthopsychiatry*, 51, 465-478.

Lipton, M.I. (1994). *Post-traumatic stress disorder: Additional perspectives*. Springfield IL: Charles C. Thomas Publishers.

Maslow, A. H. (1970). *Motivation and personality*. NY: Harper & Row.

McCarthy, M. (1988). Stressed employees look for relief in workers' compensation claims. *Wall Street Journal*, , April 7, pp, 34.

Mc Gee, R.K. (1974). *Crisis intervention in the community*. Baltimore: University Park Press.

McGeer, E. & McGeer, P. (1988). Excitotoxins and animal models of disease. In C. Galli, L. Manzo, and P. Spencer (Eds.), *Recent Advances in Nervous System Toxicology* (pp. 107-131). NY: Plenum.

Meichenbaum, D. (1994). *A clinical handbook /practical therapist manual for assessing and treating adults with post-traumatic stress disorder (PTSD)*. Waterloo, Ontario, Canada: Institute Press.

Miller, A., et al. (1988, April 25). Stress on the job. *Newsweek*, pp.40-41.

Miller, S. (1994). Reaching Out to Our Own. *Marines*, June, 9-10.

Mitchell, J. T. (1976). Rescue crisis intervention. *EMS News*. Baltimore, MD: 4(3), 4.

Mitchell, J. T. (1981, November). "Acute stress reactions and burnout in prehospital emergency medical services personnel". Paper presented at the First National Conference on Burnout. Philadelphia, PA.

Mitchell, J. T. (1982). The psychological impact of the Air Florida 90 disaster on fire-rescue, paramedic and police personnel. In R A. Cowley, S. Edelstein and M. Silerstein (Eds.), *Mass casualties: A lessons learned approach , accidents, civil disorders, natural disasters, terrorism.* Washington, D.C.: Department of Transportation (DOT HS 806302).

Mitchell, J. T. (1983).When disaster strikes ...The critical incident stress debriefing process. *Journal of Emergency Medical Services,* 8(1), 36-39.

Mitchell, J. T. (1983). Guidelines for psychological debriefings. *Emergency management course manual.* Emmitsburg, MD: Federal Emergency Management Agency, Emergency Management Institute.

Mitchell, J. T. (1986) Teaming up against critical incident stress. *Chief Fire Executive,* 1(1), 24; 36; 84.

Mitchell, J. T. (1988). The history, status and future of critical incident stress debriefings. *Journal of Emergency Medical Services,*13(11), 49-52.

Mitchell, J. T. (1988). Development and functions of a critical incident stress debriefing team. *Journal of Emergency Medical Services,* 13(12), 43-46.

Mitchell, J. T. (1988, July). "CISD Introductory Remarks". Workshop handout Baltimore MD: University of Maryland Baltimore County.

Mitchell, J. T. (1992). Comprehensive traumatic stress management in the emergency department. The Emergency Nurses Association: Monograph series. 1(8), 3 - 15.

Mitchell, J. T. (1991). Law enforcement applications of critical incident stress teams. In James T. Reese (Ed.), *Critical incidents in policing revised.* Washington, DC: US Department of Justice: Federal Bureau of Investigation.

Mitchell, J. T. (1991). Demobilizations. *Life Net,* vol. 2, (1).

Mitchell, J. T. (1992). Protecting your people from critical incident stress. *Fire Chief,* 36(5), 61-64.

Mitchell, J.T. (1994). Too much help too fast. *Life Net,* a publication of the International Critical Incident Stresss Foundation, Inc., 5(3), 3-4.

Mitchell, J. T. and Bray, G. P. (1990). *Emergency services stress, guidelines for preserving the health and careers of emergency services personnel.* Englewood Cliffs, NJ: Brady Publishing.

Mitchell, J.T. and Dyregrov, A. (1993). Traumatic stress in disaster and emergency personnel: Prevention and intervention. In J.P.Wilson and Beverly Raphael (Eds.), *International handbook on traumatic stress syndromes.* New York: Plenum Press.

Mitchell, J.T. and Everly, G.S. (1993). *Critical incident stress debriefing (CISD): An operations manual for the prevention of traumatic stress among emergency services and disaster workers,* First Edition. Ellicott City, MD: Chevron Publishing.

Mitchell, J. T. and Resnik, H. L. P. (1981). *Emergency response to crisis*. Bowie, MD: Brady Publishing. (republished Ellicott City, MD: Chevron Publishing, 1986).

Moran, C. and Britton, N.R. (1994). Emergency work experience and reactions to traumatic incidents. *Journal of Traumatic Stress*, 7(4), 575-585.

Nakanomiya, J. (1975). History of war medicine in Japan. *National Defense Medical Journal*, 22, 67-73.

Norman, E. and Getek, D. (1988). Post-traumatic stress in victims of psysicsl trauma [Abstract]. *Proceedings of the 15th Annual National Teaching Institute of the American Association of Critical Care Nurses*, (p.671). Newport Beach, CA: AACCN, 671.

Noy, S. (1991). Combat stress reactions. In R. Gal and A.D. Mangelsdorff (Eds.), *Handbook of military psychology*. Chichester, U.K.: John Wiley and Sons.

Ochberg, F. M. (1991). Post traumaitc therapy. *Psychotheraphy*, 28, 5-15.

Olney, J.W. (1978). Neurotoxicity of excitatory amino acids. In E. McGeer, J. Olney, and P. Mcgeer (Eds.), *Kainic acid as a tool in neurobiology*, (pp. 95-122) NY: Raven.

Orner, R. (1994). *Intervention strategies for emergency response groups: A new conceptual framework*. Paper presented at the NATO conference on Stress, Coping and disaster in Bonos, France.

Parad, H. (Ed.). (1965). *Crisis intervention: Selected readings*. New York: Family Service Association of America.

Patrick, P. K. S. (1981). *Health care worker burnout, what it is, what to do about it*. Chicago, IL: Inquiry Books (Blue Cross/ Blue Shield, Assoc.).

Pennebaker, J.W. (1985). Traumatic experience and psychosomatic disease. *Canadian Psychologist*, 26, 82-95.

Pennebaker, J. W. (1990). *Opening up: The healing power of confiding in others*. New York: Avon.

Pennebaker, J.W. and Beall, S. (1986). Confronting a traumatic event. *Journal of Abnormal Psychology*, 95, 274 - 281.

Pennebaker, J. and Susman, J. (1988). Disclosure of traumas and psychosomatic processes. *Social Science, and Medicine*, 26, 327-332.

Post, R. (1992). Transduction of psychosocial stress onto the neurobiology of recurrent affective disorder. *American Journal of Psychiatry*, 149, 999-1010.

Pugliese, D. (1988, May). Psychological pressures, media: Israeli Defense Forces confronts soldiers' frustrations. *Armed Forces Journal International*, 28.

Pynoos, R.S, Goeenjian, A. and Steinberg, A.M. (1994). Strategies of disaster intervention for children and adolescents. Paper presented at the NATO conference on stress, coping and disaster in Bonos, France.

Raphael, B. (1986). *When disaster strikes: How individuals and communities cope with catastrophe*. New York: Basic Books, Inc. publishers.

Raphael, B. and Wilson, J.P. (1993). Theoretical and intervention consider-ations in working with victims of disaster. In J.P. Wilson and B. Raphael (Eds.), *International handbook of traumatic stress studies*. New York: Plenum Press.

Rapoport, L. (1965). The state of crisis: Some theoretical considerations. In Howard J. Parad, (Ed.). *Crisis intervention: Selected readings*. New York: Family Service Association of America.

Ravenscroft, T. (1994). *Going critical: GMB/Apex and T&G Unions 1994 survey of occupational stress factors in accident and emergency staff in the London Ambulance Service*. London: GMB/Apex and T&G Unions.

Reese, J. T. (1987). *A history of police psychological services*. Washington, DC: U.S. Department of Justice, Federal Bureau of Investigation.

Reese, J. T., Horn, J. M. and Dunning, C. (Eds.) *Critical incidents in policing - revised*. Washington, DC: US Government Printing Office, 1991.

Reese, J.T. (Ed.). (1991). *Critical incidents in policing, revised*. Washington, DC: U.S. Department of Justice: Federal Bureau of Investigation.

Robinson, R. (Ed.). (1986, August). "Proceedings from a conference on dealing with stress and trauma in emergency services", Melbourne, Australia.

Robinson, R. (Ed.). (1991). "Discussion paper, Australian Critical Incident Stress Association, Team accreditation". Melbourne: Victoria, Australia.

Robinson, R. C. and Mitchell, J. T. (1993). Evaluation of psychological debriefings. *Journal of Traumatic Stress*, 6(3), 367 - 382.

Robinson, R. (1994). *Follow-up study of health and stress in ambulance services Victoria, Australia, Part I*. Melbourne, Australia: Victorian Ambulance Crisis Counselling Unit.

Roemer, L. and Borkovec, T. (1994). Effects of suppressing thoughts about emotional material. *Journal of Abnormal Psychology*, 103, 467 - 474.

Rogers, O. (1992). "An examination of critical incident stress debriefing for emergency service providers". Unpublished doctoral dissertation, University or Maryland.

Rosenman, I. (1984). Cognitive determinants of emotion. In P. Shaver (Ed.), *Human Stress* (p. ix-xi). New York: AMS Press.

Roth, S. and Newman, E. (1993). The process of coping with incest for adult survivors. *Journal of Interpersonal Violence*, 8, 363-377.

Rubin, J. G. (1990). Critical incident stress debriefing: Helping the helpers. *Journal of Emergency Nursing*, 16 (4), 255-258.

Rueveni, U. (1979). *Networking families in crisis: Intervention strategies with families and social networks*. New York: Human Sciences Press.

Salmon, T. W. (1919). War neuroses and their lessons. *New York Medical Journal*, 109, 993-994.

Sapolsky, R., Krey, L. and McEwen, B. (1984). Stress down regulates corticosterone receptors in a site specific manner in the brain. *Endocrinology*, 114, 287-292.

Schnitt, J.M. (1993). Traumatic stress studies: What's in a name? *Journal of Traumatic Stress*, 6, 405 - 408.

Scurfield, R. M. (1985). Post trauma stress assessment and treatment: Overview and formulation. In C.R. Figley (Ed.), *Trauma and its wake: The study and treatment of post-traumatic stress disorder*. New York: Brunner Mazel.

Selye, H. (1956). *The stress of life*. New York: McGraw-Hill.

Selye, H. (1974). *Stress without distress*. Philadelphia: Lippincott.

Selye, H. (1976). *Stress in health and disease*. Boston: Butterworth.

Selye, H. (1980). The stress concept today. In I.L. Kutash and L.B. Schlesinger (Eds.), *Handbook on stress and anxiety: Contemporary knowledge, theory and treatment*. San Francisco: Jossey-Bass Publishers.

Shalev, A.Y. (1994). Debrifing following traumatic exposure. In R.J. Ursano, B.G. McCaughey and C.S. Fullerton (Eds.), *Individual and community responses to trauma and disaster: The structure of human chaos.* Cambridge, UK: Cambridge University Press.

Silver, R.L., Boon, C. and Stones, M.H. (1983). Searching for meaning in misfortune: Making sense of incest. *Journal of social issues*, 39, 81 - 102.

Sinyor, D.S., Schwartz, S., Peronnet, F., Brisson, G., and Seraganian, P. (1983). Aerobic fitness level and reactivity to psychosocial stress. *Psychosomatic Medicine*, 45, 205-217.

Slaikeu, K. A. (1984). *Crisis intervention: A handbook for practice and research*. Boston, MA: Allyn and Bacon, Inc.

Sloan, I.H., Rozensky, R.H. Kaplan, L. and Saunders, S.M. (1994). A shooting incident in an elementary school: Effects of worker stress on public safety, mental health and medical personnel. *Journal of Traumatic Stress*, 7(4), 565 - 574.

Smith, J.R. (1985). Rap groups and group therapy for Vietnam veterans. In A.S. Blank, S.M. Sonnenberg, and J. Talbott (Eds.). *Psychiatric problems in Vietnam veterans*. Washington, DC: American Psychiatric Press.

Smith, K.J. and Everly, G.S. (1992, Dec). "A structural model and configural analysis of the relationship between stressors and disease among accountants." Paper presented to the Second NIOSH/APA Conference on Occupational Stress, , Washington DC.

Solomon, Z. (1986). Front line treatment of Israeli combat stress reaction casualties: An evaluation of its effectiveness in the1982 Lebanon War. *Israeli Defense Forces Journal*, 3(4), 53-59.

Staff report. (1984, July). Glenn Srodes, 79 dies, Chief of Staff of Hospital. *Pittsburgh Post Gazette*. Pittsburgh, PA.

Sternbach, R. (1966). *Principles of psychophysiology*. New York: Academic Press.

Taplin, J.R. (1971). Crisis theory: Critique and reformulation. *Community Mental Health Journal, 7*, 13-23.

Taylor, A.J.W and Frazer, A.G. (1982). The stress of post disaster body handling and victim identification work. *Journal of Human Stress, 8*(12), 4-12.

Thompson, J. and Suzuki, I. (1991). Stress in ambulance workers. *Disaster Management, 3*(4), 193-197.

Trimble, M. (1981). Post-truamatic neurosis. New York:Wiley.

Tindall, J.A. and Gray, H.D. (1985). *Peer power: Becoming an effective peer helper.* Muncie, IN: Accelerated Development, Inc.

Tritt, P. (1984). *Mayflower (Denver, CO) Critical incident stress debriefing team protocols.* Denver Colorado Swedish Hospital System, Paramedic Training Program.

Tritt, P. (1986). *Considerations in developing a critical incident stress debriefing team* (handout material for team training). Denver Colorado: Mayflower CISD Team.

Turner, S.W., Thompson, J., and Rosser, R.M. (1993). The kings cross fire: Early implications for organizaing a "phase - two" response. In J.P. Wilson and B. Raphael (Eds.), *International handbook of traumatic stress syndromes.* New York: Plenum Press.

van der Hart, O., Brown, P. and van der Kolk, B. (1989). Pierre Janet's treatment of post-traumatic stress. *Journal of Traumatic Stress, 2*, 379 - 396.

Viney, L. L. (1976). The concept of crisis: A tool for clinical psychologists. *Bulletin of the British Psychological Society, 29*, 387 - 395.

Wagner, M. (1979). Airline disaster: A stress debriefing program for police. *Police Stress.* 2(1), 16 - 20.

Wagner, M. (1979). Stress debriefing - Flight 191: A department program that worked. *Police Star,* 4 - 8.

Weller, D. and Everly, G. (1985). Occupational health through physical fittness programming. In G. Everly and R. Feldmen (Eds.), *Occupational health promotion* (pp.127 - 146). New York: Macmillan.

Williams, T. (1993). Trauma in the workplace. In J.P. Wilson and B. Raphael (Eds.), *International handbook of traumatic stress syndromes.* New York: Plenum Press.

Wilson, J.P., Harel, Z., and Kahan, B. (Eds.). (1988). *Human adaption to extreme stress: From the holocaust to Vietnam.* New York: Plenum Press.

Wilson, J.P. and Raphael, B. (Eds.). (1993). *International handbook of traumatic stress syndromes.* New York: Plenum Press.

World Health Organization. (1992). *International classification of diseases,* tenth edition. Geneva: United Nations.

Yandrick, R. (1990, January). Critical incidents. *EAPA Exchange,* pp.18 - 23.

Yalom, I. (1970). *The theory and practice of group psychotherapy.* New York: Basic Books.

Index

Crisis Intervention Counseling: 62.

Crisis Response Team: 9, 215. *(see also CRT)*

Critical Incident: 1 - 5, 7 - 9, 11 - 17, 45 - 46, 49 - 51, 54 - 57, 61, 66, 77, 79, 80, 94, 133, 147, 153 - 154, 168, 173, 184 - 185, 189 - 190, 204, 209, 216, 222, 224 - 225, 231, 233, 237 - 244, 248, 252, 259, 267 - 268, 273, 276, 277, 279, 281, 283.

Critical Incident Response Team: 9.

Critical Incident Stress: 1, 2, 3, 4, 5, 7, 8, 9, 11, 12, 17, 45, 46, 49, 50, 54, 55, 57, 61, 66, 77, 79, 94, 133, 147, 153, 154, 168, 173, 184, 185, 189, 190, 204, 209, 216, 222, 224, 225, 231, 233, 237, 238, 240, 241, 242, 243, 244, 248, 252, 259, 267, 268, 273, 276, 277, 279, 281, 283.

Critical Incident Stress Debriefing: 1, 3 - 5, 9, 12, 15, 17, 45, 50 - 51, 54 - 56, 77, 79 - 80, 133, 154, 168, 173, 184 - 185, 190, 222, 276 - 277, 279, 283. *(see also CISD; Debriefing)*

Critical Incident Stress Intervention: 4, 10.

Critical Incident Stress Management: 3, 5, 9, 11, 13, 16 - 17, 45 - 46, 49 - 50, 54, 56, 57, 66, 77, 147, 153 - 154, 168, 185, 189, 204, 216, 225, 240, 241, 243, 248, 252, 267, 268, 273, 277. *(see also CISM)*

Critical Incident Stress Management Team: 11, 216, 241, 252.

Critical Incident Stress Team: 9 - 11, 169, 230, 279.

CRT: 5, 11, 65, 77 - 79, 82, 84 - 85, 184, 204, 215, 222, 241, 251 - 253. *(see also Crisis Response Team)*

Cultural Difference: 89.

Cumulative Stress: 61, 179, 236, 238.

D

Debriefing: 1, 3 - 5, 8 - 16, 41, 46, 48, 51, 53 - 56, 62, 63, 77 - 144, 149, 151, 153, 156 - 160, 164, 168 - 178, 182 - 186, 190, 194 - 203, 206 - 213, 221 - 223, 226, 229, 235, 238 - 246, 250, 252 - 266, 269 - 270, 275, 279, 281, 283. *(see also CISD; Critical Incident Stress Debriefing)*

Defusing: 2, 12 - 14, 16, 41 - 42, 48, 56, 63, 82, 85 - 87, 121 - 135, 138, 142, 143, 149, 151, 153, 157 - 158, 161, 166, 168, 175, 178, 184, 186, 190, 192, 201, 207, 208, 211, 226, 236, 242, 250, 264, 265.

Demobilization: 3, 5, 12 - 14, 16, 48, 86, 126, 131, 133 - 144, 157, 186, 190, 192, 207 - 208, 238.

Denial: 87, 124, 161, 200, 201, 209.

Disaster: 1 - 4, 8, 11 - 13, 15, 32, 34, 42, 44 - 45, 50 - 51, 54, 56, 59, 63 - 65, 67, 69, 71, 78, 79 - 80, 86 - 88, 126, 131, 133 - 140, 143 - 144, 163, 168, 172 - 174, 179 - 184, 187, 189 - 192, 204 - 212, 222, 229, 241, 245, 252, 256, 262, 267 - 268, 274 - 281, 283.

Disaster Drill: 137, 262.

Disaster Worker: 1, 4, 11, 42, 50, 54, 78, 134, 140, 181, 182, 204, 209, 241, 279.

Disorders of Arousal: 26.

Distress: 4, 7 - 9, 13 - 15, 19, 25, 33, 35, 48 - 49, 59, 61, 67, 68, 77 - 80, 85, 89, 95, 97 - 102, 105, 109, 111 - 115, 117, 124, 127, 129 - 130, 143 - 151, 155, 160, 162, 174, 180, 185, 190, 194, 195, 198 - 199, 204 - 205, 219, 220, 225 - 226, 247, 254 - 255, 258, 260, 262.

E

Emergency Medical: 4, 8, 11, 54, 56, 78, 81, 97, 122, 140, 145, 182, 184, 216, 219, 241, 248.

Emergency Service Personnel: 1, 4, 42, 44, 105, 143, 144, 171, 179, 255.

Emergency Services Support Unit: 9.

Emotional Integration: 22.

M

Maladaptive Coping: 28, 68.
Mass Disaster: 15, 87, 179, 180, 181, 184.
Mental Health Professionals: 4, 9 - 11, 42, 56, 58 - 59, 62, 64 - 65, 67, 69, 76, 78, 80 - 82, 87, 89, 97 - 100, 124 - 125, 135, 147, 150, 152, 163, 174, 191 - 192, 196, 215 - 217, 220 - 226, 234, 237, 239 - 244, 248, 252, 258, 261, 269.
Military: 4, 10, 47, 48, 49, 54, 56, 58, 142, 169, 192, 241, 269.

N

Neuroanatomy: 22.
Neuromuscular Nervous System: 23.
Neurotransmitter: 39, 40.
Nurse: 1, 4, 10, 11, 50, 54, 122, 145, 169, 171, 184, 194, 216, 221, 225.

O

Occupational Stress: 1, 22, 220, 281.
On-Scene Support: 14, 42, 143, 145, 146, 147, 151, 152, 186, 242, 265.

P

Paramedic: 4, 10, 51, 54, 122, 182, 216, 241, 279.
Parasympathetic Nervous System: 23.
Peer Counseling: 12, 54, 61, 63, 226.
Peer Counselor: 60, 61, 62, 67, 69, 71, 163, 196.
Peer Support: 8 - 10, 12, 14 - 15, 42, 47, 53, 55, 56, 58 - 60, 62, 65, 76, 78, 81 - 82, 89, 93, 96, 98 - 100, 114, 119, 124 - 125, 147, 152, 163, 192, 196, 201, 208, 212, 216, 222 - 223, 225, 227, 234 - 235, 239 - 240, 242 - 244, 248, 264.
Personality Change: 7, 35.
Physical Illness: 7, 38, 41.
Physician: 1, 4, 8, 21, 50, 216, 242.
Police Officer: 4, 10, 50, 51, 52, 53, 122, 169, 174, 176, 182, 216, 225, 278.
Post Debriefing: 114, 115, 200.
Post-trauma Disorder: 1.
Post-traumatic Stress: 1 - 3, 15, 31 - 33, 36 - 37, 40 - 44, 64 - 65, 158, 165 - 166, 173, 179, 184, 274 - 278, 282 - 283.
Post-Traumatic Stress Disorder: 5, 31, 44, 166, 173, 187, 224, 235. *(see also PTSD)*
Pre-Incident Stress Education: 60.
Prevention: 1, 2, 15, 41, 44, 56, 62, 64, 68, 80, 133, 157, 158, 164, 166, 168, 173, 184, 211, 252, 254, 261.
Primary Victim: 2, 11, 79, 147, 166, 186.
Primary Victims: 2.
Professional Support Personnel: 5, 9 - 11, 124, 222.
Protective Barrier: 159, 187, 189.
Psyche: 7, 19, 50.
Psychiatrists: 10, 48, 49, 221.
Psychophysiological Disease: 19.
Psychosomatic: 19.
Psychotherapy: 14, 15, 68, 75, 78, 93, 103, 114, 130, 150, 184, 192, 211, 217, 238, 246, 269.
Psychotraumatology: 32, 268.
PTSD: 7, 31 - 42, 44, 79 - 80, 158, 165 - 166, 173, 179, 184, 187 - 189, 276 - 278. *(see also Post-traumatic Stress Disorder)*
Public Safety Personnel: 1, 2, 215.

R

Reaction Phase: 8, 109, 110, 112, 182, 195, 199, 201, 206.
Record Keeping: 238.
Recovery Process: 36, 79, 156, 173, 192, 202, 212.
Red Cross: 11, 65, 82, 140, 181, 220, 241, 252.
Referral: 14, 63, 80, 87, 98, 114, 115, 118, 130, 175, 184, 187, 193, 220, 221, 222, 223, 225, 226, 234, 236, 239.
Referral System: 184, 234.
Research: 22, 40, 49 - 50, 52 - 53, 56, 65 - 66, 153, 162, 168, 169, 171, 173, 176, 177, 178, 218, 220, 233, 261, 262, 263, 264.
Revocation: 265.

S

School: 4, 9, 10, 15, 58, 77, 78, 82, 122, 168, 215, 237.
Secondary Victim: 2, 79.
Shock: 2, 24, 31, 33, 47, 63, 65, 87, 124, 125, 149, 162, 200, 201, 204, 209.
Significant Other: 3, 12, 14, 62, 154, 166, 194, 202, 236, 253, 254, 255, 265.
Significant Other Support: 12, 62, 194, 265.
Social Worker: 10, 54, 220.
Somatoform Disorder: 19.
Specialty Debriefing: 5, 9, 16, 239, 265.
Stress: 1 - 65, 67 - 89, 92, 95, 97 - 102, 105, 109, 111 - 115, 117, 122 - 124, 127, 129, 130 - 137, 139, 141, 143 - 151, 154 - 160, 162 - 166, 168 - 177, 179 - 185, 190, 194 - 196, 198 - 199, 204 - 205, 211, 215 - 216, 219 - 220, 222, 225 - 230, 233, 235 - 243, 246 - 255, 258, 260 - 263, 265, 268, 273 - 283.
Stress Education: 53, 59, 60, 62, 63, 81, 82, 86, 112, 157, 164, 196, 228, 246, 253.
Stress Management: 3, 11, 12, 26, 42, 46, 54, 56, 57, 60 - 65, 67, 70, 71, 76, 86, 100, 112, 135, 143, 154, 163, 175, 181, 195, 220, 240, 242, 243, 248, 250, 251, 268, 279.
Stress reaction: 3, 6, 7, 9, 29, 31, 47, 48, 51, 62, 64, 78, 79, 111, 134, 135, 139, 145, 155, 157, 170, 173, 190, 216, 233, 251, 255.
Stress Response: 7, 18 - 24, 26 - 29, 79, 166, 172.
Stressor: 6, 17, 18, 20, 21, 22, 26, 27, 28, 33, 35, 46, 86, 158, 238, 239, 273, 282.
Suicide: 52, 61, 68, 76, 85, 166, 170, 236.
Supervision: 11, 59, 61, 62, 124, 257.
Sympathetic Nervous System: 23, 27.
Symptom Phase: 162.
Symptom Phase: 8, 110, 111, 129, 156, 210.

T

Target Organ Arousal: 24.
Target Organ Strain: 5 - 6.
Teaching phase: 8, 98, 100, 111, 112, 113, 198, 199, 200, 201.
Team Call Out Procedures: 82.
Team Development: 231, 232, 238, 259.
Team Evaluation: 264.
Team Leader: 8, 10, 82, 89, 90, 92, 96, 97, 98, 100, 101, 105, 108, 127, 195, 218, 238, 265.
Team Liaison: 222, 228.
Tertiary Victim: 2, 14, 79.

Thought Phase: 8, 108, 109, 116, 194, 199, 201, 210.
Transducer: 22.
Trauma: 1 - 17, 27 - 28, 31 - 49, 53 - 68, 77 - 80, 85, 87, 97, 103 - 104, 121 - 122, 125, - 131, 133 - 135, 146, 153 - 154, 157 - 170, 173 - 184, 187 - 189, 192, 194, 199 - 200, 205, 207 - 212, 215, 220, 222 - 223, 225, 227, 237, 240 - 242, 252, 263, 268, 274 - 283.
Trauma Management: 3.
Trauma Membrane: 159.
Traumatic Event: 2, 4, 7 - 9, 11 - 16, 27, 32 - 36, 48 - 49, 58 - 64, 77 - 79, 87, 97, 103 - 104, 121, 122, 125, 127, 131, 135, 146, 154, 158 - 159, 160, 163, 169, 173 - 177, 180, 187, 189, 192, 194, 199, 207, 211 - 212, 223, 225, 241 - 242, 263.
Traumatic Stress: 1 - 4, 7, 12, 15 - 16, 27, 31 - 44, 46 - 47, 49, 54, 56 - 60, 62 - 65, 78, 122, 131, 157 - 158, 164 - 166, 168, 173, 175, 179, 183 - 184, 215, 227, 237, 240 - 242, 252.
Traumatologist: 41, 160.

V

Ventilating the Stress Response: 26, 27.
Victim: 1, 2, 11, 13 - 14, 31 - 32, 36 - -37, 40, 46, 50 - 51, 59, 79, 80, 85, 147, 158 - 159, 164 - 168, 173 - 174, 176, 186, 190 - 191, 205, 208 - 209, 222, 241, 262.
Violent Crime: 64.
Volunteer: 1, 41, 69, 146, 258, 267.

W

Weak Organ Theory: 25.
Weltanshuuang: 160.
Wild Land Fire Fighter: 4, 11, 217.
Worldview: 188.